BAUDELAIRE
THE CRITIC

Margaret Gilman

BAUDELAIRE
THE CRITIC

"Je considère le poëte comme le meilleur de tous les critiques."—Richard Wagner et Tannhäuser
à Paris

1971

OCTAGON BOOKS
New York

Reprinted 1971

by special arrangement with Columbia University Press

OCTAGON BOOKS

A DIVISION OF FARRAR, STRAUS & GIROUX, INC.

19 Union Square West

New York, N. Y. 10003

LIBRARY OF CONGRESS CATALOG CARD NUMBER: 74-159245

ISBN-0-374-93088-0

Printed in U.S.A. by

NOBLE OFFSET PRINTERS, INC.

NEW YORK 3, N. Y.

PREFACE

THIS BOOK is the fruit of an interest in Baudelaire as a critic that was awakened in me some ten years ago. I remember well, at a time when Baudelaire's critical work was practically unknown to me, coming across a quotation which arrested my attention and sent me straight to the *Curiosités esthétiques* and the *Art romantique*. The enthusiasm which I felt then for the sureness and felicity of Baudelaire's judgments, my conviction of the enduring validity of the principles on which they are based, have increased with many re-readings, and I have attempted here, in Baudelaire's own phrase, to "transformer ma volupté en connaissance."

When I first became interested in the subject, comparatively little attention had been paid to Baudelaire as a critic. There were exceptions indeed; even among Baudelaire's contemporaries his value as a critic was not entirely neglected, and later critics have devoted memorable pages to it. But only in recent years has its significance begun to be fully realized, and to be emphasized by nearly all those who have written on Baudelaire. What, when I first approached it, seemed almost a desert island, now bears the footprints of many a man Friday.

I have tried first of all to dig down to the roots of Baudelaire's criticism, to find out how and why he came to be a critic, what in his temperament, his experience, his reading, set his feet in that path, and then to follow his critical work from its beginnings to its full flowering. The observance of a fairly strict chronological order has seemed to me essential; only thus are apparent contradictions understandable, only thus is the development of Baudelaire's originality perceptible.

For, original as his thought is in its final form, it is an originality which is formed slowly. At the beginning, and for a
long time indeed, he was greatly influenced by Delacroix, by
Stendhal, by De Maistre, by Poe, to cite only the chief of his
masters. By following his work year by year one realizes
how the various strands, each plainly perceptible at first, are
slowly woven into a pattern that is Baudelaire's own. So I
have ignored the time-honored classification of his criticism
into artistic, literary, and musical. Not only does the chronological development seem to me more important than such
a classification, but also Baudelaire's criticism has an underlying unity that suffers from this somewhat artificial division
into categories. The chronological method can, it is true, lead
all too easily to an artificiality of a different sort, the division
of an author's work into too sharply defined periods. I have
tried to the best of my ability to avoid this, and to emphasize
the continuous development of Baudelaire's thought. The
chapter divisions are milestones, not frontiers.

I have, however, not followed the chronological order
slavishly. To group together certain articles which present
common problems, a common interest, has seemed to me more
important, particularly in the later years, when Baudelaire's
thought has taken shape, than following his work month by
month, or even year by year. For the exact sequence of the
articles, the reader is referred to the table at the end of the
book.

In studying Baudelaire's criticism, one of the things that
have struck me most is the significance of certain words, a
significance that often changes through the years, as a word
takes on new value, new emphasis, new weight. I have tried
to follow the history of what seemed to me the most important of these words, taking each one up at the moment when
it seems most significant for Baudelaire and retracing its history with, again, a certain lack of respect for chronology.

Throughout, remembering Baudelaire's defense of the "I"
in critical writing, I have drawn largely on my personal ex-

perience, the enlarging of my own critical horizons by this critic who wrote of his contemporaries with the sure discernment which is usually the happy lot only of posterity, and in the twenty years over which his critical articles extend evolved a way of criticism which we may do well to follow.

Much that has been written on Baudelaire's criticism has been helpful and suggestive to me, as the notes will bear witness; M. André Ferran's encyclopaedic *Esthétique de Baudelaire* has been particularly valuable. And I have contracted many a debt of gratitude in the writing of this book: to those master Baudelaireans, M. Jacques Crépet and M. Yves-Gérard Le Dantec, for their kindness and interest; to M. Paul Hazard for his always generous help; to Professor Henri Peyre, who read the book in manuscript, and made many valuable and helpful suggestions; to many colleagues and friends with whom I have had lengthy discussions on one point or another; and last, but by no means least, to the Bryn Mawr students who have listened patiently and helpfully to the Protean stages through which this book has passed.

M. G.

Bryn Mawr, Pennsylvania
April 20, 1942

CONTENTS

LIST OF ABBREVIATIONS

The following abbreviations are used for works frequently cited. Unless otherwise indicated, the work is by Baudelaire and the place of publication is Paris.

I, II *Œuvres*, ed. Y.-G. Le Dantec. 2 vols., Editions de la Pléiade, 1931-32.

A.R. *L'Art romantique*, ed. Jacques Crépet. Conard, 1925.

C.E. *Curiosités esthétiques*, ed. Jacques Crépet. Conrad, 1923.

Corr. I *Œuvres complètes*, ed. F.-F. Gautier and Y.-G. Le Dantec: *Correspondance*, Vol. I (1841-1863). Nouvelle Revue Française, 1933.

Crépet Eugène Crépet. *Charles Baudelaire*, rev. Jacques Crépet. Messein, 1907.

D.L.M. *Dernières Lettres inédites à sa mère*, ed. Jacques Crépet. Editions Excelsior, 1926.

J.I. *Journaux intimes*, ed. Jacques Crépet. Mercure de France, 1938.

Juvenilia *Juvenilia, Œuvres posthumes, Reliquiae*, I, ed. Jacques Crépet. Conard, 1939.

L.M. *Lettres inédites à sa mère*, ed. Jacques Crépet. Conard, 1918.

Lettres *Lettres, 1841-1866*. Mercure de France, 1907.

O.P. *Œuvres posthumes*. Mercure de France, 1908.

Poe Edgar Allan Poe. *Histoires*, trans. Charles Baudelaire, ed. Y.-G. Le Dantec. Editions de la Pléiade, 1932.

Chapter One

THE DISCIPLE OF DELACROIX

Goût permanent depuis l'enfance de toutes les représentations plastiques.—Note autobiographique.

IN BAUDELAIRE'S own eyes, his critical work seems to have been hardly less important than his poetry. Through the twenty years of his literary activity the two run parallel, and his letters and papers show him constantly revising and arranging the critical articles, in view of their publication in volume form. In one of his letters from Belgium he writes: "Bien que ces articles, inconnus pour la plupart, aient paru à de très longs intervalles, ils sont reliés entre eux par une pensée unique et systématique. J'ai une assez vive envie de montrer ce que j'ai su faire, en matière de critique."[1] But the two volumes containing the greater part of the critical articles, *Curiosités esthétiques* and *L'Art romantique*, appeared only after his death, in the edition of his works published by Michel Lévy in 1868-1869. In 1887 the *Œuvres posthumes* edited by Eugène Crépet gathered in some of the articles that had been omitted from the two Lévy volumes, and more appeared in the *Œuvres posthumes* of 1908. Since then successive editors of Baudelaire's work have added still other articles and fragments.[2]

On the very threshold of his critical work Baudelaire pauses to consider the function of criticism and the position of the critic. The first chapter of the "Salon de 1846" is entitled "A quoi bon la critique?" Baudelaire answers: "Je crois sincèrement que la meilleure critique est celle qui est amusante et poétique. . . . Ainsi, le meilleur compte rendu d'un tableau pourra être un sonnet ou une élégie" (II, 64). Baudelaire himself gives us many an example of this last kind of criticism; "Sur le Tasse en prison," "Bohémiens en voyage," "Une Martyre," "Le Masque," to mention only a few, are translations and interpretations of a painting, a print, a drawing, a statue. So Baudelaire is thinking first of all of criticism as closely allied to poetry, as the translation of an experience. Properly speaking, criticism—by which Baudelaire means the reasoned analysis of the aesthetic experience, the judgment of the work of art, the deduction of rules and standards— should be partial, exclusive, yet broad in its implications. All that the critic is justified in doing is to "commander à l'artiste la naïveté et l'expression sincère de son tempérament, aidée par tous les moyens que lui fournit son métier" (II, 65). The young Baudelaire believes that a criterium for the critic can and should be found; but he realizes already that it must be a generous and comprehensive one. Later on a wider experience leads him to the conclusion that, experience being the touch- stone by which any system must be judged, no system is com- prehensive enough to cover the infinitely varied forms of beauty that life has to offer (II, 145). In the "Salon de 1859" criticism is again allied to poetry: "l'esprit du vrai critique, comme l'esprit du vrai poëte, doit être ouvert à toutes les beautés" (II, 235). The relation of critic to poet is again brought out in Baudelaire's most frequently quoted passage on criticism, in the article on "Richard Wagner et Tann- häuser à Paris," published in 1861. But in 1846 Baudelaire had thought of the critic as a kind of secondary poet, reflect- ing and translating the work of art. Here it is the poet who must inevitably move on from creation to criticism. Defend- ing Wagner against those who accused him of writing his operas *a posteriori* to prove his theories, Baudelaire asserts that it is contrary to all law, all experience, for the critic to become a poet. (As his application of poet to Wagner and,

later, to Delacroix, shows, he is using the word in its broadest
sense.)

Au contraire, tous les grands poëtes deviennent naturellement,
fatalement, critiques. Je plains les poëtes que guide le seul instinct;
je les crois incomplets. Dans la vie spirituelle des premiers, une crise
se fait infailliblement, où ils veulent raisonner leur art, découvrir
les lois obscures en vertu desquelles ils ont produit, et tirer de cette
étude une série de préceptes dont le but divin est l'infaillibilité dans
la production poétique. Il serait prodigieux qu'un critique devînt
poëte, et il est impossible qu'un poëte ne contienne pas un critique.
Le lecteur ne sera donc pas étonné que je considère le poëte comme
le meilleur de tous les critiques (II, 495-96).

One cannot but think that Baudelaire had himself in mind,
as well as Wagner and other "poets." And one is tempted, to
some extent justifiably so, to see in his criticism a prolonga-
tion and rationalization of his poetry. Chronology supports
this view; it seems unquestionable that Baudelaire's earliest
work was poetical, and that many of the *Fleurs du Mal* were
written before the "Salons" of 1845 and 1846. But in this
case criticism must be defined in the limited sense which it
has for Baudelaire in the passage just quoted. For it is undeniable that Baudelaire's most important critical work is his
art criticism, a criticism, that is, in which he is dealing not
with his own form of creative activity, but with another.
The first articles of literary criticism are founded on the
principles which Baudelaire had already developed in his first
"Salons." Indeed his whole system of criticism, if system it
can be called, seems to be discovered in his art criticism, and
later applied to literature and to music. So it would seem that
in its beginnings Baudelaire's criticism can hardly be considered an off-shoot of his writing of poetry. Rather they
seem to develop side by side, becoming more and more closely
related as time goes on. The first "Salons," admirable critical
début as they are, hardly show the hand of the poet; the
"Salons" of 1855 and 1859 could have been written only by
a poet. The experience and activity of the poet continually
enrich the work of the critic.

It seems to me that the essence of Baudelaire's criticism is to be found in a phrase which he uses towards the beginning of the Wagner article: "Je résolus de m'informer du pourquoi, et de transformer ma volupté en connaissance" (II, 489). The point of departure for Baudelaire is always an experience, something he has felt, and what he does in his criticism is first to translate this experience, then to analyze it and generalize from it. Whether the object be the painting of Delacroix, the writings of Poe or the music of Wagner, the approach is fundamentally the same. And the reason for the predominance of the art criticism may well be that the *volupté* of which Baudelaire speaks came to him most readily from the plastic arts, whereas the literary criticism, often written to order, sometimes seems to lack the impulse of the quickening experience.

Unquestionably such criticism depends greatly on the temperament of the critic. In a passage of the "Poëme du haschisch" which has generally been considered a self-portrait, Baudelaire describes "une âme de mon choix," a temperament which seems the ideal mirror for the work of art:

Un tempérament moitié nerveux, moitié bileux, tel est le plus favorable aux évolutions d'une pareille ivresse; ajoutons un esprit cultivé, exercé aux études de la forme et de la couleur; un cœur tendre, fatigué par le malheur, mais encore prêt au rajeunissement; nous irons, si vous le voulez bien, jusqu'à admettre des fautes anciennes, et, ce qui doit en résulter dans une nature facilement excitable, sinon des remords positifs, au moins le regret du temps profané et mal rempli. Le goût de la métaphysique, la connaissance des différentes hypothèses de la philosophie sur la destinée humaine, ne sont certainemènt pas des compléments inutiles,—non plus que cet amour de la vertu, de la vertu abstraite, stoïcienne ou mystique, qui est posé dans tous les livres dont l'enfance moderne fait sa nourriture, comme le plus haut sommet où une âme distinguée puisse monter. Si l'on ajoute à tout cela une grande finesse de sens que j'ai omise comme condition surérogatoire, je crois que j'ai rassemblé les éléments généraux les plus communs de l'homme sensible moderne, de ce que l'on pourrait appeler *la forme banale de l'originalité* (I, 304-5).

It is the work of art reflected in the undulating, iridescent waters of such a temperament that is the basis of Baudelaire's criticism.

The conclusion of the whole matter seems to me to be that Baudelaire is fundamentally right in his drawing together of the poet and the critic, if one thinks primarily in terms of poetic experience. The poet, as Baudelaire himself said (II, 521), is in the largest sense a translator of his experience, a translator into words, into painting, into music. The critic also is in his way a translator, the translator of what he has experienced in reading a poem, in standing before a picture, in listening to music. But the critic does not stop here; he goes on to "transformer la volupté en connaissance," to discover the underlying principles of artistic activity. Such is criticism for Baudelaire.

Given the importance of the art criticism, it is essential to try to discover why Baudelaire's earliest critical ventures were in the field of an art other than his own, what explains the sureness and authority with which the young critic speaks in his "Salons" of 1845 and 1846.

Baudelaire's début as an art critic was far from fortuitous. It was the result of an enthusiasm dating from his earliest years, as he has indicated in more than one passage in his writings. The fragmentary notes for his autobiography have: "Goût permanent depuis l'enfance de toutes les représentations plastiques" (II, 697), and in "Mon cœur mis à nu" he notes: "Glorifier le culte des images (ma grande, mon unique, ma primitive passion)" (II, 662). In the "Salon de 1859," looking back to his childhood, he writes: "très-jeunes, mes yeux remplis d'images peintes ou gravées n'avaient jamais pu se rassasier, et je crois que les mondes pourraient finir, *impavidum ferient,* avant que je devienne iconoclaste" (II, 230). The taste seems to have been at least partly inherited; Baudelaire's father painted (detestably indeed, according to his son's later judgment),[3] and one of the boy's clearest memories of

the father who died when his son was six years old was that
of their walks together in the Luxembourg garden, where
the old man would explain the statues to him.[4] His mother
also drew,[5] and among his childhood memories were those of
the furniture and pictures in his home.[6] During his school
years the love of pictures persisted, along with his awakening
enthusiasm for literature, as well as for less innocent pleasures.
Looking back on this period later he writes to his mother:
"Je me suis épris uniquement du plaisir, d'une excitation
perpétuelle; les voyages, les beaux meubles, les tableaux, les
filles, etc."[7]

Many of those who knew him in the years which followed
have noted his enthusiasm for art. Prarond, who knew him
at the Pension Bailly, described him at the time of the "voyage
aux Indes":

> "Passionné pour Michel-Ange
> Et Titien et Delacroix,
> Chercheur ayant sur lui la croix,
> Baudelaire allait voir le Gange."[8]

After his return, when he had come of age, he established
himself in an apartment in the Hôtel Pimodan, the many
descriptions of which all bear witness to his artistic tastes.
On the walls were the whole series of Delacroix's Hamlet
lithographs, a head of *La Douleur* by Delacroix, and a copy
by Deroy of Delacroix's *Femmes d'Alger*, as well as paintings
of the Italian school.[9] His frequent visits to museums and
galleries stood out in the memories of his friends. Prarond
writes: "Je l'ai suivi quelquefois au Louvre devant lequel il
passait rarement sans entrer. Il s'arrêtait alors, de préférence,
dans la salle des Espagnols. Il avait des toquades, était très
attiré par un Teotocopuli, entrait pour deux ou trois tableaux,
et s'en allait. Il commençait à discuter les modernes."[10]

All this goes to show how personal and firsthand Baudelaire's appreciation of art was. But he was not content with
an emotional enjoyment; already the desire to "transformer

la volupté en connaissance" was at work, and he was making
friends with painters, especially Boissard and Deroy, and having long talks with them.[11] Asselineau refers to "les longues
promenades au Luxembourg et au Louvre, les visites aux
ateliers, les cafés esthétiques et les soirées de l'Odéon-
Lirieux."[12] Baudelaire was often seen discussing aesthetic
questions in the cafés,[13] and it is about this time too that he
came to know Gautier. But the most stimulating, the most
illuminating of all relationships was to be that with Delacroix.

It is significant that Delacroix's name is blazoned on the
threshold of the "Salon de 1845": "M. Delacroix est décidément le peintre le plus original des temps anciens et des temps
modernes" (II, 16). The words were no idle repetition of a
commonplace. Delacroix had exhibited for the first time at
the Salon of 1824. His *Dante et Virgile* was greeted by Delécluze as "une vraie tartouillade," and the expression is characteristic of much of the criticism that followed. Even critics
of the rank of Stendhal and Gautier were far from appreciating Delacroix in these early years, and in 1845 blame was
still more familiar than praise.

But from the very beginning Baudelaire's enthusiasm was
spontaneous and unfaltering. The pictures in his Hôtel Pimodan apartment, as we have seen, were largely by Delacroix.
At least two of the *Fleurs du Mal* allude to Delacroix, "Les
Phares" and "Sur le Tasse en prison," and possibly also "Don
Juan aux enfers." And it would hardly be an exaggeration
to say that the greater part of Baudelaire's art criticism is a
glorification of Delacroix; the "Salons" of 1845 and 1846,
the "Exposition de 1855," the "Salon de 1859," the "Peintures murales de Saint-Sulpice" (1861), and "L'Œuvre et la
vie d'Eugène Delacroix" (1863).

Given this fervent and unswerving devotion, it is not surprising that the influence which more than any other colors
and dominates Baudelaire's thought in these early years should

be that of Delacroix. In the case of other influences (as for example Stendhal and Diderot) one can more readily cite chapter and verse, detect borrowings that occasionally fringe on plagiarism, but the influence of Delacroix seems to permeate Baudelaire's whole thought at this period. And it must be remembered that this influence acted upon Baudelaire in a multiplicity of ways. Later on, in the case of Poe, the influence will be purely literary. But with Delacroix the case is entirely different. His ideas were communicated to Baudelaire in part through a direct personal relationship, in conversations between the two; in part through the critical articles which Delacroix contributed to various periodicals from time to time; in part through mutual friends and acquaintances; and probably also through a general diffusion of Delacroix's ideas and their appearance in the works of other writers. And last, but far from least, there is the visual influence, the effect upon Baudelaire's thought and imagination of the study of Delacroix's paintings. Baudelaire's debt to Delacroix is allpervasive; he is seeing, as well as thinking, in terms of Delacroix. In the case of so complex an influence it is rarely possible to detect with any sureness the precise channel through which a particular idea passed from Delacroix to Baudelaire; all one can do is to point out parallels in their thought, with no attempt, except in a few instances, to decide what the means of communication was.

The chief source for our knowledge of the relations between Baudelaire and Delacroix is the article Baudelaire wrote after the painter's death in 1863.[14] Here Baudelaire says that he had known Delacroix since 1845, to the best of his recollection.[15] (It seems probable that the two met in the apartment of the painter Boissard, a neighbor of Baudelaire's in the Hôtel Pimodan. There are numerous references to Boissard, and to being at Boissard's, in Delacroix's journal and correspondence.) Later in the article he recalls his first conversation with Delacroix. He tells how, thanks to the sincerity of his admiration, he was admitted to Delacroix's studio, and had many long talks with him. The article is full of personal allusions and intimate details. One has the impression from this article of a lasting intimacy between the two, an intimacy that would be all-sufficient to explain all that Baudelaire owes to Delacroix. In the early years Baudelaire apparently took pride and delight in proclaiming such a relationship. For example in the "Conseils aux jeunes littérateurs," published in 1846, he flings out: "E. Delacroix me disait un jour. . . ." And an amusing anonymous article published in *La Silhouette* a few weeks later suggests that the phrase was often on his lips.[16]

But when we turn from Baudelaire's account to Delacroix's journal and letters, a different story is told. Delacroix rarely mentions Baudelaire, and when he does so there is no suggestion of intimacy. The only account of a meeting is dated Feb. 5, 1849: "M. Baudelaire venu. . . . Il m'a parlé des difficultés qu'éprouve Daumier à finir. Il a sauté à Proudhon qu'il admire et qu'il dit l'idole du peuple. Ses vues me paraissent des plus modernes et tout à fait dans le progrès."[17] One wonders whether it was this occasion that Baudelaire was recalling when he wrote in 1863: "Le causeur qui, devant M. Delacroix, s'abandonnait aux enthousiasmes enfantins de l'utopie, avait bientôt à subir l'effet de son rire amer, imprégné d'une pitié sarcastique; et si, imprudemment, on lançait devant lui la grande chimère des temps modernes, le ballon-monstre de la perfectibilité et du progrès indéfinis, volontiers il vous demandait: 'Où sont donc vos Phidias? où sont vos Raphaël?' " (II, 311.) Aside from the entry quoted, Delacroix's only other mentions of Baudelaire are a note of his address (Jan. 3, 1855: *Journal*, II, 307), and two references to Baudelaire's translation of Poe's *Histoires extraordinaires* and his preface to them (April 6 and May 30, 1856: *Journal*, II, 437 and 450-51). It must not be forgotten, however, that Delacroix kept no journal from 1824 to 1847, and that the journal for 1848 is missing, so that there is no record of the first three years of his acquaintance with Baudelaire.

But even so there is no evidence elsewhere of the intimacy which Baudelaire himself claimed. The few letters of Delacroix to Baudelaire are all letters of thanks, never intimate, often conventional, for his articles. Delacroix seems curiously unaware of the value of Baudelaire's appreciation of him; he writes just as warmly, often more so, to other critics. This indifference, to say the least, on the part of Delacroix is confirmed by his contemporaries. Asselineau, to be sure, says that Delacroix showed his appreciation by "la plus bienveillante amitié,"[18] but this may well be an echo of Baudelaire's own words. The general impression seems to be that Delacroix was certainly indifferent, probably discouraging, to Baudelaire's advances. Various reasons have been suggested: a distaste on Delacroix's part for Baudelaire's bohemian ways; an aloofness that kept Delacroix apart from all but his old friends; a growing distaste, in his later years, for the emphasis Baudelaire placed on the feverish and morbid elements in his work; and possibly even a fear that Baudelaire might try to borrow money from him.[19] Whatever the reasons, it seems unquestionable that in spite of all they had in common the intimacy between the two was not what Baudelaire, with his hero worship of Delacroix, would have wished it to be, nor what he implies in the 1863 article that it was. Perhaps in his heart of hearts he realized this, for towards the end of his life he writes to Jules Troubat: "J'ai été bien heureux d'apprendre le rétablissement de Sainte-Beuve. Je n'ai éprouvé d'émotions de ce genre, pour la santé d'autrui, que pour E. Delacroix, qui était pourtant un grand égoïste. Mais les émotions me viennent beaucoup de l'esprit" (March 5, 1866. *Lettres*, p. 537).

But there are other ways through which Delacroix's ideas could have reached Baudelaire. He was certainly familiar with the articles which Delacroix had published from time to time.[20] To be sure, as Baudelaire points out in 1863 (II, 306-9), Delacroix in his writings (particularly however in the later articles) tended to praise the classic qualities which he himself lacked, and to write with a prudence and moderation which made his handling of the pen very different from his handling of the brush. Nevertheless most of his significant ideas are suggested in these early articles, though not developed with the freedom and fullness of the *Journal*. It seems to me likely that Baudelaire may have been much more dependent on the published work when he was writing the "Salon de 1845," probably before he had met Delacroix, than he was by the time he was completing the "Salon de 1846." The 1845 "Salon," as we shall see, implies, rather than states the principles which were to be defined later, and it seems probable that Baudelaire knew little about Delacroix's ideas compared to what his acquaintance with Delacroix himself was to bring him.

But Delacroix's expression of his ideas was not confined to writing. Many of those who knew him, either intimately or in passing, have borne witness to his delight in conversation and his brilliant conversational powers. For example George Sand, in her *Impressions et Souvenirs*, under the date of January, 1841, records a conversation begun in Delacroix's studio and continued later at dinner in her home, with Chopin and Maurice Sand also taking part. Delacroix had begun by making fun of the so-called color of the school of Ingres, and by pointing out their lack of understanding of the whole theory of reflections. Then, in answer to a question of Maurice Sand's, he plunged into a comparison of tones in painting and sounds in music, and from that into a discussion of color and line.[21] The ideas are all familiar to readers of the *Journal*; what is interesting is the indication of the way in which these ideas were constantly appearing in Delacroix's conversation. It can hardly be doubted that Baudelaire would have been constantly on the alert to gather up, from Boissard and others, fragments of what Delacroix had said, and to add them to his own store.

Moreover, Delacroix's ideas were beginning to be sufficiently diffused for Baudelaire to meet them in a more or less disguised form. A few art critics had begun to appreciate

Delacroix, and to echo certain of his ideas, more or less faithfully, in their criticism. Then in Balzac's *Chef-d'œuvre inconnu* we have, it seems, an undoubted influence of Delacroix.[22] Baudelaire, as we know, was an enthusiastic reader of Balzac, and the *Chef-d'œuvre inconnu* may well have been for him, to his knowledge or not, an added source for Delacroix's ideas.

Baudelaire's experience of art was further supplemented and enriched by wide reading, first of art critics, both his contemporaries and the critics of the past. Of the former indeed he has little good to say: "Depuis M. G. Planche, un paysan du Danube dont l'éloquence impérative et savante s'est tue au grand regret des sains esprits, la critique des journaux, tantôt niaise, tantôt furieuse, jamais indépendante, a, par ses mensonges et ses camaraderies effrontées, dégoûté le bourgeois de ces utiles guide-ânes qu'on nomme comptes rendus de Salons."[23] So Baudelaire ends the first paragraph of his first "Salon," adding a note to except Delécluze from the general condemnation. He certainly read the "Salons" of his contemporaries, but in general they were little to his liking, and his criticism is a revolt against their methods rather than an attempt to imitate them in any way.

But the case is very different for some of the critics of the past. To Diderot, and even more to Stendhal, Baudelaire's debt is a large one, as we shall see, and it is interesting to note his preoccupation with them at this time. By 1845 about half of Diderot's *Salons* (those of 1759, 1761, 1765, 1767 and the last five letters of 1769), as well as the "Essai sur la peinture" and the "Pensées détachées sur la peinture" had been published. His reputation had been at a low ebb; Delécluze wrote in 1839: "Cette critique purement imaginaire qui ne repose sur rien mais qui impose par la hardiesse, par la singularité et quelquefois par l'éclat du style, comme les *Salons* de Diderot en fournissent l'exemple, cette critique en langage artistique, dis-je, est extraordinairement stérile."[24] It seems however that there was a revival of interest in Diderot in the forties. In 1845 Thoré refers to the "charmants *Salons*" of Diderot (*Constitutionnel*, March 15, 1845), and among the *Salons* of these years are "Diderot au Salon de 1844" (*La Chronique*, Vol. V.) and "Diderot (feu). Salon de 1849" (*L'Artiste*, Series 5, Vol. III). Baudelaire seems to have read Diderot carefully and delightedly. In a note to Champfleury, who was to review his "Salon de 1845," he says: "si vous voulez me faire plaisir, faites quelques lignes sérieuses, et parlez des *Salons* de Diderot" (*Corr.* I, 23). And in the "Salon de 1846" he writes: "Je recommande à ceux que mes pieuses colères ont dû parfois scandaliser la lecture des *Salons* de Diderot" (II, 746). We shall see how this reading of Diderot is reflected in the "Salons" of 1845 and 1846.

Stendhal is equally in the forefront of Baudelaire's mind. In 1843 he begins a letter to Sainte-Beuve: "Stendhal a dit quelque part ceci, ou à peu près: J'écris pour une dizaine d'âmes que je ne verrai peut-être jamais, mais que j'adore, sans les avoir vues" (*Corr.* I, 17). Stendhal's name occurs frequently in Baudelaire's writings during these years, in the "Maximes consolantes sur l'amour" and in the "Salon de 1846," where the *Histoire de la peinture en Italie* is quoted directly three times. All this goes to show that Baudelaire was from the very beginning a critic who both looked at pictures and thought about them. He was not content with the pure aesthetic experience, intense as it was with him, but set about informing himself, through conversations, through the reading of critics, sometimes finding them unsatisfactory, as was the case for most of his contemporaries, sometimes, as with Diderot and Stendhal, furnishing and enriching his own mind from their stores.

Up to this point I have considered only the part of Baudelaire's early experience and reading that contributed directly to his art criticism. But one cannot neglect other aspects. No one could be farther than Baudelaire from either a purely impressionistic criticism or the mere technical jargon of many professional art critics. His criticism is that of one who is remarkably sensitive to art and has taken pains to inform himself about it; it is also the criticism not of a narrow specialist but of a man of wide interests and culture, one who had himself something of that "universality" which he so much admired in Delacroix.

Baudelaire was one of whom reading had made a full man. His literary enthusiasms impressed his contemporaries quite as much as his artistic ones, and have been amusingly re-counted. Champfleury tells how one day Baudelaire would have a volume of Swedenborg under his arm; nothing in all literature would be comparable to Swedenborg, and Bronzino would be the greatest of all painters. Shortly afterwards the volume under his arm would be Wronski's algebra; Sweden-borg would be forgotten, and Van Eyck and the Flemish primitives would have toppled Bronzino from his pedestal.[25] And Baudelaire writes in "La Fanfarlo" of his Samuel Cramer, in so many ways a self-portrait,[26] that he belonged to a well-known type: "Les voilà aujourd'hui déchiffrant péniblement les pages mystiques de Plotin ou de Porphyre; demain ils ad-mireront comment Crébillon le fils a bien exprimé le côté volage et français de leur caractère. Hier ils s'entretenaient familièrement avec Jérôme Cardan; les voici maintenant jou-ant avec Sterne ou se vautrant avec Rabelais dans toutes les goinfreries de l'hyperbole" (I, 528). And again: "Il souffla résolument ses deux bougies dont l'une palpitait encore sur un volume de Swedenborg, et l'autre s'éteignait sur un de ces livres honteux dont la lecture n'est profitable qu'aux esprits possédés d'un goût immodéré de la vérité" (I, 530).

It is plain that Baudelaire's taste in literature, as in art, was extraordinarily personal and original, independent of traditional judgments and classifications. There is nothing one would like more than to know in full what his reading was during these formative years; what books his father had left, what discoveries he made in his school years, in and out of the classroom, what the successive volumes under his arm were, what those in the cupboard, on the book-cluttered divan of the Hôtel Pimodan apartment. Though it is impossible to make a list that has any pretensions to completeness, one can at least make a beginning from the indications given by Baudelaire in his correspondence and early writing, and by his contemporaries. Of Latin writers Lucan, Apuleius, Seneca, St. Augustine seem to have been his favorites. In French literature, while rejecting Montaigne, La Fontaine, and Molière as "trop sages,"[27] he admired especially the poets of the Pléiade, Racine, Boileau, Diderot, Chateaubriand, Sainte-Beuve, Hugo, Stendhal, Balzac, and Gautier. As for foreign writers, his taste was of the most eclectic; Swedenborg, Wronski, Hoffmann, Heine, Lavater, Byron, Maturin, Monk Lewis.[28] It is not possible to comment extensively on this reading; I would only emphasize once more its breadth and independence.

So we have in Baudelaire at this point, as he is embarking on his career as a critic, a young man in his early twenties, the dandy his friends have described, full of youthful zest, and of youthful intolerance too; extraordinarily sensitive to art, and well-informed about it; and with an immense store of the most varied reading. With all this there is the poet, who has already composed many of the *Fleurs du Mal,* and is constantly revising and correcting them, with that passion for perfection which was one of his chief characteristics. With such a background, what will his criticism be?

Baudelaire's very first critical articles were apparently written and published before the "Salons." There are several references to articles of his in early letters to his mother: "De plus je suis occupé à refondre mon article tout entier" (March 3, 1843. *L.M.,* p. 12); "mon premier travail étant presque une chose de science" (1844. *L.M.,* p. 20).[29] The majority of these articles, if really written and published, are buried in obscure periodicals. M. Crépet has, however, discovered and published a volume which undoubtedly contains some of them, the *Mystères galans.*[30] The problem of these articles, like that of the later *Causeries du Tintamarre*, is an interesting one, but the nature of the articles, largely ephemeral journalism, makes them unimportant for this study. Aside from them Baudelaire's criticism before 1845 is an unknown quantity, and the "Salon de 1845" marks his critical début.

In beginning his critical career with a "Salon," Baudelaire was attaching himself to a well-established tradition. The first criticism of a Salon had appeared nearly a hundred years before, the account of the Salon of 1747 by La Font de Saint-Yenne.[31] The artists took this criticism hardly, so much so indeed that there was no Salon in 1749, "par suite de l'irritation des artistes contre les critiques."[32] But the genre rapidly became popular, and when Diderot came to write his first "Salon" in 1759 the instrument was ready to his hand; he had only to make it his own, to animate it with his zest, his enthusiasm, his style. In practicing it through the years which followed, he became, from a distinctly ill-prepared art critic, the chief art critic in France, not only for his own time, but for many years after. Beginning by a strict adherence to the principle of the imitation of nature, Diderot freed himself more and more from it, and arrived at the conception of the *modèle idéal.*[33] But his taste lagged behind his theory, and, as has been said, "il veut que le soleil de l'artiste se tienne aussi près que possible du soleil de la nature."[34]

After Diderot, the "Salon" fell on evil days, and Baudelaire's immediate predecessors and contemporaries in the genre were ill-fitted to bear comparison with him.[35] The professional and technical criticism of Gustave Planche, the honest but narrow criticism of Delécluze, with its reiteration of "ce n'est pas un tableau," the picturesque and often overenthusiastic criticism of Gautier, the high-minded utilitarian "Salons" of Thoré, with their dedications to Béranger and George Sand, the anecdotal "Salons" of Champfleury, all seem remote from us. Baudelaire himself, as I have pointed out, had little good to say of them.

In his "Salon de 1845" Baudelaire keeps to the conventional pattern of the "Salon," the arrangement by genres; in the "Salon de 1846" we shall see him breaking away from this, and finding his own form, in which the criticism of individual works will be more and more subordinated to general ideas. But despite this outward conventionality this first "Salon" of Baudelaire's is remarkable for the firmness and authority of its tone. The introduction, after a word of contempt for contemporary criticism, presents the spectacle, contrary to all expectation, of Baudelaire making advances to the bourgeois, promising to discuss whatever pictures have attracted the attention of the crowd: "Tout ce qui plaît a une raison de plaire. . . . *Notre méthode de discours* consistera . . . à ranger les artistes suivant l'ordre et le grade que leur a assignés l'estime publique" (II, 16). Nothing could promise a more conventional "Salon"; and nothing could serve better to fling into sharp relief the audacious and categorical statement which immediately follows: "M. Delacroix est décidément le peintre le plus original des temps anciens et des temps modernes." It is characteristic and fitting that Baudelaire's entrance into the lists of criticism should be made with this battle cry, under the banner of the artist whom he admired above all others. Here he gives his youthful enthusiasm full rein. Later on he will justify his claims; here he flaunts them.

After this audacious beginning, the certain effect of which must have delighted him, Baudelaire proceeds on his tour of the Salon in the promised order. In the historical section he pauses long before the Delacroix paintings, demolishes Horace Vernet in a paragraph, and arrives at the painting before which he lingers longest, the *Fontaine de Jouvence* of the now completely forgotten William Haussoullier. He stops appreciatively before the Decamps pictures, and then hurries past a number of secondary painters, but with a marked effort to distinguish among them. When he comes to the portraits he is still more cursory, and with the genre paintings one feels that he is hurrying again, that the Salon is becoming something of a chore, to be dispatched as quickly as possible. With the landscapes and the admirable page on Corot he is himself again. But drawings and prints do not detain him for long, nor does sculpture. And he concludes with a paragraph which, with its plea for originality, its call for the painter of modern life, gives the keynote of the "Salon de 1846."

The "Salon de 1845" has a quality very much its own; it leaves one with the sense of having been led through the even then interminable rooms of the Salon by a guide with keen vision, great sensitiveness to beauty, sound technical knowledge and remarkable sureness of judgment. He is arbitrary, dogmatic, without fear or favor. It is the criticism of a young man, running through a gamut of different tones, from boundless enthusiasms (which sometimes tend to overflow with the abuse of such adjectives as magnificent, sublime, incomparable, prodigious, and the like) to devastating criticisms, so absolute that if Baudelaire were not so nearly infallible one would be tempted to call him cocksure. It is an uncompromising, sometimes faintly distant attitude, which easily calls up the picture of the handsome young dandy that Baudelaire then was. All in all, it is an extraordinarily personal criticism. Never was promise less well kept than that of Baudelaire's to base his criticism on the judgment of the public.

It is, here as always, before the pictures that Baudelaire admires most that he lingers longest. In general he does not give a precise vision of a picture; a few words on the subject, and the artist's conception of it, suffice. The only striking exception (not only in this "Salon" but in all Baudelaire's art criticism) is his description of Haussoullier's *Fontaine de Jouvence.* He describes the composition of it painstakingly—but immediately goes on to supplement the description by his characteristic re-creating of the atmosphere of a picture, his own impression of it: "Le sentiment de ce tableau est exquis; dans cette composition l'on aime et l'on boit, — aspect voluptueux — mais l'on boit et l'on aime d'une manière très-sérieuse, presque mélancolique. Ce ne sont pas des jeunesses fougueuses et remuantes, mais de secondes jeunesses qui connaissent le prix de la vie et qui en jouissent avec tranquillité" (II, 22). The description is very like the first part of the poem "J'aime le souvenir des époques nues," which may well have been inspired by the picture. Finally Baudelaire remarks on the technique and on the particular quality of the color, and ends with a slight reproach to the artist for suggesting Bellini and the early Venetians, a warning against the dangers of imitation. One regrets that this picture, so praised by Baudelaire, has disappeared, so that we cannot tell whether his enthusiasm, as is almost always the case, would have been ratified by posterity. Jacques Crépet has discovered a sketch for it, which he has described in an article in the *Figaro*[36] and which I have seen. Though it is hardly fair to judge from a sketch, it must be confessed that one's first feeling is of disappointment. Here is no lost masterpiece; a picture not without charm indeed, but hardly calculated to inspire one with Baudelaire's enthusiasm. One cannot but wonder whether Baudelaire's desire to be original did not lead him astray here, into overpraising an artist scarcely better known to his own time than to ours.

In other cases Baudelaire contents himself with a brief notation, half visual, half impressionistic, as in the case of the first three Delacroix paintings, and the Decamps drawings of Samson. His tendency is to note a figure, a gesture, a detail: "On reconnaît le génie de Decamps tout pur dans cette ombre volante de l'homme qui enjambe plusieurs marches, et qui reste éternellement suspendu en l'air" (II, 24). Sometimes his enthusiasm carries him away so completely that, save for the title, one has no vision whatever of the picture, as for the *Sultan du Maroc*, where the comment is a poetic glorification of the picture in half-pictorial, half-musical terms: "En effet, déploya-t-on jamais en aucun temps une plus grande coquetterie musicale? Véronèse fut-il jamais plus féerique? Fit-on jamais chanter sur une toile de plus capricieuses mélodies? un plus prodigieux accord de tons nouveaux, inconnus, délicats, charmants?" (II, 20.)

For the painters whom Baudelaire dislikes his execution is summary; Horace Vernet is disposed of in one stinging paragraph. At the beginning Baudelaire makes a conscientious effort to discriminate among the mediocre paintings, but as he goes on he becomes impatient, his comments become shorter, vaguer, and at last brief and biting, with a dry sarcasm or a sly mockery.

Much of Baudelaire's commentary in this first "Salon" is technical, dealing particularly with questions of color. Unlike many of his contemporaries, however, he is not dazzled by his own knowledge, and does not overindulge himself in the use of painter's jargon. He notes that a picture is painted with hatchings, that it has "une pâte solide et une bonne couleur"; he distinguishes between *couleur* and *coloriage*; he remarks that Planet has used only a few tones to produce a picture that delights the eye. And he is particularly sensitive to a happy harmony of colors, above all in Delacroix's painting.

This first "Salon" is weak in what will be one of Baudelaire's great merits, his admirable generalizations. There is one example—a discussion of color and line, and "drawing with color," with an admirable comparison of the drawing of Delacroix, Daumier, and Ingres (II, 19). But in general this first "Salon" suggests, rather than states, the principles on which Baudelaire's criticism is based. These are, however, fairly obvious; a constant appreciation of originality wherever he finds it, a plea for it when it is absent, and a severe criticism of the painters who depend on erudition and imitation or substitute technical skill for personal vision. On the technical side Baudelaire's constant preference for color over line is noteworthy. Although the "Salon" is kept within the limits of a banal and traditional framework, Baudelaire's independent vision and informing spirit give it a character quite its own.

The key words of the "Salon," indeed, are *originalité* and the closely related *naïveté*. Original is the highest word of praise for any artist, beginning with Delacroix. It is not a word which will play a great part in Baudelaire's later criticism; it will be absorbed into the larger conception of the imagination. But here it crystallizes the whole spirit of the "Salon." Its companion word, *naïf*, is very close to it in meaning, and it is not easy to establish a distinction between the two. It seems to me that *naïveté* is somewhat more positive, that *original* stresses the unlikeness of the artist to other artists, *naïf* his own peculiar quality. But the two seem very nearly synonymous, and between them they bring out the underlying principle of the "Salon," that the artist must be himself.

There is no denying that of all Baudelaire's "Salons," indeed of all his criticism, the "Salon de 1845" bears rereading least. The large number of artists mentioned, the pages of brief comments on names now completely unknown to us, end by tiring our minds just as walking through room after room of pictures tires one's feet. Baudelaire is too conscientious in his efforts to mention every picture conceivably worth mentioning, for good or for ill, and the conventional pattern he is following cramps his thought. But when all that has been said, the "Salon de 1845" remains of great interest. One has a sense of new wine in old bottles; a spirit of great independence contained in a conventional frame. All through one has the impression that Baudelaire is making a tremendous effort to see with his own eyes, to judge for himself. And his vision is indeed his own.

In the year between the "Salons" of 1845 and 1846 Baudelaire published several short critical articles, none perhaps of great importance, but all interesting for the light they shed on the growth of his ideas in these early years. His first venture into literary criticism was made in 1845; a brief unsigned review, in the *Corsaire-Satan*, of the *Contes normands* and *Historiettes baguenaudières* of Jean de Falaise (the pseudonym of the Marquis de Chennevières, a friend of Baudelaire's). The interest of the unpretentious, friendly comment is the testimony it brings that from the beginning the basis of Baudelaire's criticism is the same for literature as for art. He praises first of all the author's skill in handling style, and his "naïveté d'impressions toute fraîche" (II, 379), then the fact that while other authors are borrowing and copying, Jean de Falaise has produced an *original* work.[37]

Baudelaire's next art criticism was a notice of an exhibition of paintings by David, Ingres, and others of the older school, "Le Musée classique du Bazar Bonne-Nouvelle." The cover of the "Salon de 1845" had announced, "pour paraître prochainement," "David, Guérin, Girodet,"—an article which never appeared. (As Crépet has observed, Baudelaire never completed an article of any considerable length on a topic not congenial to him.) It seems very likely that some of the carefully weighed comments on David in the "Musée Bonne-nouvelle" are the fruit of Baudelaire's planning, and perhaps writing in part, the article announced the previous year.

He begins by enumerating the artists included in the exhibition, from David to Prud'hon, "ce frère en romantisme d'André Chénier," with an acid word for the young artists who have made fun of this painting of the revolutionary period, "cette peinture qui se prive volontairement du charme et du ragoût malsains, et qui vit surtout par la pensée et par l'âme, — amère et despotique comme la révolution dont elle est née" (II, 56). This leads him to a Stendhalian definition of romanticism, "cette expression de la société moderne." He then takes up the pictures by David, and describes the *Marat*, emphasizing certain details, which, he adds, are as historical and real as a novel of Balzac's. He describes the picture in terms evocative of his later criticism: "Ce qu'il y a de plus étonnant dans ce poëme inaccoutumé, c'est qu'il est peint avec une rapidité extrême, et quand on songe à la beauté du dessin, il y a là de quoi confondre l'esprit. Ceci est le pain des forts et le triomphe du spiritualisme; cruel comme la nature, ce tableau a tout le parfum de l'idéal" (II, 57). The use of the word *poëme*, the terms *spiritualisme* and *idéal* (both used here for the first time in Baudelaire's criticism) show the trend of his thought. This is the best example so far of Baudelaire's power of extracting and expressing the very essence of a picture, and it is interesting to find it applied to a picture in many ways so unlike those he admired most.

When Baudelaire comes to Ingres he shows an enthusiasm somewhat surprising after the "Salon de 1845." He particularly admires Ingres's portraits, "de vrais portraits, c'est-à-dire la reconstruction idéale de l'individu" (II, 59). He defends Ingres's color against the charge of grayness, his drawing against the charge of flatness. After a passing slap at Ary Scheffer ("c'est un poëte sentimental qui salit des toiles"), he ends with a regret that there are no Delacroix paintings in the exhibition. The article is a brief one, but I have dwelt upon it because it seems to me to bridge the gap between the "Salons" of 1845 and 1846. It is the work of a Baudelaire who has reflected more deeply, who has gained in power of expression. Moreover, it shows him in the admirable role of a critic understanding and appreciating paintings in many ways far from congenial to his own tastes and temperament.

Contemporary with this is another brief literary review, of the *Prométhée délivré* of Louis de Senneville (Louis Ménard).[38] Baudelaire's attitude towards this "poésie philosophique," is at first light, mocking, that of a Diderot-like dialogue. There is an interesting example of the way in which his standards have been formed by painting, then applied to literature:

Quand un peintre se dit: — Je vais faire une peinture crânement poétique! Ah! la poésie!! . . . il fait une peinture froide, où l'intention de l'œuvre brille aux dépens de l'œuvre: — le *Rêve du*

Bonheur, ou *Faust et Marguerite.* — Et cependant, MM. Papety et
Ary Scheffer ne sont pas des gens dénués de valeur; — mais! . . .
c'est que la poésie d'un tableau doit être faite par le spectateur.
   Comme la philosophie d'un poëme par le lecteur. — Vous y êtes,
c'est cela même (II, 380).

Poetry must be involuntarily philosophic. Even so, says Baudelaire, M. de Senneville's work deserves attention. Several of
his comments are worth noting: "M. de Senneville a esquivé
le culte de la Nature, cette grande religion de Diderot et
d'Holbach, cet unique ornement de l'athéisme," and "la
grande poésie est essentiellement *bête,* elle *croit,* et c'est ce
qui fait sa gloire et sa force. — Ne confondez jamais les
fantômes de la raison avec les fantômes de l'imagination;
ceux-là sont des équations et ceux-ci des êtres et des souvenirs" (II, 382). The article lays the foundation of Baudelaire's prolonged opposition to "philosophic art."
   Before the "Salon de 1846"[39] one other literary or semi-
literary article should be mentioned, the "Conseils aux jeunes
littérateurs." This shows a conception of literary creation
which differs at certain points from Baudelaire's later one.
The sedate bourgeois tone we have noted elsewhere is very
marked, and the statement "il n'y a pas de guignon" (II, 384)
will be contradicted by the Poe articles. The opposition of
Delacroix's methods of composition to Balzac's, and "l'inspiration est la sœur du travail journalier," is interesting. But
only in the section "De la poésie" does one quite recognize
Baudelaire.

The "Salon de 1846" is the most interesting of all Baudelaire's early criticism; it marks a stride beyond the "Salon
de 1845" which is but faintly suggested by the intervening
articles. It is quite possible however that parts of the "Salon
de 1846" are contemporary with the "Salon" of the previous
year, on the cover of which "De la peinture moderne" is
announced as "sous presse." This is evidently what Baudelaire
is referring to when he writes to his mother in 1844: "je vais

en profiter pour travailler rudement à mon livre de peinture que *l'on attend* à la *Revue de Paris*" (*D.L.M.*, p. 24). The work never appeared. As M. Crépet observes, the structure of the "Salon de 1846" suggests "un compte rendu d'actualité introduit dans un traité didactique" (*C.E.*, p. 450), and it seems very likely that Baudelaire borrowed a number of pages from the probably unfinished essay for his "Salon." As we shall see, this method of using a previous work, either published or unpublished, is to become a common one with Baudelaire. To be sure, he says in a letter to his mother (*L.M.*, p. 27) that he has only a week in which to write his "Salon," but the careful and deeply thought-out judgments and theories make such a rapid composition almost impossible and lead one to conclude that the week must have been spent in dovetailing the pictures of the Salon onto the essay on modern painting.

The "Salon" begins, like the preceding one, with a hand outstretched to the bourgeois, even more emphatically and cordially than before. At the same time he teaches them a lesson: "il faut que vous soyez aptes à sentir la beauté; car comme aucun d'entre vous ne peut aujourd'hui se passer de puissance, nul n'a le droit de se passer de poésie" (II, 62). In short, Baudelaire is preaching the gospel of art to those to whom the artistocrats have denied it. One is oddly reminded, here and there, of the preface to *Mademoiselle de Maupin*; Baudelaire's "Vous pouvez vivre trois jours sans pain; — sans poésie, jamais" echoes Gautier's "je me passerais plus volontiers de bottes que de poëmes."

Critics, remembering Baudelaire's later fulminations against the bourgeois, have often discussed his sincerity here; was he for the moment convinced of what he wrote, or was he writing with his tongue in his cheek? My own tendency is to the former view. Baudelaire was young, enthusiastic, and filled with an apostolic zeal in the cause of art. Moreover, this is not an isolated instance; we have seen examples of the same attitude elsewhere. As a conviction, it would be worth repeating; as a joke, it would be wearing a little thin. Then too, this is the period when Baudelaire, following in Stendhal's footsteps, was condemning the old-fashioned antibourgeois romanticism. And, as we know, he delighted in startling his comrades by the expression of ideas very different from the current coin of their conversation. But there is more to it than that, I believe—a serious bourgeois liberalism,[40] which was to reach its zenith in 1848, and wane with great rapidity afterwards.

The "Salon" itself breaks away from the traditional form; it is composed of eighteen short chapters, the majority of them theoretical, interspersed with chapters on the pictures in the Salon. "A quoi bon la critique?"[41] Baudelaire asks as the title of his first chapter. After a few harsh words for the professional critic he states his own creed: "Je crois sincèrement que la meilleure critique est celle qui est amusante et poétique" (II, 64). As a beautiful picture is nature reflected by an artist, so criticism should be this picture reflected by an intelligent and sensitive mind.[42] This kind of criticism, however, is for poetic readers. As for criticism properly speaking, it should be partial, exclusive, but at the same time open up as many horizons as possible. The critic's point of view should be to "commander à l'artiste la naïveté et l'expression sincère de son tempérament, aidée par tous les moyens que lui fournit son métier" (II, 65). Here is Baudelaire's fundamental formula for the artist: originality plus technical perfection. This criterium once established, "le critique doit accomplir son devoir avec passion; car pour être critique on n'en est pas moins homme." And Baudelaire ends this first chapter by allying what he has just said to his definition of romanticism, which is to be the subject of the next chapter: "Chaque siècle, chaque peuple ayant possédé l'expression de sa beauté et de sa morale, — si l'on veut entendre par romantisme l'expression la plus récente et la plus moderne de la beauté, — le grand artiste sera donc, — pour le critique raisonnable et passionné, — celui qui unira à la condition demandée ci-dessus, la naïveté,—le plus de romantisme possible" (II, 65). This, Baudelaire's first thought on criticism, combines a remarkable breadth of vision with the ardor and assurance of the young man who is convinced that he has found *the* standard of measurement. Although he was later to say that all standards had proved too rigid for him, the one which he sets up here is worth dwelling on; it puts the burden of the standard on the artist, not requiring him to conform to an artificial external standard, but to express himself, and to attain the perfection of that expression by a command of all the tools of his trade.

The second chapter asks another question, "Qu'est-ce que le romantisme?" and answers "Pour moi, le romantisme est l'expression la plus récente, la plus actuelle du beau" (II, 66). The definition, as we shall see, owes much to Stendhal. As a matter of fact, this chapter on romanticism is in a sense isolated in Baudelaire's work. Many of the ideas in it will recur again and again, but the effort to attach them to *romantisme*, to put new life into the word, is confined to this "Salon." Elsewhere the word is generally used in an unfavorable sense; in the "Salon de 1845" we have "les dernières ruines de l'ancien romantisme" (II, 28). After 1846 the word has an historical meaning rather than an actual one, as in the "Salon de 1859": "Le romantisme est une grâce, céleste ou infernale, à qui nous devons des stigmates éternels" (II, 250). Baudelaire seems very soon to have found the old label unsatisfactory for his new ideas.

The next chapter, "De la couleur," shows admirable technical knowledge and understanding, combined with poetic vision. At the end he introduces for the first time, with a quotation from Hoffmann, the idea (though not the word) of *correspondances*, which was to become so dear to him. Finally he returns to the questions of color and line which he had touched on the previous year, concluding: "Les purs dessinateurs sont des philosophes et des abstracteurs de quintessence. Les coloristes sont des poëtes épiques" (II, 72).

Romanticism and color lead Baudelaire directly to Delacroix. Of the twenty pages devoted to him, only two refer explicitly to the pictures exhibited in the Salon of 1846; the rest seem to belong to the projected work on modern painting. Baudelaire sketches Delacroix's career, and then takes up the parallel frequently drawn between him and Victor Hugo, showing its inaccuracy. With Hugo "l'excentricité elle-même prend . . . des formes symétriques," whereas Delacroix's creative genius, his "grands poëmes naïvement conçus" (II, 76), opens up new roads to the imagination. After defending Delacroix against the charge that chance plays a large part in his painting, he remarks that he is "un des rares hommes qui restent originaux après avoir puisé à toutes les vraies sources, et dont l'individualité indomptable a passé alternativement sous le joug secoué de tous les grands maîtres" (II, 77)—a description which might well be applied to Baudelaire himself. He quotes a few lines from Heine on supernaturalism in art, and says that Delacroix's guiding principle is that a picture must above all reproduce the inward thought of the artist, which dominates the model, as the creator his creation, with always the greatest care in technique, that the hand may carry out the divine orders of the mind—otherwise the ideal escapes. For Delacroix, Baudelaire says, nature is a huge dictionary; his painting, based on memory, appeals to memory. Lastly, Baudelaire discusses Delacroix's drawing and speaks of his universality, resulting from the combination of erudition and *naïveté*. His work ranges from religious painting, such as the *Pietà*,[43] to such painting as the cupola of the Luxembourg, in which Baudelaire admires the technical difficulties surmounted, but even more the spirit of the painting.

At last he comes to the pictures of Delacroix exhibited in the Salon, noticing particularly the *Enlèvement de Rebecca* and the *Roméo et Juliette*. These pages have a rapid, notelike quality very different from the careful writing of what precedes and follows. Baudelaire emphasizes "cette mélancolie singulière et opiniâtre" which makes of Delacroix *the* painter of the nineteenth century and in this way attaches him to the ideal of the "peintre de la vie moderne." Delacroix's melancholy is admirably characterized: "Cette haute et sérieuse mélancolie brille d'un éclat morne, même dans sa couleur, large, simple, abondante en masses harmoniques, comme celle de tous les grands coloristes, mais plaintive et profonde comme une mélodie de Weber" (II, 85).

This chapter is followed by "Des sujets amoureux et de M. Tassaert," and "De quelques coloristes," in which Baudelaire, coming back to the Salon again, dwells on the color of the curious painter Catlin.[44] These chapters show a gain in power of characterization, of drawing delicate distinctions. The following chapter, "De l'idéal et du modèle," to which we shall have occasion to return later, is sharply opposed to the theory of imitation. Then "De quelques dessinateurs" applies the principle to the Salon, taking Ingres as an example of the combination of ideal and model in drawing, though he has not the imaginative or creative drawing of the colorists. But Baudelaire is severe on Ingres's pupils for their pedantry, their unthinking imitation. The chapter "Du portrait" draws an interesting distinction between the historical and the fictional conception of the portrait; the former that of David and Ingres, the latter that of Rembrandt, Reynolds, and Lawrence, in which the imagination plays a large part. "Du chic et du poncif" (*chic* the abuse of memory, *poncif* the conventional and traditional in expression and gesture) leads up to a virulent attack on Horace Vernet, "the antithesis of the artist." "De l'éclectisme et du doute" is another ward in what Baudelaire calls the hospital of painting. Eclecticism in art is fatal, for art demands a constant idealization which can only be obtained at the cost of sacrifice. The eclectic fails to realize that the first duty of the artist is to substitute man for nature. Doubt has led him to seek help from other arts; hence the importation of poetry into painting, held up to ridicule in "De M. Ary Scheffer et des singes du sentiment" and "De quelques douteurs." Baudelaire here draws a fine distinction as to the relation of poetry and painting: "[la poésie] est le résultat de la peinture elle-même; car elle gît dans l'âme du spectateur, et le génie consiste à l'y réveiller" (II, 116).

The chapter "Du paysage" distinguishes different types of landscape, damning the historical landscape as "la morale appliquée à la nature,"—like classic tragedy—and regretting the absence of Théodore Rousseau, "un naturaliste entraîné sans cesse vers l'idéal" (II, 125). Then "Pourquoi la sculpture est-elle ennuyeuse?" Because it is closer to nature than painting, and unlike painting cannot have the "point de vue exclusif." Furthermore, sculpture is but a complementary art. The next chapter, "Des écoles et des ouvriers," compares the past and the present in a curious antirepublican strain. "L'individualité — cette petite propriété, — a mangé l'originalité collective" (II, 138). The last chapter, "De l'héroïsme de la vie moderne," defines Baudelaire's conception of beauty:

Toutes les beautés contiennent, comme tous les phénomènes possibles, quelque chose d'éternel et quelque chose de transitoire, — d'absolu et de particulier. La beauté absolue et éternelle n'existe pas, ou plutôt elle n'est qu'une abstraction écrémée à la surface générale des beautés diverses. L'élément particulier de chaque beauté vient des passions, et comme nous avons nos passions particulières, nous avons notre beauté (II, 133).

And the "Salon" ends with a plea for the artist who will see and utilize the beauty of modern clothes, who will do in painting what Balzac has done in literature.[45]

Naïveté, one of Baudelaire's favorite words of the "Salon de 1845," recurs again in this "Salon" of 1846; in the earlier chapters it seems one of the most significant words. It appears in Baudelaire's criterium for the critic, and is defined in a later note: "Il faut entendre par la naïveté du génie la science du métier combinée avec le g n ô t i   s é a u t o n, mais la science modeste laissant le beau rôle au tempérament" (II, 745). And again, "la naïveté, qui est la domination du tempérament dans la manière" (II, 131). Here there seems to be a kind of forcing of a definition upon a word, an attempt to deviate it from its normal significance. It is perhaps because of his consciousness of this that Baudelaire, from now on, drops the use of the word in this particular sense, and uses it with its ordinarily accepted meaning. Perhaps too the relationship between *naïf* and *nature* may have created difficulties as Baudelaire came to attack the imitation of nature more and more violently.

The really significant word in the "Salon de 1846" is *idéal*. It is used again and again, especially in the chapter "De l'idéal et du modèle." Baudelaire affirms that "l'idéal absolu est une bêtise" (II, 98), that "chaque individu a donc son idéal" (II, 99), and then defines it: "un idéal, c'est l'individu redressé par l'individu, reconstruit et rendu par le pinceau ou le ciseau à l'éclatante vérité de son harmonie native" (II, 100) —a foreshadowing of the function of the imagination. But, as with *naïveté*, the word is used much less frequently after 1846, and when it does recur, as in the Wagner article, it has returned to a more limited and conventional meaning. Again Baudelaire seems to be struggling, still unsuccessfully, to find the word broad enough, flexible enough, to contain all that he wishes to express.

It was the "Salon de 1846" which established Baudelaire's reputation as a critic among his contemporaries. Prarond writes that it seemed "un catéchisme de la peinture moderne," and Banville: "Nul mieux que lui ne sut jamais renouveler la sensation créée par une peinture et exprimer avec des mots le sens idéal d'une composition plastique."[46] The "Salon" is extraordinarily good reading today; it is youthful, eager, vigorous. Underneath the spontaneous, spirited commentary and intermingled with it are a wealth of ideas, all logically related, which are applicable to the painting of all times. The "Salon de 1846" has not perhaps the depth, the unity of the "Salon de 1859," but it has a sparkling quality all its own, that of Baudelaire's thought in its springtime freshness and zest.

These first two "Salons" are the cornerstone of Baudelaire's criticism. Remembering the "transformation de la volupté en connaissance," one might say that the "Salon de 1845," with its description of picture after picture, gives us the vision which precedes the theory of the following year; the *volupté* of 1845 is transformed into the *connaissance* of 1846. Even if the two "Salons" are to a large degree contemporary in their composition, the order is symbolical; experience precedes theorizing.

Throughout the two "Salons" Baudelaire emphasizes the changing, variable nature of beauty, a beauty different for every age and for every individual, though always with its soupçon of eternal and unchanging beauty. So every artist must express his own particular beauty. And always there is the corollary that only by possessing the most complete mastery of his technique, whatever it be, can the artist succeed in expressing his particular beauty adequately. It is a conception that has been worked out through the study of painting, but will be valid for all the arts. Baudelaire has found a basis for his criticism which, however certain aspects of it may vary, however much it will be enriched, will at bottom remain the same. It is well worth noting that here, before the fructifying contact with Poe, Baudelaire has laid the foundations of his criticism.

Much in these first "Salons" represents Baudelaire's spontaneous and independent thought, the expression of his own temperament, the outgrowth of his own experience. But they also contain many borrowed elements, and the main sources, at least, of his ideas are fairly easily distinguishable. Baudelaire, in all his writings, borrowed freely, and from many sources, ideas which little by little are fused in the crucible of his imagination and become something which is entirely his own. One can say of him what Delacroix said of Raphael; "Son originalité ne paraît jamais plus vive que dans les idées qu'il emprunte. Tout ce qu'il trouve, il le relève et le fait vivre d'une vie nouvelle."[47] But in the first "Salons" it is relatively easy to distinguish many of the elements which went into the making of his critical thought. Here they are relatively isolated; later on the attempt to separate them becomes futile and incongruous.

Let us begin with the most important of all, Delacroix. We have already seen how complex this influence is, how impossible it is to determine with any precision through what particular channel Delacroix's ideas reached Baudelaire. Close verbal resemblances are rare; such a phrase as "une grande coquetterie musicale" may perhaps echo Delacroix's "une extrême coquetterie dans le choix de ses tons" (II, 20; Œuvres littéraires, II, 160), but the great parallels are in thought, not expression.

First, most important and most difficult—impossible indeed —to fix with any precision, is the direct influence of Delacroix's painting on Baudelaire. Chronologically it almost certainly precedes all the rest. Baudelaire's vision and immediate experience of Delacroix's painting come before his conversations with him, his knowledge of his ideas. It is Delacroix's painting first of all which colors Baudelaire's criticism, and sets the standard for his judgment of other painters.

When it comes to the question of the influence of Delacroix's ideas on Baudelaire, all we can do is to compare those ideas as they have reached us, chiefly through the *Journal*, and also through the correspondence and published articles, with Baudelaire's. It is interesting to recall that Delacroix is one of the examples that Baudelaire cites of the poet, the artist, who inevitably becomes a critic. Certainly if Baudelaire could have known Delacroix's journal, it would have reinforced his opinion. Here, interspersed with the record of daily happenings, lists of pictures, technical indications for the make-up of the painter's palette, are the most admirable and stimulating reflections on art, first of all the art of painting and then art as a whole. Rarely, it would seem, has painting been accompanied by such intense and constant mental activity. Delacroix once wrote in his journal: "Le secret de n'avoir pas d'ennuis, pour moi du moins, c'est d'avoir des idées" (July 14, 1850. *Journal,* I, 385). If the *Journal* is any test, boredom can have had little chance in Delacroix's life.

The *Journal* as we possess it begins with the years 1822-24; from that time until 1847 (except for the journal of his trip to Morocco in 1832) Delacroix, absorbed in his painting, kept no journal. But once he had returned to the practice, he kept it up until shortly before his death. In it we can trace the growth of his ideas, only half formed at first, aglow with the ardor and vehemence of youth, then enriched by the experience and practice of his art between 1824 and 1847, and finally in his latter years modified by an increasing classical bent, always perceptible in Delacroix, to be sure, but gaining strength with the years.[48] Besides the *Journal* the modern reader has not only the articles which Delacroix published, but also his correspondence. In his letters, however, he deals very largely with technical questions, and with the relation of the arts (especially painting and music) to one another. There is by no means the same outpouring of his intimate thought on all subjects that we find in the *Journal.* This is, indeed, hardly to be wondered at, for rarely or never, I think, are the diarist's and the letter-writer's gift at their highest united in one person. For some the thought of a friend seems to provoke an outpouring of thought and feeling, a flow of wit and wisdom, an activity of mind and heart such as the writer never knows before the page that is destined for no eyes but his own, save possibly those of posterity. For others the imagined reader is a hindrance and an obstacle, and they reveal themselves and the fullness of their thoughts only to the discreet pages of a diary. To this latter class Delacroix unquestionably belongs.

At the root of Delacroix's thought is the belief that beauty is not one but many, not stable but changing. The earliest of his published articles, "Des critiques en matière d'art," alludes ironically to "ce beau immuable qui change tous les vingt ou trente ans" (*Œuvres littéraires,* I, 6). Twenty years later he writes to Peisse: "Ce *fameux Beau*, que les uns voient dans la ligne serpentine, les autres dans la ligne droite, ils se sont tous obstinés à ne le jamais voir que dans les lignes. Je suis à ma fenêtre, et je vois le plus beau paysage; l'idée d'une ligne ne me vient pas à l'esprit: l'alouette chante, la rivière réfléchit mille diamants, le feuillage murmure; où sont les lignes qui produisent ces charmantes sensations?" (*Correspondance* de Delacroix, II, 388.) Baudelaire has the same thought in the "Salon de 1846": "Exalter la ligne au détriment de la couleur, ou la couleur au dépens de la ligne, sans doute c'est un point de vue; mais ce n'est ni très-large ni très-juste, et cela accuse une grande ignorance des destinées particulières" (II, 64-65).

With such a conception of beauty, it is natural that Delacroix's chief reproach to his contemporaries should be that of a narrow imitation. He says in the article "Sur le *Jugement dernier*": "L'imitation de l'antique, c'est-à-dire de ce qu'il y a de plus noble dans l'invention et de plus simple dans les détails, avait conduit à l'absence entière d'invention et à l'exécution la plus étroite" (*Œuvres littéraires*, II, 223). Anything borrowed, copied, is hateful to him. In the letter to Peisse already quoted he says: "Sans idéal, il n'y a ni peintre, ni dessin, ni couleur. Et ce qu'il y a de pis que d'en manquer, c'est d'avoir cet idéal d'emprunt que ces gens-là vont apprendre à l'école, et qui ferait prendre en haine les modèles" (*Correspondance* de Delacroix, II, 388-89). And the next year he flagellates "une imitation surannée des beautés de la bonne époque, ce qui est le dernier terme de l'insipidité" (*Journal*, I, 342). We have seen how in both the first "Salons" Baudelaire's great reproach to a painter is that his work recalls that of some other painter.

What Delacroix seeks first of all is originality, *naïveté*. "Une poignée d'*inspiration naïve* est préférable à tout," he writes on September 30, 1855 (*Journal*, II, 394). And on October 1 of the same year he reiterates: "le *beau* est partout, et . . . chaque homme non seulement le voit, mais doit absolument le rendre à sa manière" (*Journal*, II, 395). Hence the necessity for the artist of reproducing, not the model before him, but the ideal within him.

Il est donc beaucoup plus important pour l'artiste de se rapprocher de l'idéal qu'il porte en lui, et qui lui est particulier, que de laisser, même avec force, l'idéal passager que peut présenter la nature, et elle présente de telles parties; mais encore un coup, c'est un tel homme qui les y voit, et non pas le commun des hommes, preuve que c'est son imagination qui fait le beau, justement parce qu'il suit son génie (*Journal*, II, 87).

The close parallel with Baudelaire's thought is evident; the emphasis on originality, the conception of the artist's inner ideal, which Baudelaire states: "Delacroix part donc de ce principe, qu'un tableau doit avant tout reproduire la pensée intime de l'artiste, qui domine le modèle, comme le créateur la création" (II, 78). Delacroix put all this in a formula which evidently struck Baudelaire when he said: "Les formes du modèle, que ce soit un arbre ou un homme, ne sont que le dictionnaire où l'artiste va retremper ses impressions fugitives ou plutôt leur donner une sorte de confirmation, car il doit avoir de la mémoire" (*Œuvres littéraires*, I, 58). Baudelaire says in 1846: "Pour E. Delacroix la nature est un vaste dictionnaire dont il roule et consulte les feuillets avec un œil sûr et profond; et cette peinture, qui procède surtout du souvenir, parle surtout au souvenir" (II, 78). The last part of the sentence emphasizes another idea dear to Delacroix, the role of memory in painting, which Baudelaire will develop many years later in the "Peintre de la vie moderne." This is closely connected with Delacroix's conception of the imagination, a conception which, judging by the *Journal*, developed slowly, and was far from having reached its height when Baudelaire first knew him. Baudelaire's own theory of the imagination was likewise to develop slowly, culminating in the great hymn to the imagination of the "Salon de 1859."

With all his emphasis on originality, Delacroix is constantly insisting on another point; that originality is inevitably cramped unless it is accompanied by perfection of technique and execution: "La bonne ou plutôt la vraie exécution est celle qui, par la pratique, en apparence matérielle, ajoute à la pensée, sans laquelle la pensée n'est pas complète; ainsi sont les beaux vers" (*Journal*, III, 44). "Nous avons dit qu'une bonne exécution était de la plus grande importance. On irait jusqu'à dire que, si elle n'est pas tout, elle est le seul moyen qui mette le reste en lumière et qui lui donne sa valeur" (*Journal*, III, 55). This is, I think, one of the most definite lessons which Baudelaire learned from Delacroix. We have seen how it is emphasized in his criterium for the critic, in his definition of *naïveté*, and in many other places.

Many of the technical questions discussed by Baudelaire, particularly in the chapter "De la couleur," of the "Salon de 1846," are among those of particular interest to Delacroix. Both were interested in the relation of color and line; Baudelaire speaks for them both when he says: "Au point de vue de Delacroix, la ligne n'est pas; car, si ténue qu'elle soit, un géomètre taquin peut toujours la supposer assez épaisse pour en contenir mille autres; et pour les coloristes, qui veulent imiter les palpitations éternelles de la nature, les lignes ne sont jamais, comme dans l'arc-en-ciel, que la fusion intime de deux couleurs" (II, 79).[49]

The chapter "De la couleur" also echoes some of the ideas which made Delacroix the forerunner of the Impressionists. He writes of the effect of the atmosphere:

Quand nous jetons les yeux sur les objets qui nous entourent, que ce soit un paysage ou un intérieur, nous remarquons entre les objets qui s'offrent à nos regards une sorte de liaison produite par l'atmosphère qui les enveloppe et par les reflets de toutes sortes qui font en quelque sorte participer chaque objet à une sorte d'harmonie générale (*Journal*, III, 41).

And Baudelaire in his turn:

Les affinités chimiques sont la raison pour laquelle la nature ne peut pas commettre de fautes dans l'arrangement de ses tons; car, pour elle, forme et couleur sont un.
Le vrai coloriste ne peut pas en commettre non plus; et tout lui

est permis, parce qu'il connaît de naissance la gamme des tons, la force du ton, les résultats des mélanges, et toute la science du contrepoint, et qu'il peut ainsi faire une harmonie de vingt rouges différents (II, 70).

Indeed most of Baudelaire's technical comment, what he says of reflections, of the use of touches, of the chemistry of colors, seems to proceed directly from Delacroix.

It is tempting to pile up the parallels; they are very numerous, but I have, I think, cited enough to show how large a part Delacroix's ideas played in the formation of Baudelaire's thought. Baudelaire's enthusiasm for Delacroix's work, his admiration for the artist himself and the readiness with which he accepted his ideas, combine to make this influence all-pervasive. It is a question not so much of finding precise parallels—although, as we have seen, these exist—as of realizing that Baudelaire's whole approach to art is colored by his preoccupation with the painting and the thought of Delacroix. It is an influence that continues throughout Baudelaire's work, shaped and modified by other influences and most of all by Baudelaire's own thought, but still keeping the place of honor. Delacroix remains a background for all Baudelaire's future work, like the background of one of his own pictures hardly noticeable at first, but on careful examination rich in color and significance.[50]

However, these first "Salons" show the trace of other influences, less pervasive, less durable, but at some points more direct and more precise. The most important of these seem to me to be those of Diderot and Stendhal. But it should be noted from the start that at many points it is difficult, impossible indeed, to disentangle these from one another and from that of Delacroix. The opinions of the three, dissimilar in some respects, agree in others. Moreover, Stendhal was a reader and admirer of Diderot, as was Delacroix of both Diderot and Stendhal, so that there is a whole cross-play of influences at work. Hence it is often impossible to decide whether Baudelaire borrowed certain ideas from one or the other, or from all of them. But in some cases the verbal resemblances are so strong as to leave no doubt; in others Baudelaire is definitely siding with one of the three against another, as when with Delacroix he defends allegory against Diderot, or with Stendhal, in opposition to Delacroix, glorifies the artistic possibilities of the modern world.

Certain likenesses between Diderot and Stendhal and Baudelaire struck contemporary readers of the "Salons." Champfleury, reviewing the "Salon de 1845," said: "M. Baudelaire-Dufays est hardi comme Diderot, moins le paradoxe; il a beaucoup d'allures, de ressemblances avec Stendhal, qui [sont] les deux hommes qui ont le mieux écrit: peinture" (*Corsaire-Satan*, May 27, 1845). And Auguste Vitu: "Il possède les allures franches, naïves, la bonhomie cruelle de Diderot, dont il a certainment étudié l'œuvre critique" (*La Silhouette*, July 20, 1845).

In the "Salon de 1845" the influence of Diderot shows itself most clearly, I think, in a tone which Baudelaire sometimes adopts; a more familiar, easy, half-smiling tone than that of the "Salon" in general.[51] Often when Baudelaire dislikes a picture he disposes of it in a fashion which he certainly learned from Diderot. One has only to compare such sentences as these of Baudelaire: "M. Decamps a fait du Raphaël et du Poussin. — Eh! mon Dieu! — oui"; "Tous leurs tableaux sont très-bien faits, très-bien peints, et très-monotones comme manière et choix de sujets"; "Jacquand fabrique toujours du Delaroche, vingtième qualité" (II, 24, 40, 43); with these of Diderot: "O mon ami, la mauvaise chose!"; "Le reste, c'est de la couleur, de la toile, et du temps perdu"; "Si vous êtes curieux de visages de plâtre, il faut regarder les portraits de Drouais."[52]

The conclusions of the "Salon de 1845" and of Diderot's "Salon de 1759" are strikingly alike:[53]

Constatons que tout le monde peint de mieux en mieux, ce qui nous

paraît désolant; — mais d'invention, d'idées, de tempérament, pas
davantage qu'avant (II, 54).

Nous avons beaucoup d'artistes, peu de bons, pas un excellent, ils
choissent de beaux sujets, mais la force leur manque. Ils n'ont ni
esprit, ni élévation, ni chaleur, ni imagination. Presque tous pèchent
par le coloris. Beaucoup de dessein, point d'idée (Diderot, X, 103).

In other cases there are decided likenesses of thought, though,
as I have suggested, it is often difficult to disentangle Diderot's
influence from that of Stendhal or Delacroix. But in the
"Salon de 1845" Baudelaire comes very close to Diderot's sub-
ordination of technique to idea. Compare for example:
"Réfléchir devant ce tableau combien une peinture excessivement savante et brillante de couleur peut rester froide quand
elle manque d'un tempérament particulier" (II, 39); and
"Il y a entre le mérite du faire et le mérite de l'idéal, la
différence de ce qui attache les yeux, et de ce qui attache
l'âme" (Diderot, XI, 238).

The influence of Diderot is, I think, at its height in the
"Salon de 1845." Baudelaire, having evidently read and pon-
dered Diderot, frequently echoes his method and tone, and is
close to many of his ideas. In the "Salon de 1846" his influence
is, except in one chapter, secondary. There are still occasional
flings in his manner, such as: "M. Lehmann ne fait plus que
des yeux trop grands, où la prunelle nage comme une huître
dans une soupière" (II, 104), which is quite in the key of:
"Monsieur Fragonard, cela est diablement fade. Belle omelette,
bien douillette, bien jaune et bien brûlée" (Diderot, XI, 296).

But the most precise example of the way in which Baudelaire's reading of Diderot had stuck in his mind occurs
where we should hardly expect to find it; in the chapter "De
la couleur," which owes so much to Delacroix. The chapter
begins with a passage which can hardly fail to strike the
reader as somewhat different in flavor from the rest.[54] The general idea and movement of this passage seem to me certainly
based on a passage in the "Pensées détachées sur la peinture"

(Diderot, XII, 111), which is a briefer variant of a passage in the "Salon de 1765" (Diderot, X, 365), in which Diderot describes the changing aspect of the landscape as the sun moves on its course through the day. The passages are too long to quote in full; I shall only indicate the portions in which the resemblance seems closest. The general movement of the two passages may be indicated by two sentences:

A mesure que l'astre du jour se dérange, les tons changent de valeur, mais, respectant toujours leurs sympathies et leurs haines naturelles, continuent à vivre en harmonie par des concessions réciproques (II, 68).

Cependant l'astre du jour a paru, et tout a changé par une multitude innombrable et subite de prêts et d'emprunts (Diderot, XII, 111).

In addition to the general idea of the passage, the very eighteenth-century expression, "l'astre du jour," also suggests a connection. I have the impression that Baudelaire had read the passage and been struck by it, and is here recalling it, perhaps unconsciously, with much that he had recently learned from Delacroix superimposed upon it. The tone is elevated and poetized, retouched with a brush dipped in Delacroix's colors.

The whole chapter contains echoes of Diderot, especially the "Essai sur la peinture" and the "Pensées détachées." I shall quote only one of the more striking parallels:

Le bleu, c'est-à-dire le ciel, est coupé de légers flocons blancs ou de masses grises qui trempent heureusement sa morne crudité, — et, comme la vapeur de la saison, — hiver ou été, baigne, adoucit, ou engloutit les contours, la nature ressemble à un toton qui, mû par une vitesse accélérée, nous apparaît gris bien qu'il résume en lui toutes les couleurs (II, 68).

Le ciel répand une teinte générale sur les objets. La vapeur de l'atmosphère se discerne au loin; près de nous son effet est moins sensible; autour de moi les objets gardent toute la force et toute la variété de leurs couleurs; ils se ressentent moins de la teinte de l'atmosphère et du ciel; au loin, ils s'effacent, ils s'éteignent; toutes

leurs couleurs se confondent; et la distance qui produit cette confusion, cette monotonie, les montre tout gris, grisâtres, d'un blanc
mat plus ou moins éclairé, selon le lieu de la lumière et l'effet du
soleil; c'est le même effet que celui de la vitesse avec laquelle on
tourne un globe tacheté de différentes couleurs, lorsque cette vitesse
est assez grande pour lier les taches et réduire leurs sensations particulières de rouge, de blanc, de noir, de bleu, de vert, à une sensation unique et simultanée (Diderot, X, 475-76).

The form of this chapter also, much more broken up and less
consecutive than is usual with Baudelaire, recalls that of the
"Pensées détachées sur la peinture." The influence, even when
Delacroix has been given the lion's share, seems to me unquestionable, and it is surprising and interesting to find it persist-
ing in this particular chapter.

The influence of Diderot seems more marked in these first
two "Salons" than anywhere else. It is an influence which
seems to me essentially suggestive; one has the impression
that Diderot has put into Baudelaire's mind a number of
ideas which he does not borrow directly nor accept entirely,
but works over in his own mind, where they meet other
ideas, and are modified by them, and are developed and
colored by Baudelaire's own originality. Baudelaire's chief
debt to Diderot is evident less in specific passages and ideas
than in the tone of his "Salons," and more than that in his
whole critical attitude, with its forthrightness, its frankness,
its exasperations and its enthusiasms. Baudelaire is more
peremptory, more categorical, more consistent in his critical
judgments than Diderot, but he is indisputably of his company.

If we compare these "Salons" of Baudelaire's with Diderot's,
we find that a "Salon" of Diderot gives us above all a sense
of intimacy with the writer, of a leisurely stroll through the
Salon in the most delightful of company. Diderot is lively,
quick-witted, good-natured, completely at his ease; he never
forgets his companion, and keeps up a stream of descriptions,
impressions, digressions, comments, and anecdotes that make
boredom impossible. He lingers longest before the pictures

which move his admiration and sympathy, thinking aloud to
us, and we understand why Sainte-Beuve calls him "le créateur
de la critique émue, empressée et éloquente,"[55] and the pre-
cursor of "la critique féconde des beautés." He describes the
pictures, often in such detail that they seem as clear to us as
to him, but the picture is above all a "prétexte à la rêverie."
"Diderot est le roi et le dieu de ces demi-poëtes qui deviennent et paraissent tout entiers poëtes dans la critique: ils n'ont
besoin pour cela que d'un point d'appui extérieur et d'une
excitation."[56] But we often pause too before less favored pictures, as Diderot exclaims "O mon ami, la mauvaise chose!"
and proceeds in swift impatience to point out to the artist
how he should have imagined and painted his picture. It is an
exasperation which vents itself in ridicule rather than in
scorn, and the scolding has a note of laughter. For Diderot,
in painting as in literature, the idea, the conception is what
matters, and technique is relatively unimportant. Indeed
Diderot, especially in his early "Salons," is weak on the technical side; later on he seems to have profited by the advice
he gives: "Voulez-vous faire des progrès dans la connaissance
si difficile du technique de l'art? Promenez-vous dans une
galerie avec un artiste, et faites-vous expliquer et montrer
sur la toile l'exemple des mots techniques" (Diderot, XII,
113). Diderot is, in short, a delightful companion, wise and
witty, sometimes overenthusiastic, never, I think, overharsh;
the ideal companion for a leisurely stroll through any gallery.
He himself has perhaps best described what we find in him:
"Pour décrire un Salon à mon gré et au vôtre, savez-vous,
mon ami, ce qu'il faudrait avoir? Toutes les sortes de goût,
un cœur sensible à tous les charmes, une âme susceptible d'une
infinité d'enthousiasmes différents, une variété de style qui
répondît à la variété des pinceaux" (Diderot, X, 160).

Baudelaire, in his first "Salons," is a less easy-going and
comfortable companion, much younger than Diderot (Diderot's first "Salon" was written when he was forty-six,
Baudelaire's when he was just twenty-four). He has the

sureness, the uncompromisingness, the impatience of youth. He is more self-conscious and tense, less at his ease. With him one sees the pictures in less detail, but with him, as with no one else, one is intensely aware of the impression made by the picture and the means by which that impression is created. And, even in 1845, where there is so little theorizing, the comments on individual painters and pictures leave us with a clear sense of the principles underlying Baudelaire's judgment. He rarely pauses for long except before the pictures for which he cares. There he displays his eager appreciation, his subtle sensitiveness to beauty in all its variations, his almost uncanny rightness of judgment. But there is little lingering over the mediocre; a trenchant comment, a peremptory gesture, and we are hurried on to the next picture. Sometimes he grows a little bored, his comments become a bit vague and repetitious, but the sight of a picture which he admires rouses him to fresh enthusiasm. His knowledge of the technique of painting is sure and competent, and he has a sense of its importance. His views have an underlying unity, which becomes evident when, in the "Salon de 1846" he breaks away from the conventional pattern. He is more passionate, more defiant, more completely coherent than Diderot, a more exciting and stimulating, if a less easy and comfortable, companion.

The influence of Stendhal on Baudelaire is more definite, more clearly marked. It can be pinned down to chapter and verse, in certain cases indeed to verbal resemblances so close that they must be qualified as plagiarism. The influence, as in the case of Diderot, is most marked in the early "Salons," but certain ideas suggested by Stendhal are of primary importance all through Baudelaire's criticism.

Reminiscences of Stendhal appear in practically all the articles that Baudelaire published in 1845 and 1846, in the two "Salons" and also in the "Maximes consolantes sur l'amour" and the "Conseils aux jeunes littérateurs."[57] I have already quoted Champfleury's indication of the parallel in his review of the "Salon de 1845." Many years later Champfleury asserted, not without a touch of malice, that Baudelaire at one time destroyed all the copies of the "Salon" he could lay his hands on, "sans doute par crainte de certains rapports d'idées avec Heine et Stendhal."[58] Without going so far as Champfleury, a reader of the "Salon" can hardly fail to be aware that Baudelaire had read his Stendhal to advantage.

There is first of all the constant emphasis on originality. Here, however, we have to reckon with the influence of Delacroix as well as that of Stendhal.[59] Then, in the conclusion of the "Salon," Baudelaire glorifies the heroism of modern life, and expresses for the first time his often to be repeated wish for the coming of a painter who should be aware of its epic quality, discern the poetry in cravats and well-polished boots. Here Baudelaire is diverging sharply from Delacroix, and following Stendhal's call for painters of the *beau moderne*.[60] The idea is only touched on here; it will be developed in the "Salon de 1846." But even in 1845 the emphasis on originality and the plea for the *beau moderne* are conspicuous. Except for this last, it is not so much the ideas of Stendhal as his attitude, his tone (quite different from that of Diderot), that we find in 1845; a decisive, authoritative, uncompromising tone, utterly independent, ready to startle and shock, and not without a flavor of impertinence. One need only compare such brief incisive sentences as: "Tout ce qui plaît a une raison de plaire" (II, 16) and "Que dans ce qui plaît nous ne pouvons estimer que ce qui nous plaît" (*Histoire de la peinture en Italie*, I, 258).

But it is in the "Salon de 1846" that Stendhal's influence is most conspicuous. The "Salon" owes much to Delacroix, something to Diderot, as well as other minor debts; yet the most tangible influence is that of Stendhal. The key word of the "Salon," as we have seen, is *idéal*, so dear to Stendhal. And the construction of the "Salon," with its short chapters and brief, often audacious titles, also suggests Stendhal, as does

the general tone—categorical, incisive, shaded with impertinence.
The parallels with Stendhal are particularly numerous and close in the second, seventh, and eighteenth chapters. Chapter II, "Qu'est-ce que le romantisme?" has as its fundamental idea that of *Racine et Shakespeare* (Chapter III, "Ce que c'est que le romanticisme"), which Stendhal had prefigured in the *Histoire de la peinture en Italie*, the work of his which Baudelaire seems to know best. This chapter is indebted chiefly to three books of the *Histoire*, (Book IV, "Du beau idéal antique," Book V, "Suite du beau antique," and Book VI, "Du beau idéal moderne"), in which Stendhal develops his conception of the beauty which varies with climate, with country, with government and with epoch, and which should be analogous to the character of the times. Baudelaire, after quoting Stendhal, "il y a autant de beautés qu'il y a de manières habituelles de chercher le bonheur," continues:

La philosophie du progrès explique ceci clairement; ainsi, comme il y a eu autant d'idéals qu'il y a eu pour les peuples de façons de comprendre la morale, l'amour, la religion, etc., le romantisme ne consistera pas dans une exécution parfaite, mais dans une conception analogue à la morale du siècle. . . . Il faut donc, avant tout, connaître les aspects de la nature et les situations de l'homme, que les artistes du passé ont dédaignés ou n'ont pas connus (II, 66).

This summarizes Stendhal's point of view, as expressed in various passages, such as: "Ou prononcez que la beauté n'a rien de commun avec l'imitation de la nature, ou convenez que, puisque la nature a changé, entre le beau antique et le beau moderne il doit y avoir une différence" (*Histoire de la peinture en Italie*, II, 104). Baudelaire's relating of color to romanticism is his own, but the opposition of the "Nord coloriste" to the "Midi naturaliste" recalls Stendhal's theory of the influence of climate.[61]
The final chapter of the "Salon de 1846," "De l'héroïsme de la vie moderne," is likewise indebted to Stendhal, particu-

larly in its earlier part. One of its paragraphs is a summary of Stendhal's ideas on the *beau antique*:

Qu'était-ce que cette grande tradition, si ce n'est l'idéalisation ordinaire et accoutumée de la vie ancienne; vie robuste et guerrière, état de défensive de chaque individu qui lui donnait l'habitude des mouvements sérieux, des attitudes majestueuses ou violentes. Ajoutez à cela la pompe publique qui se réfléchissait dans la vie privée. La vie ancienne *représentait* beaucoup; elle était faite surtout pour le plaisir des yeux, et ce paganisme journalier a merveilleusement servi les arts (II, 133; cf. *Histoire de la peinture en Italie*, II, 105-9 and *passim*).

There follows a definition of beauty; the last sentence— "L'élément particulier de chaque beauté vient des passions, et, comme nous avons nos passions particulières, nous avons notre beauté"—echoes Stendhal's "Que la beauté antique est incompatible avec les passions modernes" (Chapter CXV). A large part of the chapter treats of one of Baudelaire's favorite aspects of the *beau moderne*, modern clothes, on which Stendhal only touches. But the fundamental thought of the chapter is Stendhal's.

It is, however, in the chapter "De l'idéal et du modèle" that Baudelaire's borrowings are most direct; the incorrigible plagiarist Stendhal is tarred with his own brush. At the beginning of the chapter Baudelaire discusses color and line, and remarks that "le dessin du grand dessinateur doit résumer l'idéal et le modèle" (II, 98), which recalls Stendhal's "les grands artistes en faisant un dessin peu chargé font presque de l'idéal" (*Histoire de la peinture en Italie*, II, 97). Baudelaire then touches on an idea which he has already developed in connection with Delacroix, the relation of memory to art; "l'imitation exacte gâte le souvenir," he says, with an echo of Stendhal's "une telle imitation eût gâté le souvenir touchant qu'Adrien gardait de son ami." From here on he borrows shamelessly from some ten pages of Stendhal (*Histoire de la peinture en Italie*, II, 88-98). He says "Il y a de ces misérables peintres, pour qui la moindre verrue est une bonne fortune"; Stendhal had written "la moindre verrue est saisie comme une bonne fortune." Baudelaire's next paragraph, beginning "Trop particulariser ou trop généraliser empêchent également le souvenir; à l'Apollon du Belvédère et au Gladiateur je préfère l'Antinoüs, car l'Antinoüs est l'idéal du charmant Antinoüs," summarizes Stendhal's chapter "Du style dans le portrait," which compares the Apollo and the Antinous.[62] Two pages later Baudelaire's imitation becomes flagrant plagiarism:

> La première qualité d'un dessinateur est donc l'étude lente et sincère de son modèle. Il faut non-seulement que l'artiste ait une intuition profonde du caractère du modèle, mais encore qu'il le généralise quelque peu, qu'il exagère volontairement quelques détails pour augmenter la physionomie et rendre son expression plus claire.
> Il est curieux de remarquer que, guidé par ce principe, — que le sublime doit fuir les détails, — l'art pour se perfectionner revient vers son enfance. — Les premiers artistes aussi n'exprimaient pas les détails. Toute la différence, c'est qu'en faisant tout d'une venue les bras et les jambes de leurs figures, ce n'étaient pas eux qui fuyaient les détails, mais les détails qui les fuyaient; car pour choisir il faut posséder (II, 100).

L'artiste sublime doit fuir les détails; mais voilà l'art qui, pour se perfectionner, revient à son enfance. Les premiers sculpteurs aussi n'exprimaient pas les détails. Toute la différence c'est qu'en faisant *tout d'une venue* les bras et les jambes de leurs figures, ce n'étaient pas eux qui fuyaient les détails, c'étaient les détails qui les fuyaient. — Remarquez que pour choisir il faut posséder; l'auteur d'*Antinoüs* a developpé davantage les détails qu'il a gardés. Il a surtout augmenté leur physionomie, et rendu leur expression plus claire (*Histoire de la peinture en Italie*, II, 94-95).

Part of one sentence changes place; otherwise, except for the slightest of verbal changes, Baudelaire is simply copying Stendhal. The chapter ends with a direct quotation from Stendhal, introduced in this way: "Tout ce que je pourrais dire de plus sur les idéals me paraît inclus dans un chapitre de Stendhal, dont le titre est aussi clair qu'insolent" (II, 100).

This is the chapter "Comment l'emporter sur Raphaël?" which Baudelaire quotes in full.

It is difficult to judge how conscious Baudelaire's plagiarism was. Did he deliberately copy Stendhal's page, using the direct quotation at the end as a red herring? Or had he copied the page earlier and finding it among his notes used it without remembering that it was Stendhal's? Or had the page stamped itself upon his memory with such accuracy that he could reproduce it with only the slightest of verbal changes? The answer is perhaps to be found in Baudelaire's description of Samuel Cramer:

Un des travers les plus naturels de Samuel était de se considérer comme l'égal de ceux qu'il avait su admirer; après une lecture passionnée d'un beau livre, sa conclusion involontaire était: voilà qui est assez beau pour être de moi! — et de là à penser: c'est donc de moi, — il n'y a que l'espace d'un tiret (I, 528).

Baudelaire's debt to Stendhal in these early critical works is very great, reaching the point of plagiarism in the "Salon de 1846," as I have just shown. The general tone, the structure, the ideas on beauty, on romanticism and on the ideal, and on other less important points show how greatly Baudelaire was interested by Stendhal at this time. On the other hand he seems untouched by Stendhal's political and religious prejudices, and the utilitarian conception of art, its approximation to the *chasse au bonheur*, seem thoroughly alien to him. He has far more technical knowledge than Stendhal, he also sees as Stendhal never did. He is a much surer and more catholic critic, with almost impeccable taste and judgment, and his ideas have an informing poetic quality which Stendhal lacks. His "Salons" correspond to Stendhal's definition: "Les bons livres sur les arts ne sont pas les recueils d'arrêts à la La Harpe; mais ceux qui, jetant la lumière sur les profondeurs du cœur humain, mettent à ma portée des beautés que mon âme est faite pour sentir, mais qui, faute d'instruction, ne pouvaient traverser mon esprit" (*Histoire de la peinture en Italie*, I, 264-65). A sentence of the "Salon de 1846" seems to indicate admirably both what Baudelaire owed to Stendhal and what he added to him: "Qui dit romantisme dit art moderne, — c'est-à-dire intimité, spiritualité, couleur, aspiration vers l'infini, exprimées par tous les moyens que contiennent les arts" (II, 66-67). The assimilation of romanticism to modernity is Stendhal's; the definition of its qualities is Baudelaire's own.

It seems to me that Delacroix, Diderot, and Stendhal deserve the first place among those from whom Baudelaire exacted a contribution, large or small, to his own thought. But the list does not stop there. The frequent recurrence of Balzac's name in the writings of these early years suggests what seems certain, that Baudelaire had been reading Balzac with extraordinary interest.[63] I have already mentioned the possibility of some of Delacroix's ideas reaching Baudelaire through the *Chef-d'œuvre inconnu*. And in connection with Balzac one may note in these first *Salons* the earliest indications of the theory of correspondences, which is to become so important later. We have seen how in the "Salon de 1845" Delacroix's painting is described in musical terms (II, 20), how in 1846 Baudelaire state that "on trouve dans la couleur l'harmonie, la mélodie et le contrepoint" (II, 69). In the same chapter comes the passage so often referred to on the "gamme complète des couleurs et des sentiments," with its quotation from Hoffmann. In these first "Salons" Baudelaire is thinking chiefly of the correspondences between the various senses; the larger conception of correspondences between the natural and the spiritual, the visible and the invisible, has not yet been developed. Here we have the correspondences (although the word does not yet appear) between sound and perfume of Hoffmann, the correspondences between color and music that Balzac describes in *Massimilla Doni*: "Avec quel art ce grand peintre a su employer toutes les couleurs brunes de la musique et tout ce qu'il y a de tristesse sur la palette musicale."[64] The whole passage is of interest for the development of Baudelaire's interest in the idea of correspondences.[65] And other of Balzac's works, such as *Louis Lambert* and *Séraphita*, may well have guided Baudelaire to the interest in Swedenborg from which his larger theory of correspondences was to develop.[66]

One regrets that Baudelaire's enthusiasm for Balzac is expressed only in passing references; the apostrophe at the end of the "Salon de 1846," "et vous, ô Honoré de Balzac, vous le plus héroïque, le plus singulier, le plus romantique et le plus poétique parmi tous les personnages que vous avez tirés de votre sein!" (II, 136); the tribute in the article on *Madame Bovary* to "ce prodigieux météore qui couvrira notre pays d'un nuage de gloire, comme une aurore polaire inondant le désert glacé de ses lumières féeriques" (II, 442); and the admirable page in the Gautier article, developing the idea that "son principal mérite était d'être visionnaire, et vision-naire passionné" (II, 473). An article devoted to Balzac is among the first of the articles one would like Baudelaire to have written.

In connection with the idea of correspondences one may note too Baudelaire's interest in Lavater (so often mentioned by Stendhal), to whom he refers frequently, and, also, in a lesser degree, his interest in Gall.[67] Lavater's ideas contributed, as Baudelaire notes much later, to the whole complex system of correspondences and analogies: "Lavater, limitant au visage de l'homme la démonstration de l'universelle vérité, nous avait traduit le sens spirituel du contour, de la forme, de la dimen-sion" (II, 521).

On the other hand, Champfleury's malicious thrust about Baudelaire's fearing a comparison with Heine seems to me quite unfounded.[68] Baudelaire certainly knew Heine's "Salon de 1831"; he quotes from it in 1846. But it is far from fore-shadowing Baudelaire's "Salons"; the most that can be said is that Heine's method of passing from individual pictures to general reflections may have encouraged Baudelaire, not indeed in 1845, but in 1846, to substitute a freer and broader method for that of the traditional "Salon." But Heine's political preoccupations, his lack of any technical knowledge of painting, his lengthy criticisms of pictures he dislikes, are all alien to Baudelaire. One notes however the frequency in Heine of such phrases as: "C'est un tableau tout harmonieux, et dans la musique des couleurs règne l'unité la plus consolante" ("Salon de 1831," p. 295). And some of Heine's remarks on criticism must certainly have appealed to Baudelaire: "Chaque artiste original, chaque génie nouveau doit être jugé d'après l'esthétique qui lui est propre et qui se produit en même temps que son œuvre" (ibid., p. 306). But other sources are numerous, and closer, and had it not been for Champfleury's suggestion the relationship would hardly be worth discussing.

It is scarcely profitable to attempt to show in greater detail how these first "Salons" are filled with ideas, phrases, picked up here, there, and everywhere. I have tried to indicate the main strands with which Baudelaire weaves his pattern, picking, choosing, modifying, rejecting, and achieving something that is quite his own. One can truly say of him, as of his Samuel Cramer: "Il était à la fois tous les artistes qu'il avait étudiés et tous les livres qu'il avait lus, et cependant, en dépit de cette faculté comédienne, restait profondément original" (I, 529).

Chapter Two

THE SHADOW OF POE AND DE MAISTRE

De Maistre et Edgar Poe m'ont appris à raisonner.—
Mon Cœur mis à nu.

THE YEARS which immediately follow the publication of
the first "Salons" are both somewhat puzzling and
extraordinarily interesting in the development of Baudelaire's
critical thought. They are lean years indeed so far as published
criticism goes. There are, to our knowledge, no articles in
1847, two very brief ones in 1848 and none in 1849 or 1850.[1]
Then in 1851 the articles begin again, and we shall have the
series of articles on Poe, the "Exposition de 1855," the caricature articles and the Gautier article of 1859, to mention only
the most important. The reasons for this varying tempo are
not, I think, hard to find. Between 1846 and 1851 Baudelaire
was leading a more active life than at most other periods; he
was interested in politics and in journalism, and pure literature seems to go by the board for the moment. This too is the
period of Baudelaire's discovery of Poe and the first long
hours spent on the translation. But soon the coup d'état and
Poe's influence combine to send Baudelaire back to literature,
and after 1851 there is a period of great literary activity; a
large and varied output of critical articles, the translation and
publication of two volumes of Poe, and the composition and
revision of many of the *Fleurs du Mal*, which appeared in
volume form in 1857. In connection with his poetry a whole
group of ideas develop which are practiced first of all in the

poetry, and then bring their contribution to his critical theory—the ideas that constitute the doctrine of correspondences.

As I have already suggested, this doctrine, with all that it implies, is of primary importance for all of Baudelaire's work, poetry and criticism alike. Its formation and significance have been studied carefully and often,[2] and it has become increasingly plain that once the seed of the idea was planted in Baudelaire's mind, it was constantly enriched by new aspects, new allusions, found in his reading and incorporated into his own thought. We shall see how the idea recurs in connection with the names of Hoffmann, Swedenborg, Lavater, Fourier, Balzac, De Quincey, and still others.[3] The more one reads in the period, the more passages one comes across that Baudelaire may well have read and that may have reinforced his thinking along these lines. Certainly the idea was well rooted in his mind before *Aurélia* appeared in 1855, yet he can hardly have failed to be impressed by the great passage: "Tout vit, tout agit, tout se correspond; les rayons magnétiques émanés de moi-même ou des autres traversent sans obstacle la chaîne infinie des choses créées; c'est un réseau transparent qui couvre le monde, et dont les fils déliés se communiquent de proche en proche aux planètes et aux étoiles."[4] Except in the few cases where Baudelaire himself attaches the ideas to some name, it seems impossible to ascribe the passages concerning correspondences to some one definite source. More than any other idea—perhaps chiefly because of its close connection with the poetry—the conception of correspondences seems to have been digested and absorbed before it comes to play an important part in the criticism. Even when there is a specific connection with some name, one often feels that a previous interest in the idea had drawn Baudelaire's attention to a particular passage. But, as we shall see in the course of this chapter, the criticism from this time on is colored by the idea of correspondences, those between the various senses to some extent, but far more those between the natural and the spiritual, the visible and the invisible worlds.

There is abundant evidence that during this period Baudelaire was again reading widely. His correspondence mentions a few of his enthusiasms, Wronski again, Laclos, Barbey d'Aurevilly (*Corr.* I, 80, 143, 107). And for the latter part of the period, as in the following one, we have a document of great interest for Baudelaire's preoccupations, his reading, and the like; the so-called *Journaux intimes* (which are note-books rather than journals), made up of two parts, "Fusées" and "Mon Cœur mis à nu."[5] It seems impossible to date these with any exactness, but it is probable that "Fusées" was begun in the early fifties, "Mon Cœur mis à nu" in the late fifties, and that both represent the notes of a series of years and overlap to some extent.[6] "Fusées," it appears from the alternative title of "Fusées-Suggestions," was to be a "choix de pensées" on the order of Poe's "Fifty Suggestions" and "A Chapter of Suggestions." As for "Mon Cœur mis à nu," Baudelaire, writing to his mother on April 1, 1861, mentions "un grand livre auquel je rêve depuis deux ans: *Mon Cœur mis à nu,* et où j'entasserai toutes mes colères. Ah! si jamais celui-là voit le jour, les *Confessions de J.-J.* paraîtront pâles" (*L.M.*, p. 220). The letters of the following years mention the project frequently. But as they stand, both "Fusées" and "Mon Cœur mis à nu" are collections of notes on reading, jottings of ideas, personal memoranda, all mixed up together.

Both are of interest to the student of Baudelaire in many ways; perhaps most of all for the insight they give into Baudelaire's way of working, the fashion in which a thought jotted down in "Fusées" or "Mon Cœur mis à nu" reappears, most often in one of the critical articles, sometimes in a poem. A large number of these can be traced to their sources, though in very few cases does Baudelaire seem to have copied passages from the books he has been reading.[7] Most of them seem to have gone through a preliminary dipping, as it were, in his own mind, and plain as their origin is, they have begun to be

Baudelaire's own. And when they appear again, sometimes many years later, the process will have been completed, the idea will have become *sui generis*.

As for precise indications of what Baudelaire was reading, we have mentioned by name in "Fusées" Swedenborg, Chateaubriand, Hugo, Banville, Alphonse Rabbe, Brierre de Boismont, Poe; in "Mon Cœur mis à nu" Chateaubriand and Poe again, Emerson, De Maistre, George Sand, Gautier, as well as many of the small fry of journalists and critics. But the debts to authors mentioned and unmentioned are far more numerous than the actual references would suggest. And two names lead all the rest, the two of whom Baudelaire writes: "De Maistre et Edgar Poe m'ont appris à raisonner."

The volumes and articles dealing with Baudelaire and Poe already fill several shelves, and are being added to all the time.[8] Many aspects of the question—the general history of Poe in France, the detailed history of Baudelaire's translations, the question of their accuracy, and of the accuracy of Baudelaire's information about Poe, the extent of Poe's influence on Baudelaire's poetry—have little or no bearing on this study. What is of interest is Baudelaire's debt to Poe in so far as his critical thought is concerned. That can best be estimated by following the traces of Poe through the critical work of these years, remembering always what point Baudelaire had reached before the discovery of Poe.

The name of Poe first appeared in France in the *Revue Britannique* for November, 1845, which contained a translation of "The Gold Bug." Translations of several other tales followed, and the first criticism of Poe, by E.-D. Fargues, came out in the *Revue des Deux Mondes* of October 15, 1846. In 1847 a certain Isabelle Meunier published translations of several tales; according to Asselineau, it was through these that Baudelaire discovered Poe. Baudelaire himself wrote to Armand Fraisse in 1858:

En 1846 ou 1847, j'eus connaissance de quelques fragments d'Edgar Poe: j'éprouvai une commotion singulière. Ses œuvres complètes n'ayant été rassemblées qu'après sa mort en une édition unique, j'eus la patience de me lier avec des Américains vivant à Paris, pour leur emprunter des collections de journaux qui avaient été dirigés par Edgar Poe. Et alors je trouvai, croyez-moi si vous voulez, des poëmes et des nouvelles dont j'avais eu la pensée, mais vague et confuse, mal ordonnée, et que Poe avait su combiner à perfection (*Corr.* I, 227).

Asselineau confirms this: "Vers ce temps-là aussi [1847-48] une curiosité nouvelle s'empara de l'esprit de Baudelaire et remplit sa vie. . . . J'ai peu vu de possessions aussi complètes, aussi rapides, aussi absolues. A tout venant, où qu'il se trouvât dans la rue, au café, dans une imprimerie, le matin, le soir, il allait demandant:—Connaissez-vous Edgar Poë?"[9] And Baudelaire's long letter to his mother of Dec. 4, 1847 (*L.M.*, pp. 28-36) suggests to me that he knew something of Poe by then. The narrative of his misfortunes ("Franchement, le laudanum et le vin sont de mauvaises ressources contre le chagrin"), his insistent "je crois encore que la postérité me concerne," all have a Poe-like ring.

From this time on Baudelaire pursued anyone who could give him any information about Poe, and besieged the foreign booksellers with orders for his works. Asselineau tells one of the most amusing of these incidents:

Je l'accompagnai un jour à un hôtel du boulevard des Capucines, où on lui avait signalé l'arrivée d'un homme de lettres américain qui devait avoir connu Poë. Nous le trouvâmes en caleçon et en chemise, au milieu d'une flottille de chaussures de toutes sortes qu'il essayait avec l'assistance d'un cordonnier. Mais Baudelaire ne lui fit pas grâce: il fallut, bon gré mal gré, qu'il subît l'interrogatoire, entre une paire de bottines et une paire d'escarpins. L'opinion de notre hôte ne fut pas favorable à l'auteur du *Chat noir*. Je me rappelle notamment qu'il nous dit que M. Poë était un esprit bizarre et dont la conversation n'était pas du tout *conséquioutive*. Sur l'escalier Baudelaire me dit en enfonçant son chapeau avec violence: — 'Ce n'est qu'un yankee!'[10]

The tempting pursuit of the identity of the unfortunate thus pilloried has been a wild-goose chase for years with me. Never

had I realized what a Mecca Paris was for American men of
letters around 1850. Emerson was there in 1848, Francis J.
Child in 1849-51, Charles Eliot Norton in 1850, Lowell in
1851-52, but none of their letters and journals mention any
invasion of their boot-buying privacy. W. J. Stillman, the
painter and journalist, visited Delacroix's studio when he was
in Paris in 1852.[11] Did they talk of Poe, and did Delacroix put
Stillman in touch with Poe's admirer? If so, Stillman did not
think it worth recording. Finally, there is the Mann referred
to in a letter of Baudelaire's to Maxime Du Camp in 1852, in
which he speaks of "la nécessité de trouver un certain
M. Mann de qui dépend l'interprétation D'UNE LACUNE
et DE PASSAGES LITTERALEMENT INTRADUISIBLES" (Corr. I,
65). In "Fusées" (II, 631) M. Crépet reads "Ecrire à Mann"
where previous editors had read "Moun," which seems a
decided improvement. But M. Crépet conjectures: "Pour ma
part, je crois qu'il s'agissait de Horace Mann avec lequel une
lettre de notre auteur à Maxime du Camp (16 septembre
1852) montre qu'il fut en rapport à l'occasion de Poe" (J.I.,
p. 149). However, this cannot have been Horace Mann, who
was not in Europe after 1843. Could it have been the diplomat
Ambrose Dudley Mann (1801-89), a Virginian who had
been at West Point a few years before Poe, and who was in
Europe from 1842 to 1853? All this is conjecture, and one can
only hope that some yellowed journal or letter may one day
turn up to tell the story from the "Yankee's" side.

Baudelaire's correspondence at this time gives added proof
of his constant preoccupation with Poe.[12] In 1852 he writes to
his mother: "J'ai trouvé un auteur américain qui a excité
en moi une incroyable sympathie" (L.M., p. 52). The fruit
of this enthusiasm was to be the translation of a large part of
Poe's work—that perhaps most perfect of all translations, of
which Andrew Lang wrote to Poe in his Letters to Dead
Authors:

For your stories has been reserved a boundless popularity, and that
highest success—the success of a perfectly sympathetic translation.

By this time, of course, you have made the acquaintance of your translator, M. Charles Baudelaire, who so strenuously shared your views about Mr. Emerson and the Transcendentalists, and who so energetically resisted all those ideas of "progress" which "came from Hell or Boston."[13]

Baudelaire's first bit of translation from Poe appeared in 1848, and during the following years these translations were a major part of his labors. But he was not only translating the *Tales*; he was absorbing much that was in them, as well as in Poe's critical work. He had got hold of the *Southern Literary Messenger* for the two years of Poe's editorship (*Poe*, p. 670), and, judging from what Asselineau says, of other articles as well. He speaks with special enthusiasm of "Marginalia": "Faut-il encore citer ce petit passage qui me saute aux yeux, tout en feuilletant pour la centième fois ses amusants *Marginalia*, qui sont comme la chambre secrète de son esprit" (*Poe*, p. 702).

One needs only to turn over the pages of "Fusées" and "Mon Cœur mis à nu" to see how the name of Poe, thoughts from Poe, come cropping up. The title of the latter is borrowed from "Marginalia," Poe's suggestion that the road to fame lies before the man who would write "My Heart laid bare" (Virginia ed., XVI, 128). Crépet suggests that "Fusées" also comes from Poe: "The German '*Schwärmerei*'—not exactly 'humbug,' but 'sky-rocketing'—seems to be the only term by which we can conveniently designate that peculiar style of criticism which has lately come into fashion" (*ibid.*, XVI, 166). But would Baudelaire have borrowed a term so obviously uncomplimentary? At all events, the alternative heading, "Fusées-Suggestions" or "Suggestions," certainly comes from Poe.

The trace of Poe is all through "Fusées." His name is mentioned twice, the second time in the moving passage: "Faire tous les matins ma *prière à Dieu, réservoir de toute force et de toute justice, à mon père, à Mariette et à Poe*, comme intercesseurs" (II, 672; restored to "Fusées" in Crépet edition). And scattered through the pages are a whole series of notes which echo Poe, many of which we shall find Baudelaire using elsewhere. The spirit of perversity, the absurdity of the idea of progress, the definition of beauty, with its elements of strangeness and melancholy, are some of the points which Baudelaire has noted particularly (II, 628, 637, 640, 631, 632).

In "Mon Cœur mis à nu" there seem to be fewer specific notes on Poe; one might conclude that by then Baudelaire had absorbed his Poe, and was past the note-taking stage. His mind is still much on Poe, to be sure, as the note "Histoire de ma traduction d'Edgar Poe" (II, 649) indicates. And the doctrine of perversity, the opposition to progress, crop up more than once (II, 666, 646, 667). But "Mon cœur mis à nu," as one reads it through, is far from having the strong Poe flavor of "Fusées." The name that does come to mind on nearly every page is the one bracketed with that of Poe by Baudelaire himself—Joseph de Maistre.

Baudelaire has not indicated, as he did for Poe, the date of his discovery of De Maistre, but several facts point to its being about 1850. Asselineau recalls a conversation which took place, he says, in 1850 or 1851:

Nadar et Baudelaire s'engagèrent sur la politique et sur J. de Maistre (que Nadar, par parenthèse, avouait n'avoir pas lu). 'Mais, disait-il, dans le monde où je vis, on sait toujours ce que c'est que J. de Maistre!' — Baudelaire, couché sur le divan (c'était rue La Rochefoucauld), se dressa sur ses poings et médusa Nadar par ce mot terrible: 'As-tu lu la réfutation du système de Locke? — Non, dit Nadar, embarrassé. — Eh bien, alors!' . . . dit Baudelaire en se recouchant le dos tourné (*Crépet*, p. 285).

Among the notes for the projected periodical *Le Hibou philosophe*, of about 1852, is listed among the "ouvrages desquels on peut faire une appréciation" the "*Lettres et Mélanges de Joseph de Maistre*" (II, 425).[14] This mention suggests a possible way in which De Maistre may have been brought to Baudelaire's attention. The *Lettres et opuscules* were reviewed by Sainte-Beuve on June 2, 1851 (*Lundis*, IV, 192-216), and

Baudelaire, with his admiration for Sainte-Beuve, may well have been led to De Maistre by him, particularly as Sainte-Beuve indicates many of the aspects of De Maistre that were of special interest to Baudelaire.[15] However, Baudelaire may also have been led to De Maistre by a violent opponent of the latter, Vigny. In the 1852 article on Poe, Baudelaire says: "Alfred de Vigny a écrit un livre pour démontrer que la place du poëte n'est ni dans une république, ni dans une monarchie absolue, ni dans une monarchie constitutionnelle; et personne ne lui a répondu" (*Poe*, p. 654). He is referring, of course, to *Stello*. Now Chapter XXXII of *Stello*, "Sur la substitution des souffrances expiatoires," is an impassioned refutation of De Maistre's doctrine. If Baudelaire had read or reread *Stello* recently, this chapter, in itself, or together with Sainte-Beuve's review, may have given him the urge to read De Maistre. He was ripe for such reading; the preceding years had left him disillusioned with ideas of democracy and progress, and Poe had already oriented him in the direction of the rigid system of De Maistre.

It is evident, in any case, that by 1852 Baudelaire had read De Maistre, and with enthusiasm. The 1852 Poe article has two references to him, one immediately following the paragraph on *Stello*, a quotation from the *Soirées de Saint-Pétersbourg: "Quelle odeur de magasin!* comme disait J. de Maistre, à propos de Locke" (*Poe*, p. 654);[16] and later a mention of "la puissance de commandement et de prophétie dans l'œil jeté à l'horizon, et la solide figure de Joseph de Maistre, aigle et bœuf tout à la fois" (*Poe*, p. 666). From that time on the references to him in Baudelaire's works and correspondence are frequent. There can be no doubt of Baudelaire's continued admiration for "ce soldat animé de l'Esprit-Saint" (II, 166), "le grand génie de notre temps, — *un voyant!*" (*Corr.* I, 130-31.)[17]

In reading "Fusées" and especially "Mon Cœur mis à nu" one realizes to the full the tremendous impact of De Maistre's thought on Baudelaire. Entry after entry echoes the *Soirées*,

and "Mon Cœur mis à nu" is De Maistre's even more completely than "Fusées" is Poe's.[18] Much of this interest in
De Maistre and debt to him is beyond the scope of this
study;[19] it touches Baudelaire's whole philosophy, and its
direct bearing on his aesthetic theories is often slight. Yet
such is the coherence of his thought that to pass over his
debt, in his criticism, to De Maistre's theological, political, and
social ideas would be to falsify and narrow his whole way of
thinking.

Nearly all the great points of De Maistre's doctrine recur.
De Maistre's emphasis on original sin, "le péché originel, qui
explique tout, et sans lequel on n'explique rien" (*Soirées*,
Entretien 2: O.P., I, 73) is reiterated by Baudelaire. In his
letter to Toussenel in 1856, after speaking of De Maistre, he
inveighs against the "grande hérésie moderne . . . la sup-
pression de l'idée du *péché originel*" (*Corr.* I, 131), and in
"Mon Cœur mis à nu" we have: "Théorie de la vraie civilisation. Elle n'est pas dans le gaz, ni dans la vapeur, ni dans les
tables tournantes. Elle est dans la diminution des traces du
péché originel" (II, 659). And De Maistre's words on man,
"ses lumières qui l'élèvent jusqu'à l'ange ne servent qu'à lui
montrer dans lui des penchants abominables qui le dégradent
jusqu'à la brute" (*Soirées*, Entretien 2: O. P., I, 80) find their
echo in "Mon Cœur mis à nu": "Il y a dans tout homme, à
toute heure, deux postulations simultanées, l'une vers Dieu,
l'autre vers Satan" (II, 647).[20] In the same way De Maistre's
doctrines of pain and suffering as necessary consequences of
sin and expiation for it, of reversibility, of prayer, are all
echoed by Baudelaire.

In a study of the development of Baudelaire's philosophical
and religious thought the influence of De Maistre can hardly
be overestimated. It is clear-cut and unconfused with any
other influence; its traces are plain in the poetry and in the
prose alike. Though the connection with the criticism is not
always direct, the background is there, and sometimes, as in

the case of the doctrine of original sin, theology shows the way to criticism, as we shall see in the "Essence du rire."

In his conception of society and its organization Baudelaire again follows De Maistre, here however with Poe also as a guide. De Maistre's political and social ideas are derived—with questionable logic, we may sometimes think—from his theological ones. The hand of Providence is everywhere, guiding the nations, sometimes directly, sometimes deviously, as De Maistre explains in the second chapter of the *Considérations sur la France*, "Conjectures sur les voies de la Providence dans la Révolution française" (*Œuvres*, I, 9). Baudelaire picks up the idea in "Mon Cœur mis à nu": "Ce qu'est l'Empereur Napoléon III. Ce qu'il vaut. Trouver l'explication de sa nature, et sa providentialité" (II, 644). Already, in March, 1852, he had written to Poulet-Malassis: "Personne ne consent à se mettre au point de vue *providentiel*" (*Corr.* I, 58). For Baudelaire, as for De Maistre, there is only one right and reasonable form of government: "Il n'y a de gouvernement raisonnable et assuré que l'aristocratique. Monarchie ou république, basées sur la démocratie, sont également absurdes et faibles" (*Mon Cœur mis à nu*, II, 648. Cf. *Considérations sur la France*, *Œuvres*, I, especially Chapter IV, "La République française peut-elle durer?").

De Maistre's theological and political ideas helped to bring about a kind of conversion in Baudelaire, of which we shall see more than one trace in the critical articles. But Baudelaire also found in De Maistre ideas which had already begun to be dear to him, his cherished correspondences. In the *Soirées* De Maistre quotes Saint Paul, "Ce monde est un système de choses invisibles manifestées visiblement" (Entretien 10, *O.P.*, II, 210. *Romans*, i, 20: "For the invisible things of him from the creation of the world are clearly seen, being understood by the things that are made"). In a letter to the Vicomte de Bonald in 1814 he writes: "Le monde physique n'est qu'une image, ou, si vous voulez, une répétition du monde spirituel" (*Lettres et opuscules*, I, 242), and in *Sur les délais de la jus-*

tice he uses the word *correspondance* in a gloss to Plutarch: *"il y a entre les choses d'un ordre supérieur, comme entre les choses naturelles, des liaisons et des correspondances secrètes"* (*Œuvres*, II, 46).[21] All this could hardly have failed to attract Baudelaire even more to De Maistre, who had been connected with the *illuminés* whom Baudelaire had earlier read with such interest.[22]

As far as aesthetic and critical ideas are directly concerned, De Maistre had little to give to Baudelaire. He has little to say of beauty and art, and certainly Baudelaire can have found nothing new or congenial in the "4e Paradoxe, Le beau n'est qu'une convention et une habitude" (*Lettres et opuscules*, II, 123). Though an occasional phrase seems to have caught his attention, as we shall see, De Maistre's final definition, *"le beau,* dans tous les genres imaginables, est *ce qui plaît à la vertu éclairée"* (*Examen de la philosophie de Bacon*, O.P., IV, 300), will for Baudelaire lose the day to Poe's distinction of the Good, the True, and the Beautiful.

Turning back to the critical work, we find that the earlier articles of this period indicate a thought at many points at variance with itself, faced with new and perplexing problems. The Baudelaire who in 1846 had presented art to the bourgeois with the glorious confidence of youth that the offer had but to be made to be accepted, swings in the 1851 article on Pierre Dupont to a popular, democratic, utilitarian view of art—and then comes back the full swing of the pendulum to the aristocratic attitude of the Poe articles. This is the period most fertile for the critics who would point out the contradictions and discrepancies in Baudelaire's thought—too often without sufficiently considering their chronology. The fundamentals of Baudelaire's conception of beauty, of art, of criticism, seem to me to develop with remarkable coherence; the path from the "Salon de 1846" to the "Salon de 1859" is straight and plain to follow. Where, however, Baudelaire does seem to waver and to question is in regard to the relation of art and the artist to society. These are questions which concern literature more immediately, perhaps, than they concern the other arts, and we shall see that during this period Baudelaire's criticism is largely occupied with literature. He was making his own career as a man of letters, and was in close contact, as his journalistic ventures show, with other writers. Most of all, perhaps, the discovery of Poe, the "bain de Poe" in which he was plunged, turned his critical thinking in the direction of literature.

The two articles which bridge the gap between the first "Salons" and the articles which follow are a brief review of Champfleury's volume of *Contes*, and a note preceding the translation of Poe's "Révélation magnétique," both published in 1848. The first of these is obviously a blurb for a friend, but the criticism is meticulous and careful, though moderate and controlled, with only a mild reproach to Champfleury "de n'être pas suffisamment rabâcheur" (II, 396).

The note on "Révélation magnétique" is interesting as Baudelaire's first published word on Poe. It is, however, largely a brief essay on the method of novelists: "Je ne crois pas qu'il soit possible de trouver un romancier fort qui n'ait pas opéré la création de sa méthode, ou plutôt dont la sensibilité primitive ne soit pas réfléchie et transformée en un art certain" (*Poe*, p. 734). Here also is the term which will become dear to Baudelaire, *surnaturalisme,* opposed to the "naturalistes enragés." Poe is hardly mentioned; Baudelaire is hard away on his novelists.

Undoubtedly the article that surprises us most from Baudelaire's pen is his preface to the *Chants et chansons* of the popular poet, Pierre Dupont, published in 1851. Baudelaire had known Pierre Dupont well for some years; they were often seen together at the Brasserie des Martyrs, and Deroy painted both their portraits. The preface is certainly inspired in large part by friendship, but that alone is not enough to explain the ardor with which Baudelaire defends ideas that will presently be all that is hateful to him. The article is a lasting monument of a passing but intense phase of faith in popular democracy, the phase of Baudelaire's vociferous enthusiasm of 1848. It is one of the rare bits of Baudelaire's criticism which leave the modern reader cold; all such cases, I think, occur when either the call of friendship, enthusiasm for a cause, or the less worthy desire to gain the approbation of some man of letters cloud the crystalline clearness of his judgment. The art criticism is amazingly free from such motives; it might be that of an angelic visitant from another sphere, distributing praise and blame with entire impartiality. But the literary criticism is often that of a combatant in the arena he is judging, one whose vision is sometimes blurred by the heat and burden of the struggle.

The preface (Baudelaire's first criticism of poetry) begins with a categoric condemnation of "la puérile utopie de *l'art pour l'art*" (II, 403), preferring to it "la plainte de cette individualité maladive," Joseph Delorme; for Delorme and his author Baudelaire cherished a life-long tenderness.[23] But above the poet of the ego Baudelaire puts "le poëte qui se met en communication permanente avec les hommes de son temps, et échange avec eux des pensées et des sentiments traduits dans un noble langage suffisament correct." And he maintains that with Auguste Barbier "la question fut vidée, et l'art fut désormais inséparable de la morale et de l'utilité."

It is worth asking here, I think, whether Baudelaire's position is as alien to his previous criticism as it seems at first sight. Is it not possible to see in this glorification of the poet of his time a continuation of the search for the *beau moderne*, so eagerly wished for in the first "Salons"? Here is the poet who writes not of a remote past, not of exotic lands, but who is the voice of his own people and his own time. What Baudelaire neglects here is the originality, the mastery of technique, that in the "Salons" were his primary requisites for the artist. But all the same the connection is there.

After sketching Dupont's life,[24] and classifying his poetry, Baudelaire proclaims the superiority of such a poet, with his

love of virtue and humanity, "le goût infini de la République," to such will-of-the-wisps as René, Obermann, and
Werther, and characterizes poetry as essentially utopian, re-
bellious against evil. He ends with a statement singularly true
of his own criticism: "Il faut s'assimiler une œuvre pour la
bien exprimer" (II, 413). All through the preface there is a
tone of seriousness, of intense conviction, quite different from
the almost impertinent cocksureness of the earlier criticism.
Oddly enough, it is the tone which will presently be carried
over into the Poe articles, to express convictions of a very
different order.

The two articles which follow, "Les Drames et les romans
honnêtes," and "L'Ecole païenne" seem to be part of a scheme
noted in the project for *Le Hibou philosophe*,[25] the periodical
planned by Baudelaire together with Armand Boschet,
Champfleury, Monselet, André Thomas, and Henri Amic. In
Baudelaire's notes for it we find:

Faire à nous cinq un grand article: *la Vente des vieux mots aux
enchères, de l'Ecole classique, de l'Ecole classique galante, de l'Ecole
romantique naissante, de l'Ecole lunatique, de l'Ecole lance de Tolède,
de l'Ecole olympienne* (V. Hugo), *de l'Ecole plastique* (Th. Gautier), *de l'Ecole païenne* (Banville), *de l'Ecole poitrinaire, de l'Ecole
du bon sens, de l'Ecole mélancolico-farceuse* (Alfred de Musset)
(II, 426).

The project came to nothing, and even before it was given
up Baudelaire seems to have used his contributions as separate
articles.

The chronology of the two articles is something of a
puzzle. In these years in which the orientation of Baudelaire's thought is changing rapidly one would like very much
to know the precise dates at which the various articles were
composed. The "Drames et romans honnêtes" (*Semaine
Théâtrale*, Nov. 27, 1851) is certainly not exactly contemporary in its thought with the Pierre Dupont preface. But
does it precede it, is it a step in the swing from Baudelaire's
mildly pro-bourgeois attitude to the ultra-utilitarian and

democratic view of poetry, or does it come after, in the rebound toward what may be called the Poe attitude? In favor of the former, one may note the sharp, forthright tone, still that of the "Salons." And the attitude of disgust with bourgeois morality and philosophy, "la sotte hypocrisie bourgeoise," seems to indicate a rather recent disillusionment. On the other hand there is a reference to the Faucher decree, of Oct. 12, 1851, which would suggest that the article, very likely simmering in Baudelaire's mind beforehand, was brought to a head by this decree. However, the reference might have been added to an article already written, to give it an immediate interest. What seems very unlikely is that the article came between the Pierre Dupont preface and "L'Ecole païenne," in some ways so close in thought to the preface. I have been in many minds as to the correct chronology here, and still feel doubtful whether to place the "Drames et romans honnêtes" before the other two, or after; I incline to the former.[26]

The "Drames et romans honnêtes," a hearty damnation of bourgeois morality and sentimentality, has one particularly interesting passage on art and morality. Baudelaire is evidently seeking a *via media* between art for art's sake and art for morality's sake, and he arrives at a point of view which he never entirely abandons, and which later on leads him to amend and modify certain ideas of Poe:

L'art est-il utile? Oui. Pourquoi? Parce qu'il est l'art. Y a-t-il un art pernicieux? Oui. C'est celui qui dérange les conditions de la vie. Le vice est séduisant, il faut le peindre séduisant; mais il traîne avec lui des maladies et des douleurs morales singulières; il faut les décrire. Etudiez toutes les plaies comme un médecin qui fait son service dans un hôpital, et l'école du bon sens, l'école exclusivement morale, ne trouvera plus où mordre. Le crime est-il toujours châtié, la vertu gratifiée? Non; mais cependant, si votre roman, si votre drame est bien fait, il ne prendra envie à personne de violer les lois de la nature. La première condition nécessaire pour faire un art sain est la croyance à l'unité intégrale. Je défie qu'on me trouve un seul ouvrage d'imagination qui réunisse toutes les conditions du beau et qui soit un ouvrage pernicieux (II, 416-17).

The article on "L'Ecole païenne" (*Semaine Théâtrale*, Jan. 22, 1852), again at first very similar in tone to the early "Salons," with a turn into high seriousness at the end, deals with the opposite heresy, the fashion for paganism: "Impossible de faire un pas, de prononcer un mot sans buter contre un fait païen" (II, 421). Baudelaire condemns this fashion first of all from the artistic point of view as "pastiche, pastiche!" lacking the naïveté which he demands of the artist. The greater part of the article is light in tone, mocking, teasing. With the last pages comes a sudden seriousness, a profound distrust of beauty: "Congédier la passion et la raison, c'est tuer la littérature. Renier les efforts de la société précédente, chrétienne et philosophique, c'est se suicider, c'est refuser la force et les moyens de perfectionnement. S'environner exclusivement des séductions de l'art physique, c'est créer de grandes chances de perdition" (II, 422). The passage seems to become more and more personal, a sort of *mea culpa*: "Le goût immodéré de la forme pousse à des désordres monstrueux et inconnus. . . . Je comprends les fureurs des iconoclastes et des musulmans contre les images. J'admets tous les remords de Saint Augustin sur le trop grand plaisir des yeux." Baudelaire concludes: "Il faut que la littérature aille retremper ses forces dans une atmosphère meilleure. Le temps n'est pas loin où l'on comprendra que toute littérature qui se refuse à marcher fraternellement entre la science et la philosophie est une littérature homicide et suicide" (II, 424). The passage has all the marks of a conversion; the young dandy of 1845, with his passion for art, has become aware of other problems, and aware with a desperate earnestness. If we take the articles of this period separately, each of them seems to have the ring of decision and authority to which we have become accustomed; yet taken together they indicate a period of questioning, of uncertainty, of pondering over the whole problem of the relation of art to life, to philosophy, to religion.

One asks how Baudelaire was led in this direction; first of all, perhaps, by the bitter disillusionment which followed his brief revolutionary enthusiasm. Then too his own experience of the difficulties of the writer in society must have turned his thoughts in this direction. But literature as well as life had its part, I believe. It was about this time that Baudelaire discovered De Maistre, and it seems to me very likely that the concluding pages of "L'Ecole païenne" give us the immediate repercussion of that discovery. There are passages that recall De Maistre very specifically, as: "Le péché contient son enfer, et la nature dit de temps en temps à la douleur et à la misère: Allez vaincre ces rebelles!" (II, 423), which repeats the *Soirées*: "Toute *douleur* est un supplice imposé pour quelque crime actuel ou originel" and "Tout péché doit être expié dans ce monde ou dans l'autre" (Entretien 3, *O.P.*, I, 182, and Entretien 8, *O.P.*, II, 103). More than this, the whole tone of these pages has something of the harsh rigidity of De Maistre.[27]

Following this article, the first to show the hand of De Maistre, comes the first Poe article, "Edgar Allan Poe, sa vie et ses ouvrages" (*Revue de Paris*, March-April, 1852). The article is in large part biographical; many of the facts in it are however inaccurate, as Baudelaire was to discover later. But the biographical part is interesting for its portrait of Poe by Baudelaire, the fraternal sympathy and understanding that mark every line. Baudelaire seems to feel that Poe has illumined the dark corners of his mind, found for him the answer to many a "puzzling question." In many ways it is a melancholy enlightenment; the example of Poe brings home to Baudelaire the irreconcilable difference between the poet and the world in which he lives, the unhappy fate which must inevitably be his. Baudelaire, who a few years before had confidently asserted "il n'y a pas de guignon. Si vous avez du guignon, c'est qu'il vous manque quelque chose" (II, 384), begins this first Poe article: "Il existe des destinées fatales; il existe dans la littérature de chaque pays des hommes qui portent le mot *guignon* écrit en caractères mystérieux dans les plis sinueux de leurs fronts" (*Poe*, p. 653).[28] The poet in any society is fated to misfortune. All through his account of Poe's life, Baudelaire emphasizes the uncongenial, unfriendly atmosphere in which he lived, surrounded by critics trying to turn him into a *"making-money author."* It is a far cry from the Pierre Dupont Preface to the arraignment of democracy, of the tyranny of popular opinion, to which Baudelaire gives vent here. He seems to be finding his own true opinions; after the gropings and searchings indicated by the previous articles Poe has opened his eyes to truths that experience had slowly been forcing upon him.

When he comes to Poe's "Poetic Principle," Baudelaire makes what amounts to a formal recantation of much that he had said in the Pierre Dupont Preface: "Il y a, depuis longtemps déjà aux Etats-Unis, un mouvement utilitaire qui veut entraîner la poésie comme le reste. Il y a là des poëtes humanitaires, des poëtes du suffrage universel, des poëtes abolitionnistes des lois sur les céréales, et des poëtes qui veulent faire bâtir des *work-houses*" (*Poe*, p. 662). Baudelaire's declaration that he means no allusion to France is quite unconvincing. But it is of the greatest interest that Baudelaire, even here at the height of his enthusiasm for Poe, still feels it necessary to limit his ideas, to bring certain modifications, in a way which one only realizes by a careful comparison of Baudelaire's text with Poe's.

After Poe's life, Baudelaire traces his portrait, his character, and then comes to his work, treating successively the critic, the poet, and the writer of tales. The first two are dismissed in somewhat summary fashion. The critic has only a few sentences: "D'où partait une idée, quelle était son origine, son but, à quelle école elle appartenait, quelle était la méthode de l'auteur, salutaire ou dangereuse, tout cela était nettement, clairement et rapidement expliqué" (*Poe*, p. 670). The poet is somewhat more fully treated, and summed up in one of

Baudelaire's terse formulas; "Sa poésie, profonde et plaintive, est néanmoins ouvragée, pure, correcte et brillante comme un bijou de cristal."

But Baudelaire's great enthusiasm is for Poe's tales, "des bouffonneries violentes, du grotesque pur, des aspirations effrénées vers l'infini, et une grande préoccupation du magnétisme." The particular characteristic of the tales is "le conjecturisme et le probabilisme" (*Poe*, p. 672). Baudelaire analyzes a number of the tales, with a rare skill in the retelling. At the end he sums up Poe's method and characterizes his style, "serré, *concatené*; la mauvaise volonté du lecteur ou sa paresse ne pourront pas passer à travers les mailles de ce réseau tressé par la logique. Toutes les idées, comme des flèches obéissantes, volent au même but" (*Poe*, p. 677). And he describes what seem to have been his own sensations in reading Poe: "Dans cette incessante ascension vers l'infini, on perd un peu l'haleine. L'air est rarefié dans cette littérature comme dans un laboratoire" (*Poe*, p. 678). Baudelaire's final word is an apology for Poe's drunkenness, and a curious epitaph, with the suggestion of Poe as intercessor, which occurs in the pages of "Mon Cœur mis à nu."

This article was severely criticized by Poulet-Malassis in the *Journal d'Alençon* for Jan. 9, 1853: "la partie biographique est particulièrement brillante, mais la partie philosophique entièrement à refaire."[29] Baudelaire wrote to Poulet-Malassis about this review on Dec. 16, 1853:

Vous dites de plus que mes catégories, mes explications psychologiques sont inintelligibles, — et même, autant que je peux me rappeler, — que je n'ai aucun esprit philosophique. — Il est possible que je sois un peu obscur dans des travaux faits à la hâte, sous la pression du besoin, et gêné par des brutes romantiques; mais le nouveau travail, — augmenté du double, et qui paraîtra en Janvier, — vous démontrera que je me suis parfaitement compris (*Corr.* I, 83).

This first Poe article is interesting above all as showing the state of breathless enthusiasm to which Baudelaire had been brought by Poe. The biographical part is a kind of Stend-halian *cristallisation* of the beloved object, in the course of which its very faults become virtues. Baudelaire is absorbed by his sympathy with Poe the man and his sufferings. As for Poe's ideas, what he seems to have accepted whole-heartedly at this point is the scorn of democracy, of materialism, of all that made the pitiless America that treated Poe so ruthlessly. But it must not be forgotten that De Maistre was urging him in the same direction. Poe's poetic theories are accepted with some reservations, which recall the passage I have quoted from the "Drames et romans honnêtes." Baudelaire explains Poe's "heresy of *The Didactic*," affirms that poetry is ad-dressed solely to the sense of beauty, and adds: "Que la poésie soit subséquemment et conséquemment utile, cela est hors de doute, mais ce n'est pas son but; cela vient *par-dessus le marché!*" (*Poe*, p. 663.) In a word then, complete enchant-ment with Poe the man, and consequent condemnation of the political and moral environment which caused his sufferings; enthusiasm above all for the *Tales*; and a still resisted urge towards the poetic theory.

The years immediately following have little to offer in the way of published criticism. The "Morale du joujou," of 1853, shows plainly the effect of Baudelaire's reading of Poe. It is the same sort of essay as Poe's "Philosophy of Furniture" (of which Baudelaire had published a translation in 1852), though with a Baudelairean motif. It is amusing to note that Baudelaire has caught from Poe the "abus du je" which he mentions the previous year; the first person singular occurs some twenty times in the half-dozen pages of the "Morale du joujou"—about five times as often as in the first half-dozen pages of the "Salon de 1846." Here again it seems that Baude-laire found in Poe something fundamentally congenial to him, which needed only encouragement. And the last words of the article (added in 1855 when it was reprinted) are a borrow-ing from Poe; "*Puzzling question*"—the words of Sir Thomas

Browne which Poe uses as the epigraph of the "Murders in
the Rue Morgue" and often quotes elsewhere.

The following year brings only a moving dedication to
Maria Clemm of the *Histoires extraordinaires*. One would like
to know whether it ever reached her, whether she found
someone to translate it for her, and whether she answered it
in any way. All this time Baudelaire was absorbed in his labor
of translation. In spite of admitting as he does in his note to
"Hans Pfaall" in 1855: "Moi-même j'ai souri plus d'une fois
en surprenant les dada de mon auteur," his devotion is un-
flagging.

These years are not however so exclusively occupied with
Poe as one would at first imagine. The *Fleurs du Mal* were
beginning to appear in various reviews, with the attendant
labor of revision and minute proof-reading. And, although
the published articles are few, three important articles published later, "De l'essence du rire" (1855), "Quelques caricaturistes français" and "Quelques caricaturistes étrangers"
(1857) were certainly written about this time. A note to
"Quelques caricaturistes français" states; "Ce fragment est
tiré d'un livre resté inachevé et commencé il y a plusieurs
années" (II, 750); indeed on the cover of the "Salon de
1845" there is announced "pour paraître prochainement,"
"De la caricature." Two years later Baudelaire writes to his
mother: "Il y a à peu près huit mois que j'ai été chargé de faire
deux articles importants qui traînent toujours, l'un une *histoire de la caricature*" (*L.M.*, p. 34). In 1851 he writes that
he is sure of getting the article published (*L.M.*, p. 44), but
says later: "après tout, c'est une méchante affaire. Tu verras
quelques pages étonnantes sans doute et le reste n'est qu'un
ramas de contradictions et de divagations; quant à l'érudition,
il n'y en a que l'apparence" (*L.M.*, p. 46). In 1852 he writes:
"Je voudrais imprimer dans *Le Pays* quelques feuilletons in-
titulés: *Du Comique dans les Arts et des Caricaturistes*. . . .
Mon livre est très amusant. Il y a une partie philosophique qui

est courte; le reste est une revue des caricaturistes de talent. Mon livre est fini. Je le recopie. Il sera fini dans deux jours" (*Corr.* I, 54-55). If the calculation he makes as to the number of letters in the article is correct, the manuscript must at that time have been longer by one fourth than the three published articles. A short time later he writes: "Vous pourrez ajouter à cela: *Physiologie du rire,* qui paraîtra, prochainement, à la *Revue de Paris,* sans doute, ainsi que: *Salon des Caricaturistes* et *Les Limbes, poésies,* chez Michel Lévy" (*Corr.* I, 61). But the following year he writes to his mother, about the Poe translation: "Ce livre était le point de départ d'une vie nouvelle.—Il devait être suivi de la publication de mes poésies, de mes *Salons,* réunis à mon travail sur les *Caricaturistes,* resté chez l'abominable créature dont je te parlais, et sur lequel j'ai reçu plus de deux cents francs de la *Revue de Paris*" (*L.M.,* p. 63). This delay in publication seems to have been a byword among Baudelaire's friends; Champfleury writes in 1854: "Je citerai . . . mon ami Baudelaire, dont je veux citer un fragment inédit, tiré d'un livre sous presse depuis dix ans seulement: *De la caricature, et généralement du comique dans les arts.*"[30] In spite of Champfleury's tendency to exaggeration, we have here another confirmation of the fact that the publication of the articles is decidedly later than their composition. There seems little doubt, either, that, even though the book was never so completely finished as Baudelaire would lead us to think, the manuscript was much more extensive than the three published articles. A note, probably of 1852 or 1853, first published in the *Œuvres posthumes,* makes this plain: "Voici la troisième fois que je recopie et recommence d'un bout à l'autre cet article, enlevant, ajoutant, remaniant et tâchant de me conformer aux instructions de M. V. de Mars [secretary of the *Revue des Deux Mondes*]" (II, 213). Notes follow on the changes made, and on new passages on a large number of artists, the majority of whom are not so much as mentioned in the published articles.

It is evident from the articles themselves that they represent many years of thought. Baudelaire says at the beginning: "Ces réflexions étaient devenues pour moi une espèce d'obsession; j'ai voulu me soulager." Two notes in "Fusées" are plainly connected with the articles: "Raconter pompeusement des choses comiques," and "L'esprit de bouffonnerie peut ne pas exclure la charité, mais c'est rare" (II, 628, 629). The first article, "De l'essence du rire, et généralement du comique dans les arts plastiques,"[31] the philosophical section of the "book," was first published in Le Portefeuille in 1855, with the note: "Cet article est tiré d'un livre intitulé Peintres, Statuaires et Caricaturistes, qui paraîtra prochement à la librarie de Michel Lévy." (This was one of the titles suggested for the volume which was to become Curiosités esthétiques.) It is, says Baudelaire, "purement un article de philosophe et d'artiste," containing a carefully thought out theory of the comic. The article is a return to art criticism, and, coming back to it from the literary criticism, one can hardly fail to realize that Baudelaire reaches his greatest height in his criticism of art. This article, with its two companion pieces, is a type of the best of the critical articles, where admirable generalizations stand side by side with the most acute and discriminating judgments of individual artists.

Baudelaire's theory of the comic is fundamentally a theological one. His point of departure is a quotation: "Le Sage ne rit qu'en tremblant."[32] Why this contradiction between wisdom and laughter? he asks. Because laughter is closely allied to the fall of man; in Eden joy was not expressed by laughter. The proof of the Satanic origin of mirth lies in the fact that the "physiologistes du rire" agree that laughter comes from a sense of superiority. "Pour prendre un des exemples les plus vulgaires de la vie, qu'y a-t-il de si réjouissant dans le spectacle d'un homme qui tombe sur la glace ou sur le pavé, qui trébuche au bout d'un trottoir, pour que la face de son frère en Jésus-Christ se contracte d'une façon désordonnée, pour que les muscles de son visage se mettent a jouer subitement comme une horloge à midi ou un joujou à ressorts?"

(II, 170). The reason is an unconscious pride, the thought "*I* don't fall." And Baudelaire notes how the sneering laughter of the Satanic heroes, such as Melmoth, is entirely in line with this conception. So laughter, essentially human, is essentially contradictory, "à la fois signe d'une grandeur infinie et d'une misère infinie, misère infinie relativement à l'Etre absolu dont il possède la conception, grandeur infinie relativement aux animaux" (II, 171-72). With the increasing awareness of this contradiction brought by Christianity, the sense of the comic has increased.

But, Baudelaire continues, all the difficulties are not solved; many objects of laughter are quite innocent. However, childish laughter is an expression of joy, "une joie de plante," or something analogous to the tail-wagging of dogs or the purring of cats, although "ce rire n'est pas tout-à-fait exempt d'ambition, ainsi qu'il convient à des bouts d'hommes, c'est-à-dire à des Satans en herbe" (II, 174). Then there is the laughter caused by the grotesque, which, artistically speaking, is a creation, while the comic is an imitation. Hence the grotesque expresses a superiority, not of man over man, but of man over nature. "Il y a entre ces deux rires . . . la même différence qu'entre l'école littéraire intéressée et l'école de l'art pour l'art. Ainsi le grotesque domine le comique d'une hauteur proportionnelle" (II, 175). Baudelaire establishes the terms "comique absolu" for the grotesque, and "comique significatif" for the ordinary comic, which is more understandable, art being joined with morality, whereas the grotesque must be grasped intuitively. But it must be remembered that "le comique ne peut être absolu que relativement à l'humanité déchue, et c'est ainsi que je l'entends." After this Baudelaire proceeds to give examples of the different types of the comic in different countries, the outstanding examples of the "comique absolu" being the Pierrot of the English pantomime, and some of the tales of Hoffmann.

Baudelaire's theory of the comic, developed with closely knit logic, is in many ways original with him. But in it he has used elements drawn from varied sources, as can be seen when one finds ideas of Stendhal joined to the Satanism of Melmoth and to De Maistre's bedrock of sound Catholic theology. His point of departure is the close relationship of laughter to the Fall of Man, an immediate linking up with all the ideas De Maistre had put into his mind. De Maistre's "péché originel, qui explique tout, et sans lequel on n'explique rien" is here the explanation of the origins of laughter, of the comic. And, as has been pointed out, the theory owes much to the Satanic laughter of Melmoth.[33] Moreover, in the second chapter of *Racine et Shakespeare*, "Le Rire," Stendhal says: "Qu'est-ce que le *rire*? Hobbes répond: *Cette convulsion physique, que tout le monde connaît, est produite par la vue imprévue de notre supériorité sur autrui.*"[34] Like Baudelaire, he cites the classic example of a man falling in the street and the resulting laughter of the bystanders. But Baudelaire, instead of following Stendhal to his characteristic conclusion, "si l'on veut me faire rire . . . il faut que des gens passionnés se trompent, sous mes yeux, d'une manière plaisante, sur le chemin qui les mène au bonheur," goes off on a very different track, back to De Maistre and the Satanic origin of sin, and then, in a passage suddenly reminiscent of the *Préface de Cromwell*, to the way in which Christianity has been favorable to the development of the comic. There is an extraordinarily skillful weaving together—conscious or otherwise— of what would seem at first irreconcilable elements; Stendhal, De Maistre, and Maturin fused into one.

Baudelaire's theory, hedged about with restrictions indeed, is echoed in the concluding pages of his greatest successor as a theorist of the comic, Bergson, who writes at the end of *Le Rire*:

Le rire ne peut pas être absolument juste. Répétons qu'il ne doit pas non plus être bon. Il a pour fonction d'intimider en humiliant. Il n'y réussirait pas si la nature n'avait laissé à cet effet, dans les meilleurs d'entre les hommes, un petit fonds de méchanceté, ou tout au moins de malice. Peut-être vaudrait-il mieux que nous n'approfondissions pas trop ce point. Nous n'y trouverions rien de très flatteur pour nous. Nous verrions que le mouvement de détente ou d'expansion n'est qu'un prélude au rire, que le rieur rentre tout de suite en soi, s'affirme plus ou moins orgueilleusement lui-même, et tendrait à considérer la personne d'autrui comme une marionnette dont il tient les ficelles. Dans cette présomption nous démêlerions d'ailleurs bien vite un peu d'égoïsme, et, derrière l'égoïsme lui-même, quelque chose de moins spontané et de plus amer, je ne sais quel pessimisme naissant qui s'affirme de plus en plus à mesure que le rieur raisonne davantage son rire.[35]

Bergson is more cautious than Baudelaire, but the cloven hoof shows itself even in this great modern theory of the comic, "du mécanique plaqué sur du vivant."

For my own part, I find Baudelaire's theory very stimulating and in many ways convincing. To my mind he over-emphasizes—and his subsequent restrictions show that he realized it—the diabolic origin of laughter. That there is diabolic laughter, there can be no question. But, aside from the laughter of pure joy and the relatively innocent laughter caused by the grotesque, there can be, I feel sure, a laughter that results not from the sense of one's own superiority, but rather of one's own frailty, a sudden sense of fellow feeling; "there, but for the grace of God. . . ." And even when our laughter is less personally humble, it may come from a sense of the frailty of mankind in general; the absurdity of man's weakness compared to man's high calling. But humility was not the Christian virtue with which Baudelaire was most familiar.

Whatever restrictions may seem necessary in regard to Baudelaire's *theory* of the comic, one can feel nothing but admiration, amazement indeed, in reading "Quelques cari-caturistes français" and "Quelques caricaturistes étrangers." Baudelaire's gift of re-creating a work of art, of making his readers both see it and experience his own impression of it, his power of drawing subtle distinctions, of so characterizing each artist that no confusion is possible, are shown at their highest here. To individualize caricaturists who are often contemporary, who often treat the same subjects, is a tour de force worth pausing over. How does Baudelaire achieve it? How does he give such clarity to our vision, our conception of Charlet, Daumier, Monnier, Grandville, Gavarni, of Hogarth, Cruikshank, Goya, Brueghel? The pattern is much the same for each artist; a general characterization of the subjects treated, the artist's attitude towards them, the particularities of his technique, the description of a few works and the summing-up of all this in a few happy formulas, which often recall the beautiful poetic precision of the stanzas of "Les Phares." But there is nothing rigid about the pattern; sometimes one aspect, sometimes another is emphasized, and anecdote and reminiscence enliven many pages. Here, as always in his art criticism, Baudelaire is entirely frank. He does not hesitate to attack Charlet (to whose defense Delacroix came shortly) and his great reputation: "Cependant il faut avoir le courage de dire que Charlet n'appartient pas à la classe des hommes éternels et des génies cosmopolites. Ce n'est pas un caricaturiste citoyen de l'univers; et, si l'on me répond qu'un caricaturiste ne peut jamais être cela, je dirai qu'il peut l'être plus ou moins. C'est un artiste de circonstance, et un patriote exclusif, deux empêchements au génie" (II, 185-86). This quality of cosmopolitanism is something which we shall find Baudelaire emphasizing more and more; the breadth of vision of the artist, his opening up of new horizons. And Charlet, like Baudelaire's other *bêtes noires*, Béranger and Horace Vernet, is local, narrow-minded, forever playing up to the public. "Il a décalqué l'opinion, il a découpé son intelligence sur la mode. Le public était vraiment son *patron*." And, though he admits that Charlet had once done one good bit of work, he concludes with a scathing denunciation of this "fabricant de niaiseries nationales, commerçant patenté de proverbes politiques."

At the other end of the scale for Baudelaire is Daumier. Here, as in many other cases, his verdict has been ratified by posterity; Charlet's name is little heard now, while Daumier exhibitions, books and articles on Daumier (often quoting Baudelaire) are the order of the day. Baudelaire sketches Daumier's career, beginning with the period of the ferocious political caricatures, in which the pear-headed Louis-Philippe always has the part of an ogre, an assassin, a Gargantua. Then comes the description of other series of caricatures. One instance of Baudelaire's power of evocation must suffice:

Le Dernier Bain, caricature sérieuse et lamentable. — Sur le parapet d'un quai, debout et déjà penché, faisant un angle aigu avec la base d'où il se détache comme une statue qui perd son équilibre, un homme se laisse tomber roide dans la rivière. Il faut qu'il soit bien décidé; ses bras sont tranquillement croisés; un fort gros pavé est attaché à son cou avec une corde. Il a bien juré de n'en pas réchapper. Ce n'est pas un suicide de poëte qui veut être repêché et faire parler de lui. C'est la redingote chétive et grimaçante qu'il faut voir, sous laquelle tous les os font saillie! Et la cravate maladive et tortillée comme un serpent, et la pomme d'Adam, osseuse et pointue! Décidément, on n'a pas le courage d'en vouloir à ce pauvre diable d'aller fuir sous l'eau le spectacle de la civilisation. Dans le fond, de l'autre côté de la rivière, un bourgeois contemplatif, au ventre rondelet, se livre aux délices innocentes de la pêche (II, 192-93).

A sharp visual image, with the salient details of form and gesture; the imagination at work on what is behind the image; the response in the mind of the spectator; the addition of the final detail which underlines the irony of the caricature; all these combine to create an unforgettable picture. I have never seen this particular Daumier, but it is far more vivid to me than many that I have seen.

Finally Baudelaire sums up Daumier as an artist and as a moralist: "Comme artiste, ce qui distingue Daumier, c'est la certitude. Il dessine comme les grands maîtres. Son dessin est abondant, facile, c'est une improvisation suivie; et pourtant ce n'est jamais du *chic*. Il a une mémoire merveilleuse et quasi-divine qui lui tient lieu de modèle. Toutes ses figures sont bien d'aplomb, toujours dans un mouvement vrai." As for Daumier the moralist, he is not unlike Molière; he goes straight to the mark, the meaning is immediately clear. "Sa caricature est formidable d'ampleur, mais sans rancune et sans fiel. Il y a dans toute son œuvre un fond d'honnêteté et de bonhomie" (II, 196).

The other French caricaturists are treated with the same perception, the same discrimination. Monnier is condemned for his lack of creative power; Monsieur Prudhomme was taken from life. "Après l'avoir étudié, il l'a traduit; je me trompe, il l'a décalqué." As for Grandville, he turned nature upside down, but lacked the ability to express himself. Gavarni, on the other hand, is important, though less of an artist than Daumier. Lastly Baudelaire considers the work of some minor caricaturists, always with the same discrimination, the same power of finding "ce je ne sais quoi qui distingue toujours un artiste d'un autre, quelque intime que soit en apparence leur parenté" (II, 205).

When he comes to the foreign caricaturists, Baudelaire discusses half a dozen, somewhat arbitrarily chosen, it seems. England is represented by Hogarth, "singulier et minutieux moraliste," Seymour, and Cruikshank, with his "abondance inépuisable dans le grotesque," a grotesque which is constituted by "la violence extravagante du geste et du mouvement, et l'explosion dans l'expression." Then comes the admirable discussion of Goya,[36] with his peculiar fantastic atmosphere, like that of the chronic dreams to which we are subject. After re-creating some of Goya's works for us Baudelaire concludes: "Le grand mérite de Goya consiste à créer le monstrueux vraisemblable. Ses monstres sont nés viables, harmoniques. Nul n'a osé plus que lui dans le sens de l'absurde possible" (II, 208-9).

Pinelli is hardly a caricaturist at all, according to Baudelaire, who attacks the disorderly life of the artist, pointing out that often the most eccentric and surprising artists are the most orderly in their lives: "N'avez-vous pas remarqué souvent que rien ne ressemble plus au parfait bourgeois que l'artiste de génie concentré?"—a comparison which certainly comes, not from Poe, but from Delacroix. Finally Baudelaire takes up the fantastic work of Brueghel le Drôle, with its extraordinary hallucinatory power, only to be explained by "une espèce de grâce spéciale et satanique," coinciding with the famous "épidémie des sorciers."

This group of articles seems to me to have a place among the very best of Baudelaire's work, and one regrets the loss of the unpublished parts of it. The logical and stimulating theory of the comic is exemplified in the works of the caricaturists. Yet Baudelaire never forces his artists into a preconceived pattern; the connection between example and theory is flexible and never overstrained. Daumier "s'élèverait difficilement au comique absolu"; Cruikshank has as his special merit "une abondance inépuisable dans le grotesque"; while Goya "n'est précisément rien de spécial, de particulier, ni comique absolu, ni comique purement significatif, à la manière française." Always the system is subordinated to the particular artist in question, stretched, if need be, to meet his particular case.

Baudelaire's next critical work was the "Exposition universelle de 1855"; it was destined to be a complete account of the paintings exhibited, but only the introduction and the sections on Ingres and Delacroix were published. The first section was meant particularly to serve as an introduction to the foreign paintings, and is headed "Méthode de critique.— De l'idée moderne du progrès appliquée aux beaux-arts.— Déplacement de la vitalité." It shows how Baudelaire's conception of criticism has developed, what new ideas have been added in the nine years since he first wrote directly of criticism, in the "Salon de 1846." One striking thing is the frequent use of the first person singular, which I have already noted as something almost certainly caught from Poe. But the phraseology and tone alike are De Maistre's, as are the emphasis on the role of Providence in art, the belief in order and hierarchy. To this Baudelaire attaches his own aesthetic convictions, and from De Maistre himself derives a refutation of what the latter says: "Le beau européen est nul pour l'œil

asiatique, et nous-mêmes nous ne savons pas nous accorder"
(*Lettres et opuscules*, II, 137).

One of the main themes here is the necessity for the critic
to acquire "cette grâce divine du cosmopolitisme."[37] Baudelaire's point of departure has a curious quasi-mystical tinge;
the statement of his belief in order and hierarchy,[38] the fore-
ordination of certain nations by Providence for a definite
end, according to "l'immense analogie universelle," and "leur
égale utilité aux yeux de CELUI qui est indéfinissable, et le
miraculeux secours qu'elles se prêtent dans l'harmonie de
l'univers" (II, 143). What, asks Baudelaire, would a modern
Winckelmann do, faced with some bizarre product of Chinese
art? It is an example of universal beauty, but to understand
it the critic must carry out a mysterious transformation
within himself, and, by an act of the will on the imagination,
learn to feel at home in the unfamiliar environment which
gave birth to this work of art, and thus acquire, in a measure
at least, "cette grâce divine du cosmopolitisme." Although the
solitary traveler is perhaps best equipped to grasp "l'admirable,
l'immortel, l'inévitable rapport entre la forme et la fonction,"
still any intelligent man of the world, transplanted to a foreign country, will acquire a whole new world of ideas which
will accompany him, as memories, throughout his life. (Baudelaire is evidently thinking of himself and his brief "voyage
aux Indes," which furnished some of the chief themes of the
Fleurs du Mal.) But the pedant, "l'insensé doctrinaire du
Beau," will reject all such unfamiliar beauties; "les doigts
crispés, paralysés par la plume, ne peuvent plus courir avec
agilité sur l'immense clavier des *correspondances!*" (II, 145.)

This is one of the points at which, as I suggested at the
beginning of this chapter, Baudelaire's poetic experience and
his critical doctrine are closely allied. Perhaps the most important move in all his poetic development was the growth, from
1846 on, of this idea of correspondences. Here cosmopolitanism is seen primarily as a perception of correspondences not
through a "known and familiar landscape" but a strange and

unfamiliar one. This cosmopolitanism (which is above all an aesthetic cosmopolitanism) is also closely related to another idea which Baudelaire had emphasized in 1846; the variety and diversity of beauty. He says here that he had tried more than once to settle down to a system, but in vain: "J'avais beau déplacer ou étendre le criterium, il était toujours en retard sur l'homme universel, et courait sans cesse après le beau multiforme et versicolore, qui se meut dans les spirales infinies de la vie" (II, 145).[39] He concludes: "je suis revenu chercher un asile dans l'impeccable naïveté . . . mon esprit jouit maintenant d'une plus abondante impartialité."

In 1846 Baudelaire had considered particularly the variations of beauty in time; the plea for the *beau moderne* centers on this. Here with his *cosmopolitisme* he emphasizes the variations of beauty in space. Both chronology and geography contribute to the perpetually changing aspects of beauty.

The variety of beauty leads Baudelaire to another statement, often quoted by critics, and too often quoted without the reservations which follow immediately upon it. "*Le beau est toujours bizarre.* Je ne veux pas dire qu'il soit volontairement, froidement bizarre, car dans ce cas il serait un monstre sorti des rails de la vie. Je dis qu'il contient toujours un peu de bizarrerie, de bizarrerie naïve, non voulue, inconsciente, et que c'est cette bizarrerie qui le fait être particulièrement le Beau. C'est son immatriculation, sa caractéristique. Renversez la proportion et tâchez de concevoir un *beau banal!*" (II, 146.) The simple statement is a direct borrowing from Poe, who again and again quotes Bacon: " 'There is no exquisite beauty,' says Bacon, Lord Verulam, speaking truly of all the forms and *genera* of beauty, 'without some *strangeness* in the proportion.' "[40]

Baudelaire then announces that he intends to treat the exhibition without pedantry, without studio jargon. "Je préfère parler au nom du sentiment de la morale et du plaisir. . . . Il m'arrivera souvent d'apprécier un tableau uniquement par la somme d'idées ou de rêveries qu'il apportera dans

mon esprit" (II, 147). This leads him to consider another
error, the idea of progress, which, following in Poe's footsteps,
he damns heartily.[41] He takes up and develops—very much
in his own words here—the ideas on progress, on democracy,
that are found throughout Poe's works, particularly in "Some
Words with a Mummy" and "The Colloquy of Monos and
Una." Baudelaire emphasizes the absurdity of the idea of progress in the realm of the imagination, noting the spontaneous,
individual quality of great works of art, and also the way in
which artistic vitality moves from one nation to another.

This introduction would lead Baudelaire naturally to the
English paintings in the exhibition, but he says "Je retarde
pour mieux faire," and begins with Ingres and Delacroix.
With Ingres, so uncongenial to him in many ways, he is
plainly ill at ease; he writes to Armand Dutacq on June 9,
1855: "Puis, le père Ingres m'a donné un mal de chien"
(Corr. I, 116). Yet he makes a heroic effort to penetrate and
understand his mind and temperament, comparing him with
the great painters of the Revolution. But "l'imagination, cette
reine des facultés, a disparu," he affirms sadly. He enquires
what Ingres's ideal is, and answers: "Je croirais volontiers que
son idéal est une espèce d'idéal fait moitié de santé, moitié de
calme, presque d'indifférence, quelque chose d'analogue à
l'idéal antique, auquel il a ajouté les curiosités et les minuties
de l'art moderne" (II, 154). As for Ingres's drawing, it is
that of "un homme à système," with rearrangements of nature
contrary to all we have learned from Lavater. Baudelaire
particularly criticizes some of Ingres's large paintings for
their "absence totale de sentiment et de surnaturalisme." He
says in conclusion that what has made Ingres what he is, is
"un immense abus de la volonté."

Passing from Ingres to Delacroix, Baudelaire seems to
breathe a sigh of relief. All his old enthusiasm is here, all the
ardent championship of his hero. (The abundance of exclamation points, in general far from common with Baudelaire,
emphasizes the eager tone.) There were thirty-five paintings

by Delacroix in the exhibition, and Baudelaire looks at all of them with delight. Much of what he says is the development, even the repetition of what he had said in 1845 and 1846, about Delacroix's color, his drawing, his "literary" quality. But it is said in new terms, and certainly experienced and felt anew. Baudelaire recalls a passage from Poe: "Edgar Poe dit, je ne sais plus où, que le résultat de l'opium pour les sens est de revêtir la nature entière d'un intérêt surnaturel qui donne à chaque objet un sens plus profond, plus volontaire, plus despotique."[42] Such hours may come without opium, and Delacroix's painting is the translation of them: "Comme la nature perçue par des nerfs ultra-sensibles, elle révèle le surnaturalisme" (II, 164).

The "Exposition de 1855," while it contains admirable passages, lacks unity from the very fact of being incomplete. The Ingres and Delacroix sections are companion pieces, but the introductory part belongs not to them but to the unwritten section on the English painters. The great interest is in this introduction, where Baudelaire seems to pause and take stock of his aesthetic beliefs. They are not at bottom new, as I have pointed out; the idea of cosmopolitanism and the carefully hedged-in apology for the bizarre are alike developments of the "variations du beau." And Baudelaire ties to this the anti-progress ideas he has learned from Poe and De Maistre. But the most important development is, I think, the predominance of the word, and the idea, of *surnaturalisme*, so closely connected with the doctrine of correspondences.

This same year 1855 is marked by the publication of "De l'essence du rire," and also by an article on the actor Philibert Rouvière, whom Baudelaire greatly admired. In this case we cannot, as is so often possible, test Baudelaire's verdict by that of posterity, and pronounce him right and his contemporaries wrong. The cinema and the phonograph will preserve something of the actors of our day for posterity to judge afresh, but the actors of the past must stand or fall by the judgment of their contemporaries.

To this period belong also three articles or fragments of articles published recently for the first time by M. Crépet. Two of them, the unfinished "Jules Janin et le *Gâteau des rois*," and the brief review of a *Histoire de Neuilly* are of little interest. But the third, "Puisque réalisme il y a," is worth pausing over. It was apparently called forth by the Courbet exhibition of 1855 (in which the *Atelier du peintre*, with Baudelaire's portrait, was included), and the publication of Champfleury's "Sur Courbet, lettre à Madame Sand," in *L'Artiste* on September 2. Baudelaire had been interested in the realist movement in its early days, indeed sympathetic with it, but had quickly realized how alien it was to his own convictions about art. The title of his article evidently comes from a letter from Courbet to Champfleury, describing his picture, of which he says: "ce qui fera voir que je ne suis pas encore mort et le réalisme non plus, puisque réalisme il y a."[43] It seems then that Baudelaire had considered putting his break with realism on record, but, as M. Crépet suggests, perhaps decided that his just-published "Exposition de 1855" made his position sufficiently clear, and so gave up finishing and publishing his protest.

The article—hardly more than a string of notes—consists mainly of a violent attack on Champfleury and Courbet, "le Machiavel maladroit de ce Borgia." But then comes:

> Cependant, *if at all*, si Réalisme a un sens — discussion sérieuse.
> Tout bon poëte fut toujours *réaliste*.
> Equation entre l'impression et l'expression.
> Sincérité.
> Prendre Banville pour exemple.[44]

Then comes an admirable definition of poetry:

> La Poésie est ce qu'il y a de plus réel, c'est ce qui n'est complètement vrai que dans *un autre monde*.
> Ce monde-ci, dictionnaire hiéroglyphique.[45]

and finally the suggestion: "(*Analyse de la Nature, du talent de Courbet, et de la morale.*)" The outlined article is interesting as expressing more vigorously than any of Baudelaire's published articles his reaction against realism, and the suggestive phrases of the latter part make one regret that it was carried no further.

The next two years saw the publication of Baudelaire's two major articles on Poe; "Edgar Poe, sa vie et ses œuvres," published in the translation of the *Histoires extraordinaires* in 1856, and the "Notes nouvelles sur Edgar Poe," published in the *Nouvelles histoires extraordinaires* in the following year. The first of these is in part a condensation and revamping of the earlier sections of the 1852 article; though Baudelaire writes to his mother on March 15, 1856, when sending her the *Histoires extraordinaires*: "— Lisez la notice; — ce n'est pas celle que vous connaissez. — Il n'est pas resté cinquante lignes de la première. — Celle-ci est faite de manière à faire hurler" (*L.M.*, pp. 113-14). Many passages of the earlier article are cut out, and there are relatively few additions, the most important being the long paragraph at the end of the first section anathematizing America and progress (*Poe*, pp. 684-85), and the defense of Poe's drunkenness as "un moyen mnémonique, une méthode de travail, méthode énergique et mortelle, mais appropriée à sa nature passionnée" (*Poe*, p. 696). On the other hand the last section, on Poe's works, is almost entirely new.[46]

The whole article shows the most careful labor; the changing of words, of phrases, of construction, the transposition of sentences, all go to show that Baudelaire expended the same untiring labor on his critical work as on his poetry. A comparison of the two texts is illuminating; let me take as an example only the first few sentences of each:

1852: Il existe des destinées fatales; il existe dans la littérature de chaque pays des hommes qui portent le mot *guignon* écrit en caractères mystérieux dans les plis sinueux de leurs fronts. Il y a quelque temps, on amenait devant les tribunaux un malheureux qui avait sur le front un tatouage singulier: *pas de chance.* Il portait ainsi toujours avec lui l'étiquette de sa vie, comme un livre son titre, et l'interrogatoire prouva que son existence s'était conformée à cet écriteau. Dans l'histoire littéraire, il y a des fortunes analogues (*Poe,* p. 653).

1856: Dans ces derniers temps, un malheureux fut amené devant nos tribunaux, dont le front était illustré d'un rare et singulier tatouage: *Pas de chance!* Il portait ainsi au-dessus de ses yeux l'étiquette de sa vie, comme un livre son titre, et l'interrogatoire prouve que ce bizarre écriteau était cruellement véridique. Il y a, dans l'histoire littéraire, des destinées analogues, de vraies damnations, — des hommes qui portent le mot *guignon* écrit en caractères mystérieux dans les plis sinueux de leur front (*Poe,* p. 682).

The effect of the passage is far more dramatic in 1856, with the anecdote put at the beginning and the interpretation following. The minor changes all tend towards a greater precision: "dans ces derniers temps" instead of "il y a quelque temps"; the added emphasis of "*rare et* singulier tatouage"; the precision of "au-dessus de ses yeux" as compared to "avec lui"; and the added force and terseness of "ce bizarre écriteau était cruellement véridique" which replaces "son existence s'était conformée à cet écriteau." The study of successive versions of a Baudelaire text, whether poetry or prose, is as good a lesson in style as is to be found anywhere; he is always changing, modifying, and one can nearly always see that the change is for the better, and why.[47]

There are occasional passages which show how Baudelaire's opinions had changed; in 1852 his praise of Poe's first volume of poetry had been faint, but here he says: "Pour qui sait sentir la poésie anglaise, il y a là déjà l'accent extraterrestre, le calme dans la mélancolie, la solennité délicieuse, l'expérience précoce, — j'allais, je crois, dire *expérience innée,* — qui caractérisent les grands poëtes" (*Poe,* p. 687). Baudelaire's very brief final section on Poe's work shows further meditation, and a constant comparison of Poe with himself, as when he speaks of the way in which Poe has treated "les *exceptions* de la vie humaine et de la nature; — les ardeurs de curiosité de la convalescence; — les fins de saisons chargées de splendeurs énervantes, les temps chauds, humides et brumeux où le vent du sud amollit et détend les nerfs comme les cordes d'un instrument, où les yeux se remplissent de larmes qui ne viennent pas du cœur" (*Poe*, p. 698). It is the very mood not only of Poe's "Shadow" but of Baudelaire's "Causerie" and "Ciel brouillé." Again, in the comparison of Poe and Delacroix which was so little to the latter's taste, Baudelaire creates an atmosphere which is Poe's indeed, but also his own. But the major part of the article is biographical; Baudelaire himself described it to Sainte-Beuve:

La première préface que vous avez vue, et dans laquelle j'ai essayé d'enfermer une vive protestation contre l'américanisme, est à peu près complète, au point de vue biographique. On fera semblant de ne vouloir considérer Poe que comme *jongleur*, mais je reviendrai à outrance sur le caractère surnaturel de sa poésie et de ses contes. Il n'est Américain qu'en tant que *jongleur*. Quant au reste, c'est presque une pensée *antiaméricaine*. D'ailleurs, il s'est moqué de ses compatriotes le plus qu'il a pu (*Corr.* I, 138-39).

The "Notes nouvelles sur Edgar Poe" are described by Baudelaire in an earlier letter: "Vous verrez, à la fin de la Notice (laquelle contredit toutes les opinions à la mode sur les *Etats-Unis*), que j'annonce de nouvelles études. Je parlerai plus tard des opinions de cet homme singulier, en matière de science, de philosophie et de littérature" (*Corr.* I, 137). And, a week later: "La deuxième préface contiendra l'analyse des ouvrages que je ne traduirai pas, et surtout l'exposé des opinions *scientifiques* et *littéraires* de l'auteur" (*Corr.* I, 138). The composition of this preface was not without its difficulties; a little later Baudelaire writes to his mother: "Ma seconde notice me donne un mal de tous les diables. Il faut parler *religion* et *science*; tantôt c'est l'instruction suffisante qui me manque, tantôt l'argent, ou le calme, ce qui est presque la même chose" (*L.M.*, p. 116). And months later he writes to

Godefroy: "Je suis en train d'en écrire la préface, et, comme je n'accouche que douloureusement, cela pourrait bien durer quelque temps" (*Corr.* I, 141).

The "Notes nouvelles" are devoted almost entirely to Poe's literary theories, his "poetic principles." Baudelaire draws very largely, as we shall see, on the "Poetic Principle" and also on "Marginalia," from which a large number of passages are quoted.[48] He begins with a protest against the glib phrase, "littérature de décadence," which leads to his favorite theme of the "variations du beau" from age to age. But Baudelaire's antiprogress ardor is never a wistful looking back to the good old times; it never conflicts with the idea of the *beau moderne.* Here, for example, one of Baudelaire's chief diatribes against the doctrine of progress follows immediately on his defense of the "littérature de décadence."

Baudelaire notes Poe's emphasis on the natural wickedness of man: "la Perversité naturelle, qui fait que l'homme est sans cesse et à la fois homicide et suicide, assassin et bourreau" (*Poe,* p. 702). He is thinking especially of the "Spirit of PERVERSENESS" of "The Black Cat," and the story "The Imp of the Perverse." In reading what Baudelaire says, and comparing it with Poe's text, one realizes how the conception has been colored and deepened by the doctrine of original sin; it is no surprise to find De Maistre's name on the next page, where Baudelaire says of the "Colloquy of Monos and Una": "ces admirables pages . . . eussent charmé et troublé l'impeccable De Maistre." The transformation of Poe's thought is symbolized by Baudelaire's translation of "The *Imp* of Perverseness" by "Le *Démon* de la Perversité."

Then Baudelaire goes back to Poe's denunciation of Progress, "cette grande hérésie de la décrépitude." All his antidemocratic zeal, his anti-Americanism, is given full vent here. Poe's literary theories, Baudelaire continues, are a revolt against the literary errors inevitably engendered in such surroundings. He divides the world of the spirit into "intellect pur, goût et sens moral"; for him, "l'imagination est la reine des facultés" (*Poe*, p. 707). In the domain of the imagination, the short story was particularly dear to Poe, for reasons which he has often given, and which Baudelaire repeats. As for poetry, Baudelaire gives a long quotation from Poe on the "*genus irritabile vatum*," and then rehearses Poe's theories, noting his emphasis on technique: "Il affirmait que celui qui ne sait pas saisir l'intangible n'est pas poëte; que celui-là seul est poëte qui est le maître de sa mémoire, le souverain des mots, le registre de ses propres sentiments toujours prêt à se laisser feuilleter" (*Poe*, p. 709).

The rest of the article is drawn largely, with or without quotation marks, from the "Poetic Principle."[49] There is no surer test, I think, of the degree of Baudelaire's acceptance of Poe's poetic doctrine than a careful comparison of the two texts. Baudelaire begins by quoting approvingly Poe's condemnation of that "contradiction in terms," the long poem. He notes also, with Poe, that *too* short a poem is also faulty, in that its effect is not profound or enduring. Skipping Poe's examples of this, Baudelaire comes to the "heresy of *The Didactic*," the idea that the object of Poetry is Truth, and every poem should inculcate a moral. Paraphrasing Poe he concludes: "La poésie, pour peu qu'on veuille descendre en soi-même, interroger son âme, rappeler ses souvenirs d'enthousiasme, n'a pas d'autre but qu'elle-même; elle ne peut pas en avoir d'autre, et aucun poëme ne sera si grand, si noble, si véritablement digne du nom de poëme, que celui qui aura été écrit uniquement pour le plaisir d'écrire un poëme" (*Poe*, p. 710). But at this point Baudelaire seems unwilling to go all the way with Poe, and he adds two sentences which have no counterpart in the "Poetic Principle": "Je ne veux pas dire que la poésie n'ennoblisse pas les mœurs, — qu'on me comprenne bien, — que son résultat final ne soit pas d'élever l'homme au-dessus du niveau des intérêts vulgaires; ce serait évidemment une absurdité. Je dis que, si le poëte a poursuivi un but moral, il a diminué sa force poétique; et il n'est pas imprudent de parier que son œuvre sera mauvaise." Baudelaire, while opposing, with Poe, any direct utilitarian aim, is keeping to his position of 1851 (in the "Drames et romans honnêtes") that great poetry, great art, are indirectly, but inevitably, "useful." With this reservation, Baudelaire goes back to Poe and his distinction between Truth and Poetry, and the division of "the world of the mind" into the Pure Intellect, Taste and the Moral Sense—all of which Baudelaire reproduces faithfully, with the comment "je ne crois pas qu'il soit scandalisant de considérer toute infraction à la morale, au beau moral, comme une espèce de faute contre le rhythme et la prosodie universels."

This leads to Poe's paragraph on the sense of the beautiful, which Baudelaire introduces with a sentence of his own, allying what Poe says to his own dear doctrine: "C'est cet admirable, cet immortel instinct du beau qui nous fait considérer la terre et ses spectacles comme un aperçu, comme une correspondance du Ciel" (*Poe*, p. 711). The two paragraphs which follow are Baudelaire's distillation of the quintessence of Poe's somewhat diffuse pages on Beauty and Poetry. He returns to the distinction of the Poetic Sentiment from Truth and Passion; Baudelaire comments: "Car la passion est *naturelle*, trop naturelle pour ne pas introduire un ton blessant, discordant, dans le domaine de la beauté pure, trop familière et trop violente pour ne pas scandaliser les purs désirs, les gracieuses mélancolies et les nobles désespoirs qui habitent les régions surnaturelles de la poésie" (*Poe*, p. 711). Here Baudelaire leaves the "Poetic Principle," the last half of which is chiefly illustrations drawn from various poets of what has preceded.

There is no question but that Baudelaire accepted wholeheartedly many of Poe's ideas. But it seems equally true that he kept his independence, that he refused to go all the way with Poe and cut every bond between life and poetry. What he leaves out is significant too; Poe's underlined definition of Poetry as "*The Rhythmical Creation of Beauty.*" In these pages, where critics have tended to see Baudelaire's most complete subjugation to Poe, his omissions and additions alike show his own mind constantly at work. Even when he follows Poe's thought all the way, he makes it his own in form again and again, crystallizing Poe's scattered and dash-littered sentences into terse formulas of incomparable beauty.

Baudelaire notes next in Poe what is akin to what he has often said of Delacroix: "Cette extraordinaire élévation, cette exquise délicatesse, cet accent d'immortalité qu'Edgar Poe exige de la Muse, loin de le rendre moins attentif aux pratiques d'exécution, l'ont poussé à aiguiser sans cesse son génie de praticien" (*Poe*, p. 711). The partisans of inspiration would be shocked, he says, by Poe's analysis, in the "Philosophy of Composition," of his writing of "The Raven," "avec une légère impertinence que je ne puis blâmer." Baudelaire defends Poe, but with, I think, a shadow of uneasiness which will be accentuated two years later in his prefatory note to his translation of "The Raven" and the "Philosophy of Composition" (*Revue Française*, April 20, 1859). The note begins: "La poétique est faite, nous disait-on, et modelée d'après les poëmes. Voici un poëte qui prétend que son poëme a été composé d'après sa poétique." But Baudelaire questions the principle:

Il avait certes un grand génie et plus d'inspiration que qui que ce soit, si par inspiration on entend l'énergie, l'enthousiasme intellectuel, et la faculté de tenir ses facultés en éveil. Mais il aimait aussi le travail plus qu'aucun autre; il répétait volontiers, lui, un original achevé, que l'originalité est chose d'apprentissage, ce qui ne veut pas dire une chose qui peut être transmise par l'enseignement. Le hasard et l'incompréhensible étaient ses deux grands ennemis. S'est-il fait, par une vanité étrange et amusante, beaucoup moins inspiré qu'il ne l'était naturellement? A-t-il diminué la faculté gratuite qui était en lui pour faire la part la plus belle à la vanité? Je serais assez porté à le croire.[50]

So though Baudelaire insists that the *amateurs du délire* would do well to consider how art profits by deliberation, he still resists Poe's theory in this extreme form, which is funda-

mentally opposed to his deepest convictions as to the relation
between practice and theory, poetry and criticism.

The "Notes nouvelles," after discussing Poe's theories, go
on to characterize his poetry: "C'est quelque chose de profond
et de miroitant comme le rêve, de mystérieux et de parfait
comme le cristal" (*Poe*, p. 712). And Baudelaire ends on a
note already struck in the "Poetic Principle," "l'hérésie
moderne capitale, — l'enseignement."

The Poe articles—especially the parts that are Baudelaire's
rather than Poe's—are still good reading, even though posterity has dealt somewhat less gently with Poe than with
many of Baudelaire's enthusiasms. But Baudelaire's eagerness
is so compelling, his devotion to his subject so overwhelming
that he creates for us, in all honesty, a Poe greater than our
own. There is a tone in Baudelaire's writings—a tone of
mingled respect and affection, born of the most intense
admiration—that is reserved for Delacroix and Poe alone.

To this period belong also the notes for an article on *Les
Liaisons dangereuses*, interesting as showing Baudelaire's
method in writing an article. The notes are divided into three
parts: I, *Biographie*—notes on Laclos' life, with indications of
their sources; II, *Notes*—a miscellaneous jotting down of all
sorts of things that had come into Baudelaire's mind during
his reading, from anathemas on George Sand to a note on
"Puissance de l'analyse racinienne. . . . Talent rare aujourd'hui, excepté chez Stendhal, Sainte-Beuve et Balzac";
III, *Intrigue et Caractères*—largely quotations. Although
Baudelaire's correspondence for 1856 and 1857 indicates a
continued interest in Laclos, the article was unfortunately
never completed. There are many notes and phrases one would
like to see developed, such as those on the differences in man-
ners and morality between the eighteenth and nineteenth cen-
turies, and on the pre-Byronic note in Laclos: "Car Byron
était *préparé*, comme Michel-Ange. Le grand homme n'est
jamais aérolithe." Moreover the article would show us Bau-

delaire dealing, for almost the only time in his criticism, not with a contemporary work, but with a work of the past.

The best of all Baudelaire's literary criticism, to my mind, is the short article on *Madame Bovary*, published in October, 1857. The correspondence between Flaubert and Baudelaire shows a sincere mutual admiration.[51] In 1861, at the time of his candidacy for the Academy, Baudelaire writes to Flaubert: "Comment n'avez-vous pas deviné que Baudelaire, ça voulait dire: Auguste Barbier, Th. Gautier, Banville, Flaubert, Leconte de Lisle, c'est-à-dire *littérature pure*?" (*Corr.* I, 411). And to the end of his life Baudelaire sees in Flaubert one of the few exceptions to the "racaille moderne."

The article, after thanking the magistrates for their acquittal of Flaubert, indicates his position among contemporary novelists, and suggests how *Madame Bovary*, "une gageure, une vraie gageure, un pari, comme toutes les œuvres d'art," was conceived and created. Baudelaire suggests that Madame Bovary is Flaubert himself, endowed by her creator, perhaps unconsciously, with all the virile virtues; the imagination taking the place of the heart, the rapid energy in action, the "goût immodéré de la séduction"—"le tout se résumant en deux mots: dandysme, amour exclusif de la domination."

All this sounds like a development of Flaubert's "Madame Bovary, c'est moi"—but when, if ever, did Flaubert say these words? All through his letters he is maintaining quite the opposite: "*Madame Bovary* n'a rien de vrai. C'est une histoire *totalement inventée*; je n'y ai rien mis ni de mes sentiments ni de mon existence."[52] That "Madame Bovary, c'est moi," seems to have been realized—or at least admitted—by Flaubert only after the publication of the novel. It appears that a certain Mademoiselle Bosquet having asked Flaubert where he had got the character of Emma, he replied: "Madame Bovary, *c'est moi; — d'après moi*."[53] Was this said, one wonders, after Baudelaire's article had appeared and brought home to Flaubert a truth which he had not admitted even to himself? Or had the realization come of its own accord? At all events,

Flaubert found the article entirely to his liking, writing to
Baudelaire on October 21: "Votre article m'a fait le plus *grand*
plaisir. Vous êtes entré dans les arcanes de l'œuvre, comme si
ma cervelle était la vôtre. Cela est senti et compris *à fond.*"[54]

One appreciates the article fully only when one compares
it with the many other reviews of *Madame Bovary*, including
Sainte-Beuve's. Sainte-Beuve analyzes the novel and its background carefully and conscientiously, recognizes many of its
great qualities, and finds many an apt phrase. But Baudelaire's
article possesses in the highest degree the qualities of penetra-
tion, of getting at the very heart of a matter with an almost
breath-taking sureness, that marks Baudelaire at his best. The
whole analysis of *Madame Bovary*, too long to quote, is
admirable in its insight and expression. Baudelaire ends with
a few words on the *Tentation de Saint-Antoine*: "M. Gustave
Flaubert a volontairement voilé dans *Madame Bovary* les
hautes facultés lyriques et ironiques manifestées sans réserve
dans la *Tentation*, et . . . cette dernière œuvre, chambre
secrète de son esprit, reste évidemment la plus intéressante
pour les poëtes et les philosophes" (II, 450).

Baudelaire's admiration for Flaubert's later work is shown
in a letter to Poulet-Malassis of December 13, 1862: "Quant
à *Salammbô*, grand, grand succès. Une édition de 2.000 en-
levée en deux jours. *Positif.* Beau livre, plein de défauts, et
qui met en fureur tous les taquins, particulièrement Babou.
*Il y en a qui reprochent à Flaubert les imitations des auteurs
anciens.* Ce que Flaubert a fait, lui seul pouvait le faire. Beaucoup trop de bric-à-brac, mais beaucoup de grandeurs, épiques, historiques, politiques, animales même. Quelque chose
d'étonnant dans la gesticulation de tous les êtres" (*Corr.*
I, 425-26).

Another piece of literary criticism is the article on Asselineau's volume of short stories, *La Double Vie*, published in
1858.[55] Baudelaire's praise of the work of his friend and
future biographer is discreet and perceptive, and when one
has blown the dust off the Bibliothèque Nationale's copy of

La Double Vie it does not seem exaggerated. The little volume has freshness and charm; as Baudelaire says: "Ce charmant petit livre, personnel, excessivement personnel, est comme un monologue d'hiver, murmuré par l'auteur, les pieds sur les chenets" (II, 456).

Here, as so often, one notes what riches Baudelaire pours into a brief review, how whatever he has been reading and thinking brings its contribution. Thus the article is built up on the idea of the *homo duplex*, the title of a chapter of Buffon's.[56] We are reminded too that Baudelaire was working on the *Confessions d'un mangeur d'opium* by his use of the phrase "touched with pensiveness" and, at the end, the exclamation, "Thou art the man," which occurs in the *English Opium-Eater* and is also the title of a story of Poe's.[57]

Perhaps the most interesting thing connected with this book is the discovery of the proof sheets of Asselineau's preface (which Baudelaire does not mention), with annotations by Baudelaire in the margin.[58] There are a large number of typographical corrections, and such acid stylistic and grammatical comments as "toute la phrase affreusement embourbée." Most interesting perhaps is his annotation to Asselineau's attack on the *école du bon sens*: "En passant, voici l'histoire du mot. Je causais avec St-Alme d'un ouvrage de ce genre et je dis: faut-il être bête pour croire qu'on fait une comédie avec du bon sens! St-Alme se tordit de joie. Il trouva ma folie si grande qu'il fit de notre conversation une nouvelle à la main. Par Viard, Champfleury, etc. . . . , qui adoptèrent le mot, le mot est resté." As M. Crépet points out, a very similar note is found in the "Drames et romans honnêtes" (II, 759-60), where many of Asselineau's ideas are to be found. One has the impression very decidedly that the marginal notes are far from being Baudelaire's first contribution to the Preface. What Asselineau says of an author's difficulties in dealing with editors, his defense of art for art's sake ("Faire le bien est le domaine de la morale; bien faire est la mission de l'artiste"), his attack on the *école du bon sens* and on *l'art*

philosophique all have a very familiar ring, and seem almost
certainly to be the fruit of much conversation with Baudelaire,
if not actually dictated by him.

The following year, 1859, brings Baudelaire's most ambitious effort in the way of literary criticism, the "Théophile
Gautier." The sincerity of the article has been the object of
much discussion;[59] I should like to recall first of all the more
significant mentions of Gautier in Baudelaire's work up to
this time. The "Salon de 1845" has a word of very moderate
praise: "M. Th. Gautier, quand les œuvres vont bien à son
tempérament et à son éducation littéraires, commente bien
ce qu'il sent juste" (II, 19). But in the "Salon de 1846" the
comment is acid: "Je ne sais pourquoi M. Théophile Gautier
a endossé cette année le carrick et la pèlerine de l'*homme
bienfaisant*: car il a loué tout le monde, et il n'est si malheureux barbouilleur dont il n'ait catalogué les tableaux"
(II, 105). The criticism is indeed tempered with praise: "La
nature a doué M. Gautier d'un esprit excellent, large et
poétique. Tout le monde sait quelle sauvage admiration il a
toujours témoignée pour les œuvres franches et abondantes"
(II, 106). But the "Conseils aux jeunes littérateurs" of the
same year refer to "les feuilletons souvent médiocres de
Théophile Gautier" (II, 389). (The "souvent médiocres" is
deleted in the first edition of *L'Art romantique*.) However
the "Caricaturistes étrangers" refers to Gautier's "excellent
article" on Goya, and 1857 brings the dazzling dedication to
Gautier of the *Fleurs du Mal*: "au poëte impeccable, au parfait magicien ès lettres françaises." It would seem that up to
the dedication Baudelaire has felt no great urge to praise
Gautier (it must not be forgotten, however, that the previous
allusions are all to Gautier's critical work, not to his poetry).

As for the Gautier article itself, Baudelaire seems to have
hesitated about writing it, for a letter to him of January 31,
1859, from Edouard Houssaye, then the director of *L'Artiste*,
says: "Décidément, voulez-vous faire l'étude sur Gautier? Si

oui, donnez-la cette semaine; si non, je vais la faire faire par un autre ami de Gautier" (*Crépet*, p. 375). But the article once finished, Baudelaire seems pleased with it; he writes to Poulet-Malassis on February 13: "J'ai fini l'étude sur Gautier. Je crois qu'il sera content, ainsi que vous et tous nos amis" (*Corr.* I, 234). A letter to Gautier's son, on February 27, is perhaps more revealing: "si je me suis appliqué, c'est non seulement pour être agréable à Théo, mais aussi pour la satisfaction de ma vanité" (*Corr.* I, 244).

The article is to my mind the least satisfactory of all Baudelaire's criticism. Not only does Baudelaire's Gautier seem magnified to unduly heroic proportions to a generation that knows not Gautier; but also one suspects that Baudelaire himself was not unaware of the exaggeration. I have already suggested that Baudelaire's literary criticism seems sometimes to lack the fine flavor of complete disinterestedness that is the hallmark of the art criticism; here, more than anywhere else, one is uncomfortably conscious that Baudelaire is writing about a contemporary whose opinion and influence might be of great use to him. I am far from denying Baudelaire's admiration for Gautier, especially in his early years, or Gautier's influence on his poetry.[60] It seems to me however that in this article the ashes of a youthful enthusiasm are not fanned into flame without conscious effort. The very fact that, more than any other article, it is a patchwork product, is significant; it contains not only two direct quotations from the "Notes nouvelles sur Edgar Poe," one of them a very long one,[61] but also a passage which borrows largely from the "Drames et romans honnêtes,"[62] and a page which also appears, with only slight variations, in the "Salon de 1859."[63] It seems as if Baudelaire had felt himself becoming a bit short-winded in his praises of Gautier, and had felt the need of padding; hence this mosaic of borrowed passages. Another curious point is the resemblances one notices here and there between Baudelaire's Gautier and his Poe. The same phrases recur about both, as for example "il n'était jamais dupe"

(II, 480; *Poe*, p. 701). The mantle of Poe seems to have
fallen on Gautier.

From the beginning the tone of the article seems forced;
one has only to compare what Baudelaire says of Gautier's
"Salons," "si calmes, si pleins de candeur et de majesté," of
Gautier as "un critique incomparable et indispensable" (II,
458), with his previous comments on Gautier's criticism.
Gautier has now become for him the figure of the antidemocratic poet, unappreciated by the public. "En littérature
comme en morale, il y a danger, autant que gloire, à être
délicat. L'aristocratie nous isole" (II, 460).

Baudelaire recalls his first visit to Gautier and looks back
wistfully to the great days of the romantic movement when
"Chateaubriand, toujours plein de force, mais comme couché
à l'horizon, semblait un Athos qui contemple nonchalamment
le mouvement de la plaine" (II, 463). In connection with
Mademoiselle de Maupin he reiterates what he had said of the
heresy of didacticism in the "Notes nouvelles." It is by his
exclusive devotion to the Beautiful that Gautier excels, and
by the marvels of his style. Then comes a curious passage in
which Baudelaire, without giving chapter and verse, dis-
covers in Gautier a master of correspondences:

Si l'on réfléchit qu'à cette merveilleuse faculté Gautier unit une
immense intelligence innée de la *correspondance* et du symbolisme
universels, ce répertoire de toute métaphore, on comprendra qu'il
puisse sans cesse, sans fatigue comme sans faute, définir l'attitude
mystérieuse que les objets de la création tiennent devant le regard
de l'homme. Il y a dans le mot, dans le *verbe*, quelque chose de
sacré qui nous défend d'en faire un jeu de hasard. Manier savamment
une langue, c'est pratiquer une espèce de sorcellerie évocatoire (II,
470-71).[64]

Baudelaire then discusses Gautier's novels and short stories,
with their "grâce *sui generis*." (Much later he writes to his
mother: "Et le *Fracasse* t'amuse-t-il? Il y a des beautés étonnantes.") Here is included the admirable passage on Balzac
which I have quoted earlier. When Baudelaire comes to the
poetry, he characterizes Gautier's muse excellently:

Ainsi va, dans son allure variée, cette muse bizarre, aux toilettes multiples, muse cosmopolite douée de la souplesse d'Alcibiade; quel-quefois le front ceint de la mitre orientale, l'air grand et sacré, les bandelettes au vent; d'autres fois, se pavanant comme une reine de Saba en goguette, son petit parasol de cuivre à la main, sur l'élé-phant de porcelaine qui décore les cheminées du siècle galant (II, 475).

It is particularly when Baudelaire comes to Gautier as a critic that the reader, remembering his previous strictures on Gautier's "Salons," feels ill at ease on reading that Gautier is "un auteur critique tout à fait à part." But the very vagueness of the terms is significant, and Baudelaire turns quickly to a disquisition on the non-artistic nature of the French public. This leads him to the statement that France is not poetic either, and so to Gautier's poetry and the hyperbolic state-ment: "Nos voisins disent: Shakspeare et Goethe! nous pou-vons leur répondre: Victor Hugo et Théophile Gautier" (II, 478).[65] But Baudelaire's page on Gautier's poetry is one of his best, noting on the one hand its melancholy, continuing the romantic tradition but with a character of its own, "plus positif, plus charnel, et confinant quelquefois à la tristesse antique," and on the other hand a new quality, "la consola-tion par les arts." "Ténèbres," "prodigieuse symphonie," is a poem which he admires particularly. One of the epigraphs of the 1856 Poe article is taken from it, and in this same year of 1859 Baudelaire refers to it in "La Genèse d'un poëme" as "ce chapelet de redoutables concetti sur la mort et le néant, où la rime triplée s'adapte si bien à la mélancolie obsédante" (Eureka, p. 155).

Baudelaire's final prophecy, that "devant la postérité, il sera un des maîtres écrivains, non-seulement de la France, mais aussi de l'Europe," is still unfulfilled; indeed the figure of Gautier has singularly diminished, and it seems unlikely that it will ever attain the heroic stature foretold for it. How far Baudelaire's judgment is an honest, if mistaken one, how far it was dictated by self-interest, it is difficult to tell. The truth certainly lies between the two extremes. Baudelaire's admiration for parts, at least, of Gautier's work, are too precisely expressed not to be truthful; on the other hand, the vagueness of the hyperbolic terms of admiration makes one doubt their authenticity and question the enthronement of Gautier as "UN PARFAIT HOMME DE LETTRES" (II, 481). The phrase is however significant; is not Baudelaire using Gautier as a kind of lay figure on which to hang his conception of the man of letters, partly borrowed from Poe, partly wrought out of his own experience? The delightful porcelain figure of a poet that Gautier is for us is overlaid with the bronze of immortality, and the weight seems too heavy for it to bear.

The article was republished in pamphlet form the same year, with the added panoply of a letter-preface by Victor Hugo. Baudelaire's letter to Victor Hugo asking him to write this preface contains a passage which seems to bear out what I have suggested:

Relativement à l'écrivain qui fait le sujet de cet article et dont le nom a servi de prétexte à mes considérations critiques, je puis avouer confidentiellement que je connais les lacunes de son étonnant esprit. Bien des fois, pensant à lui, j'ai été affligé de voir que Dieu ne voulait pas être absolument généreux. Je n'ai pas menti, j'ai esquivé, j'ai dissimulé. Si j'étais appelé à témoigner en justice, et si mon témoignage, absolument véridique, pouvait nuire à un être favorisé par la nature et aimé par mon cœur, je vous jure que je mentirais avec fierté! parce que les lois sont au-dessous du sentiment, parce que l'amitié est, de sa nature, infaillible et ingouvernable. Mais, vis-à-vis de vous, il me semble inutile de mentir (*Corr.* I, 274).

The sincerity of this paragraph, as well as that of the article, might be questioned. But however much Baudelaire may be trying to win Hugo's favor, as he may well have been trying to win Gautier's in the article, the letter seems to me to have the truer ring.

I have somewhat arbitrarily, I must confess, brought this period of Baudelaire's criticism to an end with the Gautier article, almost contemporary with the "Salon de 1859," with which I shall begin what seems to me the period of Baudelaire's supreme critical activity. It is not merely that the Gautier seems to me unworthy to be classed with the articles that follow; it also appears to mark the close of the long period in which we feel that the shadow of Poe lies over nearly all that Baudelaire writes. So this seems the moment to look back over the thirteen years since the first "Salons" and see what changes they have brought.

Most noticeable of all, I think, is the development of Baudelaire's power of expression, his ability to render with marvelous precision the particular quality of the picture, the book, the artist, the author he is discussing. He says in the Gautier article "j'avais été pris très-jeune de lexicomanie" (II, 461), and the power over words, the ability to make them convey an atmosphere, an impression, is one of his greatest critical gifts. Whether it be the various caricaturists, the temperament of Ingres, Poe's tales, Gautier's poetry, there is always the right word, the subtle distinction.

When one turns to Baudelaire's critical ideas, there is much to note. First of all, his preoccupation with the artist, both in relation to his own work and to society. All this is closely bound up with Baudelaire's religious and social views, his ultra-orthodox theology and his artistocratic, antidemocratic, antiprogressive position. Also, Baudelaire's conception of the poet, the artist, has altered—or at least enlarged—from that of the artist who depends on an inner ideal, on temperament, on *naïveté*, to that of the artist who is above all a visionary, one who perceives analogies and correspondences. Not that there is a sharp break between the two; but the earlier conception is gradually spiritualized and elevated to supernatural regions. (The frequent use of the word *surnaturel* is one of the key notes of this period.) The conception of the imagination rises to higher levels, to culminate in the great glorification of the imagination in the "Salon de 1859." Baudelaire's criticism has been greatly enriched in these years, and in the process he has laid many a source under contribution.

Baudelaire's debt to De Maistre is theological and philosophical rather than directly aesthetic and critical; De Maistre's writings affect his whole thought and touch his poetry as much as his criticism, if not more. But in the critical work one is aware of a unified thought, a closely reasoned correlation of ideas that is very typical of De Maistre. On the purely aesthetic side Baudelaire has nothing to learn from De Maistre; what he does is to relate his own aesthetic beliefs to a theological system, as when he derives his theory of the comic from the doctrine of original sin, his cosmopolitanism of art from the workings of Providence.

It is in Baudelaire's conception of society, and his ideas on the relation of the artist to society that De Maistre's influence shows itself most clearly, though here Poe must not be forgotten. But with Poe much of the reaction against democracy is the fruit of personal experience; De Maistre contributes a closely knit reasoning in favor of aristocracy which evidently had a large part in Baudelaire's gradual abandonment of the bourgeois, his conviction that art too must be aristocratic. This influence of De Maistre seems an entirely impersonal one. Whereas with Poe and Delacroix, later with Wagner, all Baudelaire's sympathy and enthusiasm are engaged, making of him a partisan of the man as much as of the artist, with De Maistre the man hardly seems to exist for him; his head, not his heart is touched. The way has been prepared by Poe, by the disillusionment of the years immediately after 1848; De Maistre brings a structure of reason which holds together the multicolored riches of the imagination. But whereas De Maistre's reasoning is rigid, unbending, Baudelaire's is supple, flexible.

With Poe, on the other hand, the personal element is of the first importance. The attraction is to the man as much as to the work, if not indeed more so. And the immense personal attraction certainly had its share in Baudelaire's immediate and whole-hearted acceptance of many of Poe's ideas.

The question of the extent of Poe's influence on Baudelaire has been so much discussed, with opinion ranging from giving the credit to Poe for Baudelaire's whole aesthetic system to denying him all but the most trifling part in it, that one can only go back to the texts once more, keeping in mind what we found in Baudelaire before the contact with Poe, noting what the articles of the following years bring that is new, and determining how much of that is due wholly or in part to Poe.

The constant emphasis on originality in the first "Salons" frees Baudelaire from the count of any debt on that score. Poe's reiteration that "the leading sin is the sin of imitation— the entire absence of originality"[66] must have been for Baudelaire the echo of his own ideas, one of the things which made him find in Poe a spiritual brother, not a startling new discovery. Again Poe's passage on the universal quality of great genius[67] is what Baudelaire had already remarked of Delacroix in the "Salon de 1846." And in discussing the "Salons" of 1845 and 1846 I have noted more than one curious coincidence between Baudelaire and Poe—details which, together with the larger ideas, explain the sense of rediscovery of himself that Baudelaire felt and emphasized years later in a letter to Thoré on Manet's supposed *pastiches* of Spanish painting. Baudelaire says that Manet had seen practically no Spanish painting:

Vous doutez de ce que je vous dis? Vous doutez que de si étonnants parallélismes géométriques puissent se présenter dans la nature. Eh bien! on m'accuse, moi, d'imiter Edgar Poe! Savez-vous pourquoi j'ai si patiemment traduit Poe? *Parce qu'il me ressemblait.* La première fois que j'ai ouvert un livre de lui, j'ai vu, avec épouvante et ravissement, non seulement des sujets rêvés par moi, mais des PHRASES, pensées par moi, et écrites par lui, vingt ans auparavant (*Lettres*, p. 362).

But when all this has been said there seems no doubt that

at certain points Baudelaire's thought was deeply touched and modified by Poe's—to a certain extent in the purely aesthetic domain, far more so in regard to certain philosophical and social questions. All along, in the later articles as well as in those we have just been considering, there seems to be on Baudelaire's part a certain amount of resistance, which breaks down only slowly, and never completely, to part at least of Poe's aesthetic theory. But where Poe's influence is unquestionable is in Baudelaire's political and social attitude—antiindustrialism, antidemocracy, antiprogress—even though here, as I have noted, the influences of Poe and De Maistre are difficult to disentangle. In the early "Salons" Baudelaire is making overtures to the bourgeois and attaching his theory of romanticism to the philosophy of progress, in 1848 he is full of revolutionary ardor, and we have seen how all that is swept away. The reason of this complete conversion is not, I think, hard to find. Baudelaire's mind was ground ready and prepared for Poe and De Maistre at this point; the general disillusionment that followed 1848, as well as his personal difficulties and trials, made him ready to welcome a whole new set of ideas. Then too in his early years his preoccupations had been largely artistic and literary, and his early liberalism was not, I think, a deeply reasoned system, nor indeed a system at all. So De Maistre's and Poe's reasoning made a particular appeal to Baudelaire's keen intelligence, and we may well underline "De Maistre et Poe m'ont appris à *raisonner*."

All these changes inevitably bring in their wake a change in the conception of the relation of the artist to society, of art to life. Here again the Baudelaire who in 1846 wanted above all to be hand in hand with the bourgeois, who proclaimed that "le guignon n'existe pas," has learned from Poe's experience, as well as from his own, that society has no place for the poet, that they are eternally at odds. Poe's question, "When *shall* the artist assume his proper situation in society—

in a society of thinking beings?"[68] is sadly echoed by Baudelaire.

For Poe the isolation of art is complete; there are no connections between the Good, the True, and the Beautiful. Any attempt on the part of Art to teach, to be of any use, is demeaning and hateful. There is no question that the Baudelaire who in the Pierre Dupont Preface had defended the utility of art was here again struck by Poe's reasoning, and brought to consider as "l'hérésie moderne capitale, — l'enseignement." But the conversion is not perhaps so complete or so extreme as would appear at first sight. Baudelaire's position in 1851 had been a temporary swing in the other direction, and his fundamental attitude is rather that of the passage in the "Drames et romans honnêtes" to which I have already called attention. And he never goes all the way with Poe, as his modifications of the "Poetic Principle" show. For him, as for Poe, the utilitarian intention is wrong; but for Poe the ultimate utility of art is inacceptable, for Baudelaire it is inevitable.

In this domain of art, though many a detail can be referred back to Poe, Baudelaire's ideas are already well grounded. His conception of beauty remains in large measure his own; the definition of 1859, as we shall see, is but the full flowering of that of 1846. It is a conception that, while valid for all the arts, has its roots in painting, whereas Poe constantly tends to define beauty in mathematical and musical terms: "that merely mathematical recognition of *equality* which seems to be the *root of all Beauty*."[69] But much that Poe says, as we shall see in greater detail when we come to Baudelaire's later defining of *le beau*, is in line with Baudelaire's own conception. The great thing that Poe contributes, I think, is a more unearthly, ethereal, half-mystical conception of Beauty, a "supernal Beauty," whereas Baudelaire's Beauty has been, and never entirely ceases to be, of this earth. But in these years, in the criticism as in the poetry, it seems to become less terrestrial, to reach out into the infinite and take on a supernatural character. Here the whole doctrine of correspondences comes in, in which Poe has his part, noting again and again how "the material world . . . abounds with very strict analogies to the immaterial."[70]

For Poe, poetry, "the rhythmical creation of Beauty," must have the same unearthly quality: "Passion proper and poesy are discordant. Poetry, in elevating, tranquillizes the *soul*. With the *heart* it has nothing to do."[71] Here again, although Baudelaire is far from following Poe all the way, his conception of poetry is tinged with this unearthly hue. The great quality of the poet is the imagination, and Baudelaire, when he writes the "Salon de 1859" around his conception of the imagination, will use Poe's ideas, along with many others. And he also finds in Poe the exaggeration—in the "Philosophy of Composition" the *reductio ad absurdum* indeed—of his own mistrust of so-called inspiration, his belief in the sovereign importance of intelligence and technique. But nowhere, I think, in the purely artistic domain, do we find an unqualified adherence to Poe's tenets. This is in large measure because Baudelaire's own thought, in so many ways completely congenial with Poe's but by no means entirely so, is firmly founded before his discovery of Poe. There is no surer proof of Baudelaire's independence of judgment than the way in which, even in the white heat of his enthusiasm for Poe, he brings many a reservation to his hero's thought.

There are indeed questions on which Baudelaire is definitely opposed to Poe. Their apparent divergence on the use of allegory is not, I think, fundamental. To be sure, Poe writes "In defense of allegory (however, or for whatever object, employed,) there is scarcely one respectable word to be said,"[72] while for Baudelaire in 1845 "l'allégorie est un des plus beaux genres de l'art" (II, 30), and in 1860, "tout pour moi devient allégorie" ("Le Cygne"). But Poe is undoubtedly thinking of the outworn conventional allegory so dear to the eighteenth century, while Baudelaire uses *allegory, metaphor, hieroglyph, symbol* indifferently to express the doctrine of correspondences, of universal analogy. He and Poe are at odds only in the significances they attach to the word. The two conceptions of criticism do however differ fundamentally. Poe says: "we may assume, notwithstanding a vast deal of pitiable cant upon this topic, that in pointing out frankly the errors of a work, we do nearly all that is critically necessary in displaying its merits."[73] His criticism usually follows this precept. But for Baudelaire: "Rien n'est plus doux que d'admirer, rien n'est plus désagréable que de critiquer" (II, 276), and all his greatest critical articles are built up on admiration.

It seems then that Baudelaire found in Poe many ideas on art, on poetry, closely akin to his own, that in some cases they gave a new orientation to his own thought, while in others there are more or less bluntly expressed reservations. On the other hand Poe's political and social ideas were just what Baudelaire was ready for, and he accepted them unreservedly, carrying them to their farthest implications. Here the "influence," conjoined with that of De Maistre, seems unmistakable; in the aesthetic domain, to draw the line with any precision between what Baudelaire found of his own in Poe, and what he borrowed from him, seems an impossibility. Rather than talk of plagiarism, we may conclude with Coleridge: "He who can catch the spirit of an original, has it already."[74]

Finally, it is obvious that the whole complex idea of correspondences is beginning to play a part in the criticism of these years. Whereas in the first "Salons" the correspondences were synaesthetic, the larger aspect appears here. The word itself is used for the first time in the "Exposition de 1855," "l'immense clavier des *correspondances*" (II, 145). In the "Notes nouvelles sur Edgar Poe," the idea of correspondence is linked with the imagination, which is defined as the faculty of perceiving "les rapports intimes et secrets des choses, les correspondances et les analogies" (*Poe*, p. 707). We have seen how in the Gautier article Baudelaire claims for Gautier (however mistakenly) an "immense intelligence innée de la *cor-*

respondance et du symbolisme universels" (II, 470-471). And
the *Paradis artificiels* which were being composed at this time
(the "Poëme du haschisch" was published in 1858) show
Baudelaire's interest; he notes that at a certain stage of the
hashish intoxication: "Les sons se revêtent de couleurs, et les
couleurs contiennent une musique. Cela, dira-t-on, n'a rien
que de fort naturel, et tout cerveau poétique, dans son état
sain et normal, conçoit facilement ces analogies" (I, 293).
The chapter "L'Homme-Dieu," describes further this exaggeration of the idea of correspondences which hashish brings,
"où le premier objet venu devient symbole parlant." There
is little doubt, I think, that De Quincey as well as Poe
strengthened Baudelaire's interest in these ideas, which do not
until later become of primary importance for the criticism as
well as for the poetry—but the beginnings are here.

Until now Baudelaire's thought has been modified and enriched to a perceptible degree by definite influences which
can be traced with some precision. From this point on, although one can easily pick up the traces of his reading, the
criticism is more and more a synthesis of all the varied elements gathered in the preceding years, a fusion of them in the
crucible of Baudelaire's own imagination and intelligence.
And here one may well quote M. Crépet's admirable page on
Baudelaire's originality:

Baudelaire n'est pas un génie tout spontané. Plus je l'étudie, plus
je viens à cette conclusion: il a *fait* en grande partie son génie, il
l'a acquis par un exercice de son jugement, de son choix et de sa
volonté, qui est peut-être plus surprenant et plus admirable encore
que son œuvre. On a souvent énoncé qu'il était *un cas*. Je le dis à
mon tour, mais je l'entends dans un sens nouveau: Baudelaire est le
cas le plus singulier de narcissisme et de mimétisme que présentent
les lettres françaises. Baudelaire ne s'est jamais penché que sur son
moi et sur ce qui lui ressemblait ou à quoi il voulait ressembler.
C'est ce moi qu'il a cherché et chéri chez autrui, à l'inverse de tant
d'écrivains qui ne sont attirés que par leurs contraires. Il a passé sa
vie à battre le rappel des atomes épars dans l'univers, qui lui sem-
blaient propres à nourrir, fortifier et féconder sa personnalité. Et
sans doute, à les y agréger, éprouvait-il la même satisfaction qu'un
propriétaire qui rentre en possession de ses biens (*J.I.*, pp. 11-12).

Chapter Three

THE POET AS CRITIC

---

*Tous les grands poëtes deviennent naturellement, fatale-
ment critiques.*—Richard Wagner et Tannhäuser à Paris.

THE YEARS 1859 to 1861 mark the height of Baudelaire's
critical production. By then the varied strands he has
gathered here and there have been woven into a harmonious
pattern that is Baudelaire's alone. He is still reading, still
absorbing new ideas, and one still finds many an echo of
Poe and De Maistre, but these fit into an already existing
pattern without modifying it to any noticeable degree. Baudelaire's own thought has attained such a structural solidity,
such a quality *sui generis* (to use one of his favorite expressions) that any addition serves as illustration and ornament,
and brings no substantial alteration.

This period is one of great creative activity in general for
Baudelaire. A large number of the poems added to the second
edition of the *Fleurs du Mal* in 1861 were being written,
and more than one has its echo in the critical articles. Baudelaire was also thinking a great deal about poetry, as well as
writing it, as the series of notes for a preface to the *Fleurs du
Mal* show. Then too he was busy with the later translations
of Poe, who was thus still in the forefront of his mind. This
is the period too of the *Paradis artificiels*; the "Poëme du
haschisch" had been published in 1858, and the adaptation
of the *Confessions of an English Opium-Eater* was now one
of Baudelaire's chief preoccupations. It is perhaps to De

Quincey that Baudelaire owes most in the way of suggestion
and illustration for his critical work during this period. He
writes to his mother on July 9, 1857: "le *Mangeur d'opium*
est une nouvelle traduction d'un auteur magnifique, inconnu
à Paris" (*L.M.*, p. 144). In 1860, immediately after the publication, he writes to Poulet-Malassis: "De Quincey est un
auteur affreusement conversationniste et digressionniste, et
ce n'était pas une petite affaire que de donner à ce résumé
une forme dramatique et d'y introduire l'ordre. De plus il
s'agissait de fondre mes sensations personnelles avec les opinions
de l'auteur original et d'en faire un amalgame dont les parties
fussent indiscernables" (*Corr.* I, 295). This constant working
over De Quincey led Baudelaire, on the one hand, to borrow
many an idea, illustration, phrase from him, and on the other
to develop for himself many an idea for which De Quincey
gave him the first impulse. Here, as elsewhere, there is a constant interplay of all that Baudelaire is writing.

The critical work of these years consists chiefly of three
great articles, the "Salon de 1859," the "Peintre de la vie
moderne" and "Richard Wagner et Tannhäuser à Paris"—
three peaks in Baudelaire's criticism. The "Salon de 1859"
is first mentioned in a letter to Poulet-Malassis, written at
Honfleur and dated April 29, 1859: "*Salon de 1859* (fini, et
que je livre ce soir ou demain)" (*Corr.*, I, 251). But on
May 14 Baudelaire writes to Nadar: "j'écris maintenant un
Salon, sans l'avoir vu. Mais *j'ai un livret*. Sauf la fatigue de
deviner les tableaux, c'est une excellente méthode que je te
recommande. On craint de trop louer et de trop blâmer; on
en arrive ainsi à l'impartialité" (*Corr.*, I, 262). Apparently
Nadar's reply protested against the "method," for Baudelaire
writes again, two days later: "Quant au Salon, hélas! je t'ai
un peu menti, mais si peu! J'ai fait une visite, une seule, con-
sacrée à chercher les nouveautés, mais j'en ai trouvé bien peu,
et pour tous les vieux noms, ou les noms simplement connus,
je me confie à ma vieille mémoire, excitée par le livret. Cette
méthode, je le répète, n'est pas mauvaise, à la condition qu'on

possède bien son personnel" (*Corr.*, I, 265). But even if Baudelaire had spoken quite truly, and had never set foot in the Salon, the "Salon de 1859" would lose little of its interest. It stands not as a record of a not particularly noteworthy Salon, nor even as one more example of Baudelaire's discrimination, his power of separating the wheat from the intolerable deal of tares of any Salon. It is essentially a declaration of principles, the definition and glorification of the imagination in such terms that all Baudelaire's critical thought is gathered up into the word.

The "Salon" is in the form of a series of letters to Jean Morel, editor of the *Revue Française*, in which the "Salon" was first published. It begins with an expression of regret at the absence of the promised English artists, and moves into a bitter attack on the modern artist, this spoiled child, alike ignorant and uninspired.

Discrédit de l'imagination, mépris du grand, amour (non, ce mot est trop beau), pratique exclusive du métier, telles sont, je crois, quant à l'artiste, les raisons principales de son abaissement. Plus on possède d'imagination, mieux il faut posséder le métier pour accompagner celle-ci dans ses aventures et surmonter les difficultés qu'elle recherche avidement. Et mieux on possède son métier, moins il faut s'en prévaloir et le montrer, pour laisser l'imagination briller de tout son éclat (II, 218).

With the addition of the word *imagination* this is essentially what Baudelaire had said in 1846 (II, 65). Then, with some well-deserved raps at the absurd titles of some of the paintings, at the "goût du spirituel" of the French artist, Baudelaire denounces the confusion of the True and the Beautiful, and the artist who seeks to astonish by illegitimate means. (The desire to surprise is legitimate in itself, says Baudelaire, quoting Poe's *Morella*, "*It is a happiness to wonder*," but also "*it is a happiness to dream*."[1]) Thus he arrives at his *bête noire* of the moment, photography, the very antithesis, in its exact copying of nature, of all his theories of art. Like all material progress, it has contributed to the decline of art: "La poésie et le progrès sont deux ambitieux qui se haïssent d'une haine instinctive, et, quand ils se rencontrent dans le même chemin, il faut que l'un des deux serve l'autre" (II, 224). Photography is all very well as the very humble servant of science and art; but she must be kept in her place.

This brings Baudelaire to the two capital chapters of the "Salon," "La Reine des facultés" and "Le Gouvernement de l'imagination." He attacks the current catchword, "Copy nature, copy only nature," which should mean, he says, that the artist, the poet should paint only what he sees and feels. But, alas, it means rather "we have no imagination, and we decree that no one else shall." Here Baudelaire begins his attempt to define the imagination, "cette reine des facultés," sometimes like the other faculties, yet always herself.

Elle est l'analyse, elle est la synthèse; et cependant des hommes habiles dans l'analyse et suffisamment aptes à faire un résumé peuvent être privés d'imagination. Elle est cela, et elle n'est pas tout à fait cela. Elle est la sensibilité, et pourtant il y a des personnes très-sensibles, trop sensibles peut-être, qui en sont privées. C'est l'imagination qui a enseigné à l'homme le sens moral de la couleur, du contour, du son et du parfum. Elle a créé, au commencement du monde, l'analogie et la métaphore. Elle décompose toute la création, et, avec les matériaux amassés et disposés suivant des règles dont on ne peut trouver l'origine que dans le plus profond de l'âme, elle crée un monde nouveau, elle produit la sensation du neuf (II, 226).

Imagination has made the world; and rules the world.

In the next chapter, "Le Gouvernement de l'imagination," Baudelaire begins by quoting a sentence on the distinction between fancy and imagination from the curious *Night Side of Nature* of Catherine Crowe. He immediately goes on to acknowledge his debt to Delacroix in this whole question of the imagination; Delacroix who often said that nature is only a dictionary, in which painters with imagination look up what they need, while painters without imagination copy the dictionary. But the painter with imagination must spare no pains with technique, in order that "le langage du rêve soit très-nettement traduit." In a word: "Tout l'univers visible n'est qu'un magasin d'images et de signes auxquels l'imagination donnera une place et une valeur relative; c'est une espèce de pâture que l'imagination doit digérer et transformer. Toutes les facultés de l'âme humaine doivent être subordonnées à l'imagination, qui les met en réquisition toutes à la fois" (II, 232).

Even if Baudelaire had not underlined this passage by calling it "tout le formulaire de la véritable esthétique," one could hardly fail to realize the importance he attaches to this doctrine of the imagination, and the way in which it has come to embrace and symbolize his whole aesthetic creed. The constant repetition of the word *imagination* is significant; whereas it is used ten times at most, usually much less, in any of Baudelaire's other articles, in the "Salon de 1859" it occurs more than sixty times.

One wonders first of all how the imagination has acquired its full weight of meaning for Baudelaire, and one turns back through the critical work before 1859, in pursuit first of the word, then, disconcerted by its infrequent appearances, of its elements under other names. The word does not appear at all in the "Salon de 1845"; the great word of praise there is *original*,[2] the chief term of reproach *imitation* (not however imitation of nature, as in 1859, but imitation of other artists, for which Baudelaire shows a certain amount of tolerance in 1859). But *original* is the seed of the Baudelairean conception of the imagination. In the following year the word *imagination* is used twice in the "Musée Bonne-Nouvelle" (II, 58, 60), but with a very limited meaning, that of seeing a picture in one's mind. The fact that in one of these cases the word is used of Ary Scheffer, "un homme d'un talent éminent, ou plutôt une heureuse imagination," shows how little it meant to Baudelaire at this time. The article on the *Prométhée délivré* of the same year uses the word with much the same meaning. In the "Salon de 1846," the word appears half a dozen times, with varying, and sometimes rather vague and uncertain meanings; once as opposed to *positif* and allied to *pittoresque* (II, 67), once (II, 76) as referring to the spectator rather than the artist (a use which Baudelaire maintains even in 1859), twice (II, 101, 129) in the phrase "l'imagination du dessin," which is explained by "dessin imaginatif ou de création," generally the privilege only of the *coloristes*. And Baudelaire says that in the "portrait-roman," "l'imagination a une plus grande part." Here Baudelaire seems to mean by imagination the faculty of creating an atmosphere, of opening up horizons, of making a line more than an outline, a portrait more than a likeness. The word also occurs in the passage from Hoffmann which Baudelaire quotes in a note: "La véritable mémoire . . . ne consiste, je pense, que dans une imagination très-vive, facile à émouvoir, et par conséquent susceptible d'évoquer à l'appui de chaque sensation les scènes du passé, en les douant, comme par enchantement, de la vie et du caractère propres à chacune d'elles" (II, 746). The relating of imagination and memory by Hoffmann here is in its balance unlike that at which Baudelaire will arrive; for Hoffmann, memory is a "reproductive" imagination, quick to evoke the past, to make it live again, while for Baudelaire memory will be but the handmaid of the "creative" imagination. Here again in the "Salon de 1846," it is not the *word* that prefigures the *imagination* of 1859, so much as the conception expressed by the Stendhalian word *idéal*.

In the articles of the early fifties the word *imagination* still appears only rarely, and for the most part in such conventional phrases as "ouvrages d'imagination," "votre imagination curieuse" (II, 138, 139, 169, 185, 417). Even the 1852 Poe article hardly uses the word. It is only in the "Exposition de 1855" that the word begins to take on something of its later value. Beside two or three conventional uses, there is one sentence which brings a phrase often repeated later: "L'imagination qui soutenait ces grands maîtres, dévoyés dans leur gymnastique académique, l'imagination, cette reine des facultés, a disparu" (II, 153). But Baudelaire drops the idea without further development. The next year the well-known letter to Toussenel indicates that Baudelaire was thinking hard on this question of the imagination: "Il y a bien longtemps que je dis que le poëte est *souverainement* intelligent, qu'il est l'intelligence par excellence, — et que *l'imagination* est la plus *scientifique* des facultés, parce que seule elle comprend *l'analogie universelle*, ou ce qu'une religion mystique appelle la *correspondance*" (*Corr.* I, 130). The passage has a double interest; first the close alliance between the intelligence and the imagination (to which Baudelaire will return in the Wagner article), and secondly the assignment to the imagination of the role of perceiving and understanding the correspondences which are so much in the foreground of Baudelaire's thought and poetry at this time. The next year he develops the idea in the "Notes nouvelles sur Edgar Poe":

> Pour lui, l'imagination est la reine des facultés; mais par ce mot il entend quelque chose de plus grand que ce qui est entendu par le commun des lecteurs. L'imagination n'est pas la fantaisie; elle n'est pas non plus la sensibilité, bien qu'il soit difficile de concevoir un homme imaginatif que ne serait pas sensible. L'imagination est une qualité quasi divine qui perçoit tout d'abord, en dehors des méthodes philosophiques, les rapports intimes et secrets des choses, les correspondances et les analogies. Les honneurs et les fonctions qu'il confère à cette faculté lui donnent une valeur telle (du moins quand on a bien compris la pensée de l'auteur), qu'un savant sans imagination n'apparaît plus que comme un faux savant, ou tout au moins comme un savant incomplet (*Poe*, p. 707).

This same year the word occurs only twice in the *Madame Bovary* article. One might expect to meet it frequently in the Gautier article, but there are only a very few uses of it, and only one that is significant, "l'Imagination seule contient la poésie" (II, 468). One wonders whether Baudelaire realized, consciously or not, that imagination and Gautier were no running mates.

Up to the "Salon de 1859," then, the word *imagination* seems to have slowly become more important in Baudelaire's thought; at first hardly used, then with fairly conventional and superficial meanings, and in 1855 becoming, though without definition, "la reine des facultés." It is in the letter to Toussenel of 1856, and in the "Notes nouvelles" of the following year—and also in the "Poëme du haschisch" of 1858—that one of the most important functions of the imagination for Baudelaire is indicated—the power of perceiving analogies and correspondences. This brings us to the "Salon de 1859" itself, where the word takes on such primary importance, and where Baudelaire, as we have seen, struggles to find a definition which will satisfy his feeling of what the imagination is; it is more than the power of analysis or synthesis, more than sensitivity; it shows to man the hidden meaning of the visible world, and is the creator of analogy and metaphor. And finally, decomposing the world we know, it creates a new one, giving to us the sense of something hitherto unknown.

This idea of the imagination is I think less new for Baudelaire than the examination of previous uses of the *word* would indicate. The terms so dear to him in the early "Salons," *originalité, naïveté, idéal,* have the germ of the idea of freshness, newness; the *esprit cosmopolite, ouvert à toutes les beautés,* of 1855 is close to the imagination which perceives the hidden meaning of nature; and the doctrine of correspondences, to which Baudelaire attaches the imagination, has been at the heart of his thinking long since. What for me characterizes the imagination of 1859 is first that Baudelaire seems to have found in the word a synthesis of all the aesthetic ideas most significant to him, and second that certain ideas, such as that of novelty, have taken on, thus vested in the word, a more mysterious and supernatural quality. I have already spoken of this general change in the preceding period; it is emphasized here. It should be noted, however, that the many uses of the word in this "Salon" are far from carrying equally the weight of meaning with which Baudelaire has endowed it. In the first two chapters the usage is vague, perhaps purposely so, to leave the way clear for the definition and glorification of the imagination in the third and fourth chapters, where every use of the word has its full weight. From there the word occurs in varying ways; sometimes with its full significance, as when applied to Delacroix; later, in connection with other artists, with less force; it is also applied to the imagination of the spectator as well as of the artist. But the very decided tendency is to use the word with a full sense of its value and meaning.

The "Salon de 1859" marks the climax of this Baudelairean glorification of the imagination. In the "Peintre de la vie moderne," probably nearly contemporary with the "Salon," the word is also used a number of times, and with its full value. But after this, except in the Delacroix article, the uses of the word are again few, and in the majority of cases insignificant. So it seems worth asking here, having followed the growth of the conception of the imagination through Baudelaire's work, what contributed to it, how much he owed to other conceptions of the imagination.

What I felt the need of at this point, what I looked for in vain in libraries and bibliographies, and what I devoutly hope some one will write before long, is a study of the use of the word *imagination* in France. It is not, I think, essential for this study—Baudelaire has indicated plainly the main sources of *his* conception of the imagination—but it would form an interesting prelude, besides having integral value. One would like to follow in detail the history of the word, beginning with Montaigne's dangerously vivid imitative imagination, which he could only avoid, not resist,[3] and Pascal's definition: "C'est cette partie décevante dans l'homme, cette maîtresse d'erreur et de fausseté, et d'autant plus fourbe qu'elle ne l'est pas toujours; car elle serait règle infaillible de vérité si elle l'était infaillible de mensonge."[4] In the eighteenth century the distrust of the word begins to disappear, and the first foreshadowings of the conception of the creative imagination appear. Voltaire defines: "Il y a deux sortes d'imagination: l'une, qui consiste à retenir une simple impression des objets; l'autre, qui arrange ces images reçues et les combine en mille manières. La première a été appelée *imagination passive*; la seconde, *active.*"⁵ But Voltaire resists the tendency to conceive of the imagination as creative: "l'imagination active est celle qui joint la réflexion, la combinaison à la mémoire. Elle rapproche plusieurs objets distants; elle sépare ceux qui se mêlent, les compose et les change; elle semble créer quand elle ne fait qu'arranger: car il n'est pas donné à l'homme de se faire des idées; il ne peut que les modifier."⁶

My impression is—and I should much like to have it tested by a careful study of French romantic literature—that the word *imagination* played a rather small part during the romantic period in France. The battle raged round *art, poésie, génie*, and the imagination seems to have been little talked of. Joubert, in the *Pensées* which Baudelaire sent to his mother in 1860 with the comment, "un livre *magnifique* . . . je ne le connaissais pas" (*L.M.*, p. 199), has a good deal to say about the imagination: "J'appelle imagination la faculté de rendre sensible ce qui est intellectuel, d'incorporer ce qui est esprit; en un mot, de mettre au jour, sans le dénaturer, ce qui est de soi-même invisible" (*Pensées*, VI, 43). But among the great romantics the only champion of the imagination seems to have been Vigny, who exalts it—but without defining it— in *Stello* as "la première et la plus rare des facultés."⁷ But the word was certainly not one of the fashionable battle cries;⁸ the fact that Baudelaire uses it so rarely in his early writings also points in this direction. But he was hardly a pioneer in the use of the word, and he has indicated more than one of his sources.

There is first of all Baudelaire's own acknowledgment of all he owes to Delacroix; how Delacroix had taught him that nature was a dictionary, in which the painter found the elements of his picture. For Delacroix, Baudelaire says, all the different parts and techniques of art are but the servants of the one unique and dominant faculty—the imagination. He emphasizes this again in the 1863 article on Delacroix: "Il est évident qu'à ses yeux l'imagination était le don le plus précieux, la faculté la plus importante, mais que cette faculté restait impuissante et stérile, si elle n'avait pas à son service une habileté rapide, qui pût suivre la grande faculté despotique dans ses caprices impatients" (II, 300-301). He then quotes at length the passages from the "Salon de 1859" with which we have just been dealing. So one is interested, first of all, in turning to Delacroix's own writings, to see how the word imagination is used, what part it plays.

As with Baudelaire, the conception develops slowly. One of Delacroix's first uses of the word is in the *Journal* under the date of April 27, 1824: "Dimier pensait que les grandes passions étaient la source du génie! Je pense que c'est l'imagination seule, ou bien, ce qui revient au même, cette délicatesse d'organes qui fait voir là où les autres ne voient pas, et qui fait voir d'une différente façon" (*Journal*, I, 87). It is interesting to see Delacroix already thinking of imagination as the essential of genius, even though imagination is here for him primarily a vision, a way of seeing. The same idea is expressed in the article on Lawrence's portrait of Pius VII, where Delacroix says: "Le peintre qui crée un tableau le voit ou croit le voir dans son imagination" (*Œuvres littéraires*, II, 160). In a letter to Balzac written towards the end of 1832 Delacroix uses for the first time the term *imagination créatrice* (*Correspondance* de Delacroix, I, 342-45), the implications of which will not be developed until later. When the *Journal* begins again in 1847 we find Delacroix much occupied with the problem of imagination in its relation to the theatre: "Diderot, en refusant toute sensibilité à l'acteur, ne dit pas assez que l'imagination y supplée" (*Journal*, I, 170). And soon afterwards, after seeing *Don Juan*, he writes: "Je pensais à la dose d'imagination nécessaire au spectateur pour être digne d'entendre un tel ouvrage" (*Journal*, I, 185). In all these cases the imagination seems to be an inner vision or perception, surpassing in quality mere outward perception.

With time there comes an increasing respect for the importance and rights of the imagination. On April 26, 1853,

Delacroix writes: "L'indépendance de l'imagination doit être entière devant le tableau" (*Journal*, II, 26). Later in the same year the word *imagination* occurs several times in a long passage headed "De l'emploi du modèle" (*Journal*, II, 85-88). "Le vrai peintre est celui chez lequel l'imagination parle avant tout," Delacroix says. Here *imagination* is opposed to *imitation*;[9] it performs what Delacroix calls a "travail d'idéalisation," the effort of the artist to reproduce his inner vision, not the passing vision which nature offers him: "c'est son imagination qui fait le beau, justement parce qu'il suit son génie." All through this passage Delacroix is suggesting an idea which we find in Baudelaire, the relationship of memory and imagination. Delacroix returns to this in 1855, when he speaks of "*ce petit monde* que l'homme porte en lui":

> Il y a en nous un écho qui répond à toutes les impressions: ou nous avons vu cela ailleurs, ou bien toutes les combinaisons possibles des choses sont à l'avance dans notre cerveau. En les retrouvant dans ce monde passager, nous ne faisons qu'ouvrir une case de notre cerveau ou de notre âme. Comment expliquer autrement la puissance incroyable de l'imagination et, comme dernière preuve, cette puissance incroyable qui est relativement incomparable dans l'enfance? (*Journal*, II, 374.)

However Delacroix's most definite statement of the meaning of imagination for him protests against too close an approximation of memory and imagination. In 1857, defining *imagination* ("la première qualité de l'artiste") for his projected *Dictionnaire des Beaux-arts*, he says:

> Que les partisans de l'axiome des sensualistes, que *nil est in intellectu quod non fuerit prius in sensu*, prétendent en conséquence de ce principe que l'imagination n'est qu'une espèce de souvenir, il faudra bien qu'ils accordent cependant que tous les hommes ont la sensation et la mémoire, et que très peu ont l'imagination, qu'on prétend se composer de ces deux éléments. L'imagination chez l'artiste ne se représente pas seulement tels ou tels objets, elle les combine pour la fin qu'il veut obtenir; elle fait des tableaux, des images qu'il compose à son gré (*Journal*, III, 45).

Here Delacroix comes closest to the idea of the creative

imagination, finding in the imagination not merely reproductive and selective powers, but a *combining* power. Later
he returns to a more limited view: "[Les talents maniérés] ne
peuvent frapper l'imagination qui n'est en nous qu'une sorte
de miroir où la nature telle qu'elle est vient se réfléchir, pour
nous donner, par une sorte de souvenir puissant, les spectacles
des choses dont l'âme seule a la jouissance" (*Journal*, III,
48). In 1858 he is still more cautious, more classic: "Il est
bien convenu que ce qu'on appelle *création* dans les grands
artistes n'est qu'une manière particulière à chacun de voir, de
coordonner et de rendre la nature" (*Journal*, III, 222). And
in the same year he writes: "Devant la nature elle-même,
c'est notre imagination qui fait le tableau" (*Journal*, III, 232).
For Delacroix imagination was never divorced from intelligence. On February 10, 1850, he writes: "C'est la réunion
de ces deux facultés, l'imagination et la raison, qui fait les
hommes exceptionnels" (*Journal*, I, 339). And in 1855 he
says of Mozart, Molière and Racine: "leur *raison* . . . était
à la hauteur de leur *génie*, ou plutôt était *leur génie même*"
(*Journal*, II, 318). So with Delacroix we have above all, I
think, the conception of imagination opposed to imitation.
It is a reproducing but selective power, and, says Delacroix
at his boldest, a combining power, always seconded by technique and intelligence. I said earlier that Baudelaire's use of
naïveté in the earlier "Salons" had much of the connotation
of *imagination*; Delacroix also often uses *naïveté* in the
same way.

Is Baudelaire's *imagination* merely a borrowing from Delacroix? Not entirely, by any means. It certainly owes much
to it; Baudelaire's point of departure, like Delacroix's, is an
opposition of imagination to imitation; he too sees it as the
fundamental quality of the artist; and it must always be
seconded by intelligence and technical skill. But to Baudelaire
imagination is more than that; one great element in it is the
perception of correspondences, its power of crossing the bridge
from the visible world to the invisible, of not only seeing, but

seeing meanings. The Baudelairean imagination is a more magical, mysterious faculty than Delacroix's. Moreover, Baudelaire's conception of the creating, governing character of the imagination is far bolder than Delacroix's.

The only specific debt beside the one to Delacroix that Baudelaire admits in these chapters on the imagination is the surprising one to an English author unknown, I suspect, to most of us until we met her in Baudelaire's pages—Mrs. Catherine Crowe. At the beginning of Chapter IV of the "Salon de 1859," Baudelaire justifies the statement he had made in the preceding chapter, "Comme l'imagination a créé le monde, elle le gouverne," by a passage from Mrs. Crowe's *The Night Side of Nature*, that curious and badly written compendium of psychical phenomena—dreams, wraiths, haunted houses, poltergeists and the like.[10] This passage deals with the distinction between the fancy and what Mrs. Crowe calls the constructive imagination (translated by Baudelaire as *fantaisie* and *imagination créatrice*). With his uncanny sureness, Baudelaire has laid his finger on the one passage in this hotchpotch of naïve credulity that is really worth thinking about.[11] The distinction between the fancy and the imagination, the creative character of the imagination, have an interest beyond that of the authenticity of Mrs. Crowe's dubious ghost stories or the pegs of German romantic philosophy on which she hangs them.

It has been suggested that Baudelaire misunderstood the meaning and the implications of what Mrs. Crowe says of the imagination.[12] Indeed when one restores the passage he quotes to its setting one might well think so. In the chapter on "Apparitions," it appears as follows:

As I find so many people willing to believe in wraiths who cannot believe in ghosts—that is, they are overpowered by the numerous examples and the weight of the evidence for the first—it would be very desirable if we could ascertain whether these wraiths are seen before the death occurs, or after it; but, though the day is recorded, and seems always to be the one on which the death took place, and the hour about the same, minutes are not sufficiently observed to enable us to answer that question. It would be an interesting one, because the argument advanced by those who believe that the dead never are seen, is, that it is the strong will and desire of the expiring person which enable him so to act on the nervous system of his distant friend, that the imagination of the latter projects the form, and sees it as if objectively. By *imagination* I do not simply mean to convey the common notion implied by that much abused word, which is only *fancy*, but the *constructive* imagination, which is a much higher function, and which, inasmuch as man is made in the likeness of God, bears a distant relation to that sublime power by which the Creator projects, creates and upholds his universe; whilst the far-working of the departing spirit seems to consist in the strong will to do, reinforced by the strong faith that the thing can be done. We have rarely the strong will, and still more rarely the strong faith, without which the will remains ineffective. In the following case, which is strictly authentic, the apparition of Major R. was seen several hours after his death had occurred (*The Night Side of Nature,* p. 64).

The passage in its entirety is confusing indeed. The definition seems to imply the creative function of the imagination in its fullest sense, but the actual use of the word suggests a passive and reflective meaning; the will and faith of the dying person act on the imagination of the absent friend, which is the recipient, the mirror. One has the impression that the word imagination, as Mrs. Crowe used it in this limited sense, brought to her mind the Coleridgean conception, which she promptly introduced, with little or no regard to its appropriateness. It seems to me yet one more indication of Baudelaire's perception that he could spy out the significant sentence and extricate it from its inappropriate context, shaking it free of its restrictions and restoring its full meaning.

Was it the distinction between the fancy and the imagination which particularly struck Baudelaire? And did he meet it as a new idea in Mrs. Crowe's page? This brings the tantalizing question: had Baudelaire read Coleridge? There is no question that there are pages and sentences of Baudelaire which cannot fail to recall Coleridge, as when he writes of the imagination: "Elle décompose toute la création, et, avec les matériaux amassés et disposés suivant des règles dont on ne peut trouver l'origine que dans le plus profond de l'âme, elle crée un monde nouveau" (II, 226), recalling the sentence of Coleridge: "It dissolves, diffuses, dissipates, in order to re-create" (*Biographia Literaria,* Chapter XIII). But there seems to be not a shred of evidence that Baudelaire had read a word of Coleridge's critical work. He mentions Coleridge's name in a letter to Sainte-Beuve of February 21, 1859: "Je n'ai pas oublié votre *Coleridge,* mais je suis resté un mois sans recevoir mes livres, et parcourir les 2.400 pages de Poe est un petit travail" (*Corr.* I, 240). And the obituary note on De Quincey, added to the *Mangeur d'opium* in the *Revue Contemporaine* (January, 1860) mentions Coleridge several times (I, 634-35), but only in passing. Baudelaire could not have failed to know of the existence of Coleridge's work, because of Poe's many mentions of it; but there is no indication that Poe sent him to Coleridge. I think that the Coleridgean tone of some of Baudelaire's pages comes from Coleridge by way of Poe, who owed much—more perhaps than he admitted— to Coleridge.[13] It hardly seems likely that if Baudelaire, seeking support for his idea of the imagination, could have cited Coleridge, he would not have done so in preference to citing Mrs. Crowe.

It does not seem indeed, that the much-discussed distinction between Fancy and Imagination took great hold on Baudelaire. He had certainly met it in some of Poe's many discussions of the question, such as: "What we feel to be *Fancy* will be found fanciful still, whatever be the theme which engages it. No *subject* exalts it into imagination."[14] The passage in the "Notes nouvelles sur Edgar Poe" on Poe's conception of the imagination states that "l'imagination n'est pas la fantaisie," but goes on immediately "elle n'est pas non plus la sensibilité" (*Poe,* p. 707). Baudelaire does not develop the idea, nor refer to it explicitly again. Later in the "Salon de 1859" his discussion of *fantaisie* suggests, but does not state, the opposition: "[La fantaisie] est la première chose venue interprétée par le premier venu; et, si celui-là n'a pas l'âme qui jette une lumière magique et surnaturelle sur l'obscurité naturelle des choses, elle est une inutilité horrible. . . . Ici donc, plus d'analogie, sinon de hasard" (II, 250). It seems that his interest in Mrs. Crowe's passage is in the *creative* character of the imagination, rather than in the distinction between it and the fancy. More or less consciously —rather less, I suspect—he ranges himself with those, like Poe, for whom the distinction is at most one of degree or intensity.[15]

On the other hand, the creative function of the imagination is uppermost in his mind at this point.[16] But it seems hardly likely that he had found his road to Damascus in Mrs. Crowe's pages, and it is worth looking further. The conception of the creative nature of the imagination was held to some extent by Delacroix, but more definitely by Poe. In 1836 Poe was writing, obviously fresh from Coleridge, but carefully defining the meaning of creative: "Imagination is possibly, in man, a lesser degree of the creative power in God. What the Deity imagines, *is*, but *was not* before. What man imagines *is*, but *was* also. The mind of man cannot imagine what *is not*."[17] And later Poe frequently defines the work of the imagination:

The *pure Imagination* chooses, from *either Beauty or Deformity*, only the most combinable things hitherto uncombined; the compound, as a general rule, partaking, in character, of beauty, or sublimity, in the ratio of the respective beauty or sublimity of the things combined—which are themselves still to be considered as atomic—that is to say, as previous combinations. But, as often analogously happens in physical chemistry, so not infrequently does it occur in this chemistry of the intellect, that the admixture of two elements results in a something that has nothing of the qualities of one of them, or even nothing of the qualities of either. . . . Thus, the range of Imagination is unlimited. Its materials extend throughout the universe. Even out of deformities it fabricates that *Beauty* which is at once its sole object and its inevitable test.[18]

So for Poe the imagination is creative—as chemistry is creative. It is the great combining power. And he, like Delacroix,
emphasizes the close relation of imagination and intellect:
"the reasoning powers never exist in perfection unless when
allied with a very high degree of the imaginative faculty."[19]

But for Poe the imagination has another side, expressed in
a passage in "A Chapter of Suggestions": "That the imagination has not been unjustly ranked as supreme among the
mental faculties, appears from the intense consciousness, on
the part of the imaginative man, that the faculty in question
brings his soul often to a glimpse of things supernal and
eternal—to the very verge of the *great secrets*. There are
moments, indeed, in which he perceives the faint perfumes,
and hears the melodies of a happier world."[20] This quality of
the imagination—the mystic perception of correspondences
—is the great meeting place of Poe and Baudelaire. The original idea was by no means borrowed from Poe; I have tried
all along to show how fundamental it is in Baudelaire's
thought, how it is one of the roots first of his poetry and
then of his criticism. But it seems likely that the conception
of the imagination as the faculty by which correspondences
and analogies are perceived was suggested by Poe.

In conclusion, it seems to me that what Baudelaire is doing
in these chapters is to bring together under the aegis of one
word, brought to his attention by Delacroix and Poe, his
fundamental ideas of the function of the poet and the artist.
Imagination is opposed to imitation of nature and tradition
alike; it is the power of recalling impressions; it is the mystic
perception of the secrets of the invisible world, hidden beneath the forms of the visible world; and it creates, in the
sense that it brings together, combines and transforms various elements, producing something new as a result. Vision;
discovery; creation; there are its three stages. And the great
mysterious faculty seems almost personified for Baudelaire, a
companion to the strange figure of Beauty of the "Hymne à
la Beauté." Moreover, intelligence is not merely the handmaid,

but an integral part, of the imagination: "l'imagination universelle renferme l'intelligence de tous les moyens et le désir de les acquérir" (II, 233). And the insistence that imagination, to attain perfection, must always be served by craftsmanship, is never lost sight of; the poet's eye must always be served by the poet's pen.

> "The poet's eye, in a fine frenzy rolling,
>   Doth glance from heaven to earth, from earth to heaven;
> And, as imagination bodies forth
> The forms of things unknown, the poet's pen
> Turns them to shapes, and gives to airy nothing
> A local habitation and a name."
>   (*Midsummer Night's Dream*, V, i, 12-17.)

So this Baudelairean imagination is an all-embracing faculty —less mysterious, perhaps, more visible in its workings than the Coleridgean imagination—but loaded with a wealth of varied meaning. The whole conception is an example of the creative imagination itself at work, fusing many scattered elements into one Imagination.

These chapters on the imagination are at the heart of the "Salon," and all the discussion of individual painters and paintings that follows is brought into line with them. Baudelaire takes up the paintings by genres, introducing each section by some general remarks on the genre. The chapters "Religion, Histoire, Fantaisie," begin with the statement of the need for imagination in religious painting. After kindly words for Legros and Armand Gautier,[21] Delacroix is introduced with: "L'imagination de Delacroix! Celle-là n'a jamais craint d'escalader les hauteurs difficiles de la religion. . . . Son imagination, ardente comme les chapelles ardentes, brille de toutes les flammes et de toutes les pourpres" (II, 237). The pages on Delacroix show that Baudelaire's enthusiasm had in no way waned. There is the same ardent defense of Delacroix against his detractors; the difference is that whereas in the

first "Salons" Baudelaire had attempted to convert the bourgeois, he now says: "Mais à bien regarder la chose, pour les
gens qui, comme moi, veulent que les affaires d'art ne se
traitent qu'entre aristocrates et qui croient que c'est la rareté
des élus qui fait le paradis, tout est ainsi pour le mieux" (II,
239). There are comments on all the paintings by Delacroix
—"c'est toujours le vin du même tonneau, capiteux, exquis,
sui generis"—with special enthusiasm for *Ovide chez les
Scythes*, with its reminiscence of *Les Martyrs*: "L'esprit s'y
enfonce avec une lente et gourmande volupté, comme dans
le ciel, dans l'horizon de la mer, dans des yeux pleins de
pensée, dans une tendance féconde et grosse de rêverie" (II,
242). Baudelaire says: "Je tourmente mon esprit pour en
arracher quelque formule qui exprime bien la *spécialité*
d'Eugène Delacroix"; the concentrated effort to find the exact
formula, the perfect phrase, is one of the marks of Baudelaire's criticism. After feeling his way, as it were, he arrives
at: "En un mot, Eugène Delacroix peint surtout *l'âme* dans
ses belles heures."

The *école des pointus*, with its confectioner's Cupids, is the
object of a bitter attack.[22] Baudelaire has many reservations
about the paintings which were the great popular success of
the Salon, those of Gérôme: "Son originalité (si toutefois il
y a originalité) est souvent d'une nature laborieuse et à peine
visible . . . il n'a été jusqu'à présent, et ne sera, ou du moins
cela est fort à craindre, que le premier des esprits pointus"
(II, 245). The military pictures are passed over rapidly, with
one exception, when Baudelaire finds his favorite combination
of red and green in the poppy-red of uniforms against a sea
of green. The *fantaisistes* are dealt with swiftly, but surely,
with nice distinctions, and then Baudelaire pauses with pleasure before the Delacroix-inspired Fromentin.

In the next group, the portraits, Baudelaire turns violently
against the "Ame de la Bourgeoisie," which he imagines protesting against the need for imagination, and flings at it:
"*Caput mortuum*, tais-toi! . . . plus la matière est, en ap-

parence, positive et solide, et plus le besogne de l'imagination est subtile et laborieuse." And he continues: "Le portrait, ce genre en apparence si modeste, nécessite une immense intelligence" (II, 260); another example of the close alliance between intelligence and imagination. The whole passage, with its careful definitions, is admirable in its sureness: "Parce que je réclame sans cesse l'application de l'imagination, l'introduction de la poésie dans toutes les fonctions de l'art, personne ne supposera que je désire, dans le portrait surtout, une altération consciencieuse du modèle" (II, 262). Baudelaire contrasts Holbein, who knew and studied Erasmus so well that he could re-create him, with Ingres, who adds an alien poetry, borrowed from the past, to his subject.

Baudelaire, so vehement in his opposition to the imitation of nature, is here more tolerant of the imitation of the great artists of the past, which he had attacked in the first "Salons": "Car l'imitation est le vertige des esprits souples et brillants, et souvent même une preuve de supériorité" (II, 263). Anything, for the Baudelaire of 1859, is superior to the direct and photographic imitation of nature. He returns to this in the next section, on landscape, in a passage which recalls Amiel's famous "Un paysage quelconque est un état d'âme."[23] Baudelaire's passage is an application of all that he has said on the imagination to landscape:

Si tel assemblage d'arbres, de montagnes, d'eaux et de maisons, que nous appelons un paysage, est beau, ce n'est pas par lui-même, mais par moi, par ma grâce propre, par l'idée ou le sentiment que j'y attache. C'est dire suffisamment, je pense, que tout paysagiste qui ne sait pas traduire un sentiment par un assemblage de matière végétale ou minérale n'est pas un artiste (II, 264-65).

But modern artists, says Baudelaire, have tried, and all too successfully, to divorce nature from the feelings she inspires in man; "dans ce culte niais de la nature, non épurée, non expliquée par l'imagination, je vois un signe évident d'abaissement général." The landscapists, like the portraitists, instead of finding the poetry of their subject, add something alien to it. Baudelaire turns vehemently against Millet and his pedantic peasants, with their "prétention philosophique, mélancolique et raphaélesque." Théodore Rousseau and Corot are the only landscape painters for whom he has kind words, especially for the sense of proportion and harmony in the latter. But in general the role of the imagination has been sadly diminished; perhaps because the artists have distrusted their memory and copied directly from nature. Baudelaire cites as an example of the right method Boudin, who accumulated hundreds of sketches of sea and sky, knowing well that "il faut que tout cela devienne tableau par le moyen de l'impression poétique rappelée à volonté" (II, 270). Here again is a suggestion of the relationship between memory and art which we shall meet again in the "Peintre de la vie moderne." Baudelaire describes these sketches of Boudin's in one of those sentences which only he can write, compact of the very essence of a work:

A la fin tous ces nuages aux formes fantastiques et lumineuses, ces ténèbres chaotiques, ces immensités vertes et roses, suspendues et ajoutées les unes aux autres, ces fournaises béantes, ces firmaments de satin noir ou violet, fripé, roulé ou déchiré, ces horizons en deuil ou ruisselants de métal fondu, toutes ces profondeurs, toutes ces splendeurs, me montèrent au cerveau comme une boisson capiteuse ou comme l'éloquence de l'opium (II, 270).

Though Baudelaire does not miss the human element in these particular sketches, he warns painters in general to remember that, as Robespierre had said, "l'homme ne voit jamais l'homme sans plaisir" (II, 271).[24] More than the absence of seascapes, Baudelaire regrets the absence of "le paysage des grandes villes," and particularly of Meryon, whom he characterizes in a sentence that is a companion piece to the sentence on Boudin I have just quoted:

Les majestés de la pierre accumulée, les clochers *montrant du doigt le ciel*, les obélisques de l'industrie vomissant contre le firmament leurs coalitions de fumée, les prodigieux échafaudages des monuments en réparation, appliquant sur le corps solide de l'architecture leur architecture à jour d'une beauté si paradoxale, le ciel tumultueux, chargé de colère et de rancune, la profondeur des perspectives, augmentée par la pensée de tous les drames qui y sont contenus, aucun des éléments complexes dont se compose le douloureux et glorieux décor de la civilisation n'était oublié (II, 271).

This sentence, used again later in the "Peintres et aquafortistes," is Baudelaire's only published criticism of Meryon. His correspondence, however, shows how much interested he was in him. In February, 1859, he writes to Asselineau: "tâchez donc de *carotter* pour moi à Edouard Houssaye TOUTES les images de Méryon (vues de Paris), bonnes épreuves sur Chine. *Pour parer notre chambre*, comme dit Dorine" (*Corr.* I, 237-38). The next year brings a curious account to Poulet-Malassis of a visit from Meryon and his half-mad conversation (*Corr.* I, 287-89), and in February Baudelaire writes, again to Poulet-Malassis:

Et puis Méryon! Oh! ça, c'est intolérable. Delâtre me prie de faire un texte pour l'album. Bon! voilà une occasion d'écrire des rêveries de dix lignes, de vingt ou trente lignes, sur de belles gravures, les rêveries philosophiques d'un flâneur parisien. Mais M. Méryon intervient, qui n'entend pas les choses ainsi. Il faut dire; à droite, on voit ceci; à gauche, on voit cela. Il faut chercher des notes dans les vieux bouquins. Il faut dire: ici, il y avait primitivement douze fenêtres, réduites à six par l'artiste; et enfin il faut aller à l'hôtel de ville s'enquérir de l'époque exacte des démolitions (*Corr.* I, 297).

Again: "M. Méryon a repoussé, avec une espèce d'horreur, l'idée d'un texte fait de douze petits poëmes ou sonnets; il a refusé l'idée de méditations poétiques en prose" (*Corr.* I, 315-16). One cannot but feel annoyed with Meryon for depriving us of this conjunction of visions of Paris by two of its greatest artists. As Baudelaire remarks about this time: "Ce Méryon ne sait pas se conduire" (*Corr.* I, 312). But about the same time he sends the Meryon album to his mother (*D.L.M.*, p. 129), and later writes to her at length about them: "Tu te trompes en appelant cela le *Vieux Paris*. Ce sont des points de vue poétiques de Paris, tel qu'il était avant les immenses démolitions et toutes les réparations ordonnées par l'Empereur" (*D.L.M.*, p. 132).

To go back to the "Salon," Baudelaire's sad conclusion is that he has found among the landscape painters only nice little talents, and little or no imagination. He then turns to the sculpture, to which he devotes much more attention than in 1846, evoking various scenes in which sculpture plays a part, appealing to the imagination with its austere charm. But in the sculpture, as in the rest of the Salon, imagination is lacking, with the two essential conditions of unity of impression and totality of effect. Baudelaire refers particularly to Hébert's *Jamais et Toujours*, about which he had written amusingly to Nadar.[25] Again an absentee has the lion's share of praise; Christophe, for the two statues which inspired poems of Baudelaire, "Le Masque" and "Danse macabre," the latter of which Baudelaire quotes here.[26]

In the "Envoi" which ends the "Salon" Baudelaire reiterates: "Je m'étais imposé de chercher l'imagination à travers le *Salon*, et, l'ayant rarement trouvée, je n'ai dû parler que d'un petit nombre d'hommes." There is indeed a tone of weariness, of disappointment, on many pages of the "Salon." It seems, indeed, that the Salon of 1859 had relatively little to offer. If one turns for a moment to other accounts of it, one finds Delécluze tolerant of Gérôme, giving an enthusiastic aside to Ary Scheffer, but concluding: "le niveau de l'art ne s'est point élevé."[27] Gautier criticizes the Salon rather severely, protesting against the literary quality of Gérôme, the realism of Millet, and saying of Delacroix: "il s'offre au public tel qu'il est, avec ses qualités et ses défauts." But he puts Fromentin in the first rank, and praises Penguilly and Baron. Among the portraits, his praise goes to Flandrin, and among the landscapes to Corot. The whole tone is eclectic; Gautier judges the landscape painters according to what they have tried to do, with a complete absence of any guiding principle.[28] Castagnary, in his "Salon," damns Gérôme even more thoroughly than Baudelaire had done: "M. Gérôme n'est pas même un

peintre médiocre." But he is nearly as severe on Corot, whom
he puts far below Daubigny and Rousseau. All his praise is
kept for Millet, whom he qualifies as not merely a painter but
an artist, not merely an artist but a poet.[29] Dumas, whose
"Salon" Baudelaire refers to with admiration, writes enthu-
siastically of Delacroix indeed, but in general his comments
are superficial and anecdotic, with no connecting thread.[30]
Finally, Aubert's *Souvenirs du Salon de 1859*, which includes
a selection of comments culled from other "Salons" (Baudelaire's is not among them), gives a sense of dreariness and
mediocrity which is in no way relieved by the banal praises
heaped on many insignificant artists. Aubert proclaims that
he has studied the Salon without prejudice, without enthusiasm, and as impartially as possible—a completely un-Baude-
lairean attitude. But for him too the prevailing impression is
one of mediocrity, of "un réalisme qui se dégrade." He is all
too tolerant of Gérôme, however, as well as of Troyon, Penguilly, and Flandrin, and regrets the absence of Horace Vernet. His treatment of Delacroix is mild: "l'aspect de ces toiles
est étrange, mais . . . on y retrouve presque toujours les mer-
veilleuses harmonies de couleur dont ce maître a le secret."
But he ends with an apology for his first impression of the
Salon, and the statement that it was better than he had first
thought.[31]

The question again presents itself, after one has plodded
one's weary way through the arid wastes of other accounts of
the Salon: why can one read and reread Baudelaire's with re-
newed pleasure and profit? First of all, I think, because it
transcends the occasional and ephemeral character of a
"Salon"; it is not a mere analysis, it is a synthesis, centered
around the idea of the imagination, an "Essay on the Imagination, with illustrations from the Salon of 1859," if you will.
The pages on the imagination, as I have suggested, show the
creative imagination itself at work, and give food for thought
on its mysterious processes. The "Salon" is all that, but not
only that; it is an admirable account of what is significant

in the Salon itself. What is perpetually amazing in Baudelaire is his freedom from the conventional praise and blame, the hasty approximations of other critics. With him the judgment is weighed, the characterization made, with unfailing effort. Here and there a phrase suggests this constant self-surveillance: "Et puis le terrible, l'éternel pourquoi se dressa" (II, 216); "Je me dis sans cesse: *à quoi bon?*" (II, 285). There is an integrity of thought, a scrupulousness of expression that are crystallized in some of the phrases and sentences in which Baudelaire gives the very essence of a painting, of the whole work of an artist. One may miss in the "Salon de 1859" the youthful enthusiasm, the fine zest of the first "Salons," and regret the lack of opportunity for the "critique admirative" in which Baudelaire excelled; but the "Salon de 1859" is unique in its evocation of the art of a certain moment and the relating of that art to an all-embracing conception of the imagination.

The "Peintre de la vie moderne," although not published until 1863, seems to be nearly contemporary with the "Salon de 1859."[32] On November 15, 1859, Baudelaire writes to Poulet-Malassis: "Excepté *Espagnols, Allemands* et *Guys, Curiosités* est fait" (*Corr.* I, 279), and on December 28 to his mother, of a drawing by Guys he had sent to her: "ce dessin est le seul morceau oriental que j'aie pu arracher à cet homme bizarre, sur qui je vais écrire un grand article" (*L.M.*, pp. 187 88). On February 4, 1860 he writes: "J'ai profité d'une invitation de *La Presse* pour lui livrer *Monsieur G., peintre de mœurs*" (*Corr.* I, 293). But later in the year the article was transferred to the *Constitutionnel*, then to the *Pays* (*Corr.* I, 345, 348, 350, 360, 442-44), where it was held up for more than two years. It was finally published in the *Figaro* at the end of 1863, and Baudelaire writes to his mother on November 25, sending her the first instalment: "J'attache une certaine importance au travail dont je t'envoie le premier numéro" (*L.M.*, p. 290).

It seems that Baudelaire at one time was seeing this article as a part of a much more extensive one,[33] for on February 3, 1862, he writes to Sainte-Beuve: "Je vous enverrai prochainement plusieurs paquets de rêvasseries en prose, sans compter un énorme travail sur les *Peintres de mœurs* (crayon, aquarelle, lithographie, gravure)" (*Corr.* I, 415). Early in 1859 his letters to Poulet-Malassis show his interest in fashion plates (*Corr.* I, 234-35, 246, 298), and in the first chapter of the "Peintre" he writes: "J'ai sous les yeux une série de gravures de modes commençant avec la Révolution et finissant à peu près au Consulat" (II, 325). But the longer study, like so many of Baudelaire's more ambitious projects, was never realized.

The "Peintre de la vie moderne," like all Baudelaire's great critical articles, is constructed on a balance between the general and the specific, the latter serving as illustration to the former. Here, more than in many other cases (those of Delacroix and Poe for example), much of the theory seems to have been developed before the specific instance to which it is attached. The underlying thought is to be found in Baudelaire's writings long before his contact with Guys; indeed one feels that Guys was for him the long-awaited answer to his prayers for the painter of modern life. It is not surprising, then, that the personal relations between the two should have been fairly superficial, and Guys the man less significant for Baudelaire than in the cases in which the man had been in a measure responsible for the ideas.

Just when or how Baudelaire came to know Guys, we do not know. Guys, born in Holland, of French origin, in 1802, had led a vagabond life, fighting for Greek independence, joining a cavalry regiment, traveling widely, then settling down in Paris, with frequent visits to London, where he came to know Thackeray. His artistic gift developed late in life; his first sketches were made about 1845. He went out to the Crimean War as one of the correspondents of the *Illustrated London News*, and came back in a leisurely fashion through

Turkey. He then settled down in Paris, and became "l'histori-ographe du régime."[34] He and Baudelaire had many friends and acquaintances in common, among them Delacroix and Nadar, and it is somewhat surprising that they had not met earlier. Baudelaire himself says: "Pendant dix ans, j'ai désiré faire la connaissance de M. G., qui est, par nature, très-voyageur et très-cosmopolite" (II, 329-30).

The first letter indicating a personal relationship comes at the end of 1859, Baudelaire writing to Poulet-Malassis on December 23: "Je dîne, ce soir, avec M. Guys" (*Corr.* I, 284). On December 30, 1860, Guys writes to Baudelaire: "Dear Sir, Dites-moi franchement! Ça vous dérange-t-il que j'aille vous voir là où vous êtes maintenant?" (*Crépet*, p. 371.) The only other letter from Guys to Baudelaire, undated, is couched in even friendlier terms, ending "Your friendly old C. Guys" (*Crépet*, p. 372). But the friendship must have had its ups and downs, for at one point Baudelaire writes to Poulet-Malassis: "Guys et moi, nous sommes pleinement reconciliés. C'est un homme charmant, plein d'esprit, et il n'est pas igno-rant, comme tous les littérateurs" (*Corr.* I, 289). There are no letters extant of Baudelaire to Guys, but there are occa-sional mentions of him, once as "un personnage fantastique," in the 1860 letters (*Corr.* I, 290, 296, 322-23). In 1861, in the second edition of the *Fleurs du Mal*, Baudelaire adds the dedication "à Constantin Guys" to "Rêve parisien," which had appeared in the *Revue Contemporaine* the preceding year. But after that there is no indication of any further contact between the two, and it would seem that with the completion of the article Baudelaire's interest in Guys waned.[35] It is pos-sible that Baudelaire, with his motto of "Beaucoup d'amis, beaucoup de gants," found Guys too free and easy—or per-haps his interest was really only in Guys's work.

The first five chapters of the article deal largely with gen-eral ideas, in support of which Guys is introduced, after which Baudelaire devotes a series of chapters to the evocation of various aspects of Guys's work, which here and there lead him again into more general discussions. The first chapter,

"Le Beau, la mode et le bonheur," begins with a sharp attack on people who go to the Louvre, look only at Titian and Raphael, and come away saying "I know my museum,"—like people who, having once read Bossuet and Racine, know the history of literature. But, says Baudelaire, luckily there are those who realize that, together with the love of "la beauté générale," one should not neglect "la beauté particulière, la beauté de circonstance et le trait de mœurs" (II, 324). Looking at his series of fashion plates, Baudelaire finds there "la morale et l'esthétique du temps," and realizes how "même dans les siècles qui nous paraissent les plus monstrueux et les plus fous, l'immortel appétit du beau a toujours trouvé sa satisfaction." This brings him to the paragraph that is the core of this article, the theory of the Beautiful:

C'est ici une belle occasion, en vérité, pour établir une théorie rationnelle et historique du beau, en opposition avec la théorie du beau unique et absolu; pour montrer que le beau est toujours, inévitablement, d'une composition double, bien que l'impression qu'il produit soit une; car la difficulté de discerner les éléments variables du beau dans l'unité de l'impression n'infirme en rien la nécessité de la variété dans sa composition. Le beau est fait d'un élément éternel, invariable, dont la quantité est excessivement difficile à déterminer, et d'un élément relatif, circonstanciel, qui sera, si l'on veut, tour à tour ou tout ensemble, l'époque, la mode, la morale, la passion. Sans ce second élément, qui est comme l'enveloppe amusante, titillante, apéritive, du divin gâteau, le premier élément serait indigestible, inappréciable, non adapté et non approprié à la nature humaine. Je défie qu'on découvre un échantillon quelconque de beauté qui ne contienne pas ces deux éléments (II, 326).

Baudelaire says at the end of the chapter: "J'ai plus d'une fois déjà expliqué ces choses," and, as with the imagination, when he arrives at a definitive formulation of one of his essential ideas, it seems worth while to go back and trace its history. Here is the theory of *le beau*; how has Baudelaire previously written of it?

There is by no means the variation and slow development which we saw in the case of Imagination. On the contrary,

Baudelaire's first formulation of a doctrine of *le beau*, in the "Salon de 1846," is, it will be remembered, almost identical with this. In the second chapter he defines romanticism, "pour moi, le romantisme est l'expression la plus récente, la plus actuelle du beau," and in the final chapter comes the sentence which is the germ of our paragraph in the "Peintre": "Toutes les beautés contiennent, comme tous les phénomènes possibles, quelque chose d'éternel et quelque chose de transitoire,— d'absolu et de particulier" (II, 133). Immediately after comes the plea for the painter who will put this doctrine into practice, see and paint "la beauté moderne." It may be just because this wish remained ungratified for so long, because Baudelaire had to wait thirteen years for his "painter of modern life," that he clung so tenaciously to it, and that it kept its enchantment for him. Delacroix, who in every other respect satisfied Baudelaire's every requirement, was decidedly not the "Peintre de la vie moderne" and his theory was as opposed to the conception as his practice. So Baudelaire's theory has waited for a painter who should put it into practice.

In the intervening years Baudelaire's use of the term *le beau* is—almost inevitably—fairly frequent. Sometimes it has its Baudelairean meaning, more often the usage is somewhat vague and conventional.[36] A long note in "Fusées" shows Baudelaire poring over the question of *le beau*: "J'ai trouvé la définition du Beau, de mon Beau." The correction is significant; Baudelaire is defining, not a general conception, but *his* beautiful, the particular transitory elements that, with the absolute element, constitute *le beau* of one particular individual.

C'est quelque chose d'ardent et de triste, quelque chose d'un peu vague, laissant carrière à la conjecture. Je vais, si l'on veut, appliquer mes idées à un objet sensible, à l'objet, par exemple, le plus intéressant dans la société, à un visage de femme. Une tête séduisante et belle, une tête de femme, veux-je dire, c'est une tête qui fait rêver à la fois, — mais d'une manière confuse, — de volupté et de tristesse;

qui comporte une idée de mélancolie, de lassitude, même de satiété, — soit une idée contraire, c'est-à-dire une ardeur, un désir de vivre, associés avec une amertume refluante, comme venant de privation ou de désespérance. Le mystère, le regret sont aussi des caractères du Beau (II, 632).

The passage is an admirable commentary on the particular beauty of the *Fleurs du Mal*, especially of "Spleen et Idéal."

In the "Exposition de 1855" Baudelaire is again preoccupied with the question, attacking "l'insensé doctrinaire du beau," and emphasizing the endless variety of the beautiful, "le beau multiforme et versicolore, qui se meut dans les spirales infinies de la vie" (II, 145). This is followed by the insistence on "cette dose de bizarrerie qui constitue et définit l'individualité, sans laquelle il n'y a pas de beau."

Baudelaire's reading of Poe seems to have kept the question in the forefront of his mind, for it comes up often in the Poe articles of 1856 and 1857. Poe's "amour insatiable du Beau" (*Poe*, pp. 685, 699), his distinction of the Good, the True, and the Beautiful (*Poe*, p. 710) are reiterated. The imagination and the beautiful are side by side, "des procédés inconnus pour étonner l'imagination, pour séduire les esprits assoiffés du Beau" (*Poe*, p. 689). We have seen how the endless variety of beauty, the bizarre element in it, have their parallels in Poe. And a passage of the "Philosophy of Composition" makes the same connection between melancholy and beauty that Baudelaire makes in "Fusées": "Beauty of whatever kind, in its supreme development, invariably excites the sensitive soul to tears. Melancholy is thus the most legitimate of all the poetical tones."[37]

The use of the word *beau* in the Gautier article is curious. Baudelaire, who up to this point has emphasized the individuality, the variety of beauty, relapses here into an almost consistently vague and abstract notion. He sets up as Gautier's special merit "l'amour exclusif du Beau, *l'Idée fixe*" (II, 465). Here, as what follows shows, Baudelaire is thinking of the Beautiful as opposed to the True and the Good, "l'unique ambition, le but exclusif du Goût." It is this conception of the Beautiful, the purely aesthetic ideal, which is the object of Gautier's "amour immense, fécond, et sans cesse rajeuni" (II, 470). All the emphasis is on the autonomy of the Beautiful; in itself it remains curiously abstract. This conception is carried over into the earlier chapters of the "Salon de 1859," with the statement indeed that "le Beau est toujours étonnant." But before the end of the "Salon" Baudelaire is recalling his own *beau*, when he praises Fromentin for his gift "de saisir les parcelles du beau égarées sur la terre, de suivre le beau à la piste partout où il a pu se glisser à travers les trivialités de la nature déchue" (II, 255). This is the time too when in his poetry Beauty had taken on for him the living form she has in the "Hymne à la Beauté" (*L'Artiste*, October 21, 1860), a more human and familiar figure than the "sphinx incompris" of the earlier "Beauté" (*Revue Française*, April 20, 1857).

Then comes the "Peintre de la vie moderne," centered round the theory of the Beautiful. Stated in the first chapter, it is reiterated throughout the article, with various ideas attached to it; it is opposed to *la simple nature*, and in this way each varying fashion is "un effort nouveau, plus ou moins heureux, vers le beau, une approximation quelconque d'un idéal dont le désir titille sans cesse l'esprit humain non satisfait" (II, 355-56). The article closes on the note of "la beauté passagère, fugace, de la vie présente." All through it is this passing, fugitive element of beauty that is emphasized; the absolute element is taken for granted, and then forgotten or ignored.

In the later articles *le beau* appears occasionally, but rather with its more abstract meaning, whether it be apropos of Delacroix, Gautier, or Barbier. With Leconte there comes a suggestion of the more precise meaning: "le poëte a décrit la beauté, telle qu'elle posait pour son œil original et individuel" (II, 560)—a phrase which connects *le beau* with the imagination of the poet. And the relation has been plain throughout;

that it is the imagination of the artist that sees, that creates this many-colored beauty. The closer defining of *le beau* indicates to the artist, as well as to the public, what rich fodder for the imagination is to be found in the varying aspects of modern life.

For Baudelaire's conception of the Beautiful there seems to be no such complexity of sources as for the imagination; partly because, as I have pointed out, the foundation of the idea was firmly established very early. For once the name of Delacroix need not be mentioned; we are at one of the rare points where Baudelaire is at variance with him. Delacroix deliberately avoids modern subjects: "Sujets modernes difficiles à traiter avec l'absence du nu et la pauvreté des costumes" (Jan. 13, 1857. *Journal*, III, 24). The ending of the "Salon de 1845" and the whole final chapter of the "Salon de 1846" (which takes pains to point out that "le *nu*, cette chose si chère aux artistes . . . est aussi fréquent et aussi nécessaire que dans la vie ancienne") seem a direct answer to Delacroix on this point. As for the general definition of the beautiful, at times Delacroix seems not far from Baudelaire, as when he says: "le *beau* est partout, et . . . chaque homme non seulement le voit, mais doit absolument le rendre à sa manière" (Oct. 1, 1855. *Journal*, II, 395). Sometimes, however, his conception is much vaguer, more conventional. He writes on January 1, 1857: "Poussin définit le beau: la délectation. Après avoir examiné toutes les pédantesques définitions modernes . . . j'avais trouvé en moi sans beaucoup de peine la définition que je trouve dans Voltaire . . . *nous n'appelons beau que ce qui cause à notre âme et à nos sens du plaisir et de l'admiration*" (*Journal*, III, 1-2). In the projects for the *Dictionnaire des Beaux-arts* Delacroix refers back to both these passages.[38]

But this whole idea of *le beau* of Baudelaire's owes far more to Stendhal than to anyone else. We have seen how the idea is developed in connection with him in the "Salon de 1846," and if further proof is needed we have only to turn back to the "Peintre de la vie moderne" and see how the definition of beauty from which we started immediately brings Stendhal's name in its wake:

C'est pourquoi Stendhal, esprit impertinent, taquin, répugnant même, mais dont les impertinences provoquent utilement la méditation, s'est rapproché de la vérité, plus que beaucoup d'autres, en disant que *le Beau n'est que la promesse du bonheur.* Sans doute cette définition dépasse le but; elle soumet beaucoup trop le beau à l'idéal infiniment variable du bonheur; elle dépouille trop lestement le beau de son caractère aristocratique; mais elle a le grand mérite de s'éloigner décidément de l'erreur des académiciens (II, 327).

On the one hand, the passage shows the permanency of Baudelaire's debt to Stendhal, and his own recognition of it; on the other hand it shows how far beyond Stendhal he had gone, how conscious he is of Stendhal's limitations. "Esprit impertinent, taquin, répugnant même"; that aspect of Stendhal belongs to the past. But Stendhal's definition of *le Beau* has kept its merits. It lacks the beautiful balance of Baudelaire's own theory; it is not sufficiently aristocratic for him (here the influence of Poe is clearly shown); yet Baudelaire never ceases to recognize its fundamental value. He is far from having kept it integrally; it has become more independent, more varied, more personal. Stendhal's original idea is a central core which Baudelaire's experience, creative and critical alike, has adorned with rich arabesques.

From this point of departure Baudelaire moves to a particular aspect of the *beau moderne*, the *croquis de mœurs*, which, frivolous though it be, has produced monumental works: "On a justement appelé les œuvres de Gavarni et de Daumier des compléments de la *Comédie humaine*" (II, 328). Such a painter "est le peintre de la circonstance et de tout ce qu'elle suggère d'éternel." And this brings Baudelaire to Guys (referred to, by his express wish, as M. G.), "un homme singulier, originalité si puissante et si décidée, qu'elle se suffit à elle-même et ne recherche même pas l'approbation." When

Baudelaire first met Guys, he found, not an artist, in the narrow sense of the specialist, bound to his palette, but a man of
the world, a "citoyen spirituel de l'univers,"[39] inspired by the
same curiosity as Poe's convalescent "Man of the Crowd." Imagine, says Baudelaire, an artist perpetually in the state of
mind of the convalescent, and you have the key to Guys's
character.

Baudelaire then goes on to a comparison of convalescence
and childhood: "Le convalescent jouit au plus haut degré,
comme l'enfant, de la faculté de s'intéresser vivement aux
choses, même les plus triviales en apparence." Then the
famous comparison between childhood and genius:

L'enfant voit tout en *nouveauté*; il est toujours *ivre*. Rien ne ressemble plus à ce qu'on appelle l'inspiration, que la joie avec laquelle
l'enfant absorbe la forme et la couleur. J'oserai pousser plus loin;
j'affirme que l'inspiration a quelque rapport avec la *congestion*, et
que toute pensée sublime est accompagnée d'une secousse nerveuse,
plus ou moins forte, qui retentit jusque dans le cervelet. L'homme
de génie a les nerfs solides; l'enfant les a faibles. Chez l'un, la raison
a pris une place considérable; chez l'autre, la sensibilité occupe presque tout l'être. Mais le génie n'est que *l'enfance retrouvée* à volonté,
l'enfance douée maintenant, pour s'exprimer, d'organes virils et de
l'esprit analytique qui lui permet d'ordonner la somme de matériaux
involontairement amassée (II, 331).

This relation of childhood to genius is one that may have
been suggested to Baudelaire by Delacroix, who mentions it
in several passages of the *Journal*, as when, on October 9,
1849, regretting the disappearance with age of a certain
"vivacité d'impressions," he writes: "Peut-être les très grands
hommes, et je le crois tout à fait, sont-ils ceux qui ont con-
servé, à l'âge où l'intelligence a toute sa force, une partie de
cette impétuosité dans les impressions, qui est le caractère de la
jeunesse?" (*Journal*, I, 314.) At all events, Baudelaire, in his
1852 article on Poe, notes, in connection with "William
Wilson," "quelle part immense l'adolescence tient dans le
génie définitif d'un homme" (*Poe*, p. 656). But at this time
the idea was much in Baudelaire's mind, for it recurs in the

Mangeur d'opium, published in the *Revue Contemporaine* in January, 1860, just when Baudelaire was composing the "Peintre." There, after speaking of the importance of childhood experience for the future artist, Baudelaire goes on in words which are a first state of those we have just read: "Ne serait-il pas facile de prouver, par une comparaison philosophique entre les ouvrages d'un artiste mûr et l'état de son âme quand il était enfant, que le génie n'est que l'enfance nettement formulée, douée maintenant, pour s'exprimer, d'organes virils et puissants?" (I, 380.) The passage occurs in a brief chapter, "Le Génie enfant," in which Baudelaire has much abbreviated and rearranged De Quincey. This particular chapter is very largely Baudelaire's own; its point of departure is undoubtedly the passage in *Suspiria* which begins: "I maintain steadfastly that into all the *elementary* feelings of man children look with more searching gaze than adults."[40] The passage may well have recalled Delacroix's ideas to Baudelaire, so that from the fusion of the two came his own terse formula.

One might think that the word *génie* which Baudelaire is defining here would be one of the key words in his thought. But this does not seem to be the case. The word is used fairly often throughout his work, with a good many meanings, varying from that of mere temperament to the ultra-romantic conception. But at no point does Baudelaire appear to attach great importance to it. One group of qualities do seem to be attached to it—force, energy, intensity (II, 76, 86, 156). In 1846 Baudelaire's only approach to a definition is: "[La poésie] gît dans l'âme du spectateur, et le génie consiste à l'y réveiller" (II, 116). From then until the "Peintre de la vie moderne" the word occurs frequently; in its highest sense Baudelaire reserves it for such as Delacroix, while he says that Ingres is "dénué de ce tempérament énergique quit fait la fatalité du génie" (II, 156). Later, in the Wagner article, he emphasizes the rational element in genius, attacking those who "dépouillent ainsi le génie de sa rationalité, et lui assignent une fonction purement instinctive et pour ainsi dire végétale" (II, 495). But later on he reiterates:

Tout ce qu'impliquent les mots: *volonté, désir, concentration, intensité nerveuse, explosion,* se sent et se fait deviner dans ses œuvres. Je ne crois pas me faire illusion ni tromper personne en affirmant que je vois là les principales caractéristiques du phénomène que nous appelons *génie*; ou du moins, que dans l'analyse de tout ce que nous avons jusqu'ici légitimement appelé *génie*, on retrouve les dites caractéristiques (II, 509).

It seems that for Baudelaire genius at its highest is essentially will, energy, reason applied to the imagination to give it its full force. As he says in 1861 in his review of *Les Martyrs ridicules*: "le génie (si toutefois on peut appeler ainsi le germe indéfinissable du grand homme) doit, comme le saltimbanque apprenti, risquer de se rompre mille fois les os en secret avant de danser devant le public" (II, 568). This seems to be the full meaning of "l'enfance retrouvée à *volonté*"; the combination of reason and will power with imagination is the function of genius. I rather think that Baudelaire's lack of stress on the word is partly due to a dislike of the romantic tendency to confuse genius with inspiration in the purest sense. By keeping to the conception of the imagination accompanied by intelligence, by technique, he avoids this danger.

Baudelaire, returning to Guys, says that in some respects he would call him a *dandy* (which he will elaborate later on), but that by his passion for seeing and feeling he is alien to the insensibility of the *dandy*. Nor is he exactly a philosopher: "réduisons-le donc à la condition de pur moraliste pittoresque, comme La Bruyère." Baudelaire pictures Guys plunging eagerly into the crowd, "un *moi* insatiable du *non-moi*," like the Opium Eater and his "bain de multitude" (I, 348). In something over a page Baudelaire evokes the whole of Guys's work, the visions of a great city, the beauty of horses, of women of fashion (noting each slight change in style), of soldiers, of the light and color and movement of the night life of Paris. Guys sees all this, and then sits down to express it:

Et les choses renaissent sur le papier, naturelles et plus que naturelles, belles et plus que belles, singulières et douées d'une vie enthousiaste comme l'âme de l'auteur. La fantasmagorie a été extraite de la nature. Tous les matériaux dont la mémoire s'est encombrée se classent, se rangent, s'harmonisent et subissent cette idéalisation forcée qui est le résultat d'une perception *enfantine*, c'est-à-dire d'une perception aiguë, magique à force d'ingénuité! (II, 334-35.)

What is Guys looking for, Baudelaire asks, and answers: "Il cherche ce quelque chose qu'on nous permettra d'appeler la *modernité*. . . . La modernité, c'est le transitoire, le fugitif, le contingent, la moitié de l'art, dont l'autre moitié est l'éternel et l'immuable." This brings us back to the definition of *le beau* which was Baudelaire's point of departure. He points out how each painter of the past has his own modernity, the costumes, the gestures, sometimes even the smile that belong to a period, that save him from an abstract and vague beauty: "Malheur à celui qui étudie dans l'antique autre chose que l'art pur, la logique, la méthode générale! Pour s'y trop plonger, il perd la mémoire du présent; il abdique la valeur et les privilèges fournis par la circonstance; car presque toute notre originalité vient de l'estampille que le *temps* imprime à nos sensations" (II, 337). Guys began by observing life, and only later learned how to express it. For most people the fantastic element in life is dulled, but Guys has his memory and his vision full of it.

The word *mémoire* leads Baudelaire to a chapter on a subject on which he has often touched before, "L'Art mnémonique"; this art is the representation not of nature, directly, but of the image of nature in the artist's mind, the work of memory, which in its turn appeals to the spectator's memory. "Le spectateur est ici le traducteur d'une traduction toujours claire et enivrante" (II, 338). Artists such as Guys and Daumier, accustomed to work from memory, are troubled indeed by the immediate presence of the model. "Il s'établit alors un duel entre la volonté de tout voir, de ne rien oublier, et la faculté de la mémoire qui a pris l'habitude d'absorber vivement la couleur générale et la silhouette, l'arabesque du contour."[41] The passage is very close to that on Boudin in the "Salon de 1859": "il faut que tout cela devienne tableau par le moyen de l'impression poétique rappelée à volonté" (II, 270).

This is not the first time that Baudelaire has noted the role of memory in art. In the "Salon de 1846" he says of Delacroix: "cette peinture, qui procède surtout du souvenir, parle surtout au souvenir" (II, 78), and later on: "j'ai déjà remarqué que le souvenir était le grand critérium de l'art; l'art est une mnémotechnie du beau: or, l'imitation exacte gâte le souvenir" (II, 99). This connection of memory and art is most often referred to by Baudelaire in connection with Delacroix, with whom it was a favorite idea. A fragment dated September 16, 1849, approximates memory and imagination closely:

Le fait est comme rien, puisqu'il passe. Il n'en reste que l'idée; réellement même, il n'existe pas dans l'idée, puisqu'elle lui donne une couleur, qu'elle se le représente en le teignant à sa manière et suivant les dispositions du moment. . . . C'est qu'il se passe dans la pensée, quand elle se souvient des émotions du cœur, ce qui s'y passe quand la faculté créatrice s'empare d'elle pour animer le monde réel et en tirer des tableaux d'imagination. Elle compose, c'est-à-dire qu'elle idéalise et choisit (Œuvres littéraires, I, 114).

And on April 29, 1854, he writes: "En réfléchissant sur la fraîcheur des souvenirs, sur la couleur enchantée qu'ils revêtent dans un passé lointain, j'admirais ce travail involontaire de l'âme qui écarte et supprime, dans le ressouvenir de moments agréables, tout ce qui en diminuait le charme, au moment où on les traversait. Je comparais cette espèce d'idéalisation, car c'en est une, à l'effet des beaux ouvrages de l'imagination" (Journal, II, 174). And on October 12 of the same year he also notes the appeal to the memory of the spectator:

Les peintres qui reproduisent tout simplement leurs études dans leurs tableaux ne donneront jamais au spectateur un vif sentiment de la nature. Le spectateur est ému, parce qu'il voit la nature par souvenir, en même temps qu'il voit votre tableau. Il faut que votre tableau soit déjà orné, idéalisé, pour que l'idéal, que le souvenir fourre, bon gré, mal gré, dans la mémoire que nous conservons de toutes choses, ne vous trouve pas inférieur à ce qu'il croit être la représentation de la nature (*Journal*, II, 287).[42]

This whole question of the memory is closely allied to that of the imagination; it is by memory that the artist is freed from the bonds of direct imitation; it is memory that prepares his materials, as it were; it is memory that awakens the memory of the spectator, as imagination arouses his imagination. With Delacroix, particularly, it is often difficult to see where the line is drawn between memory and imagination; in the passage from the *Œuvres littéraires* quoted above the use of the word *composer*—though it is immediately qualified as *idéaliser et choisir*—seems to take memory over the border line into the realm of the creative imagination. With Baudelaire there is less of this; memory is more strictly the servant of the imagination, ready to supply it with materials. One is reminded of St. Augustine's great passage on the memory:

These fields and spacious palaces of my memory, where the treasures of innumerable forms brought into it from these things that have been perceived by the senses be hoarded up. There is laid up whatever besides we think, either by way of enlarging or diminishing, or any other ways varying of those things which the sense hath come at. . . . Out of the same store do I myself combine fresh and fresh likelihoods of things, which I have experienced, or believed upon experience: and by these do I infer actions to come, events and hopes: and upon all these again do I meditate, as if they were now present.

And later: "Doubtless therefore memory is as it were the belly of the mind."[43] In the "Notes nouvelles" Baudelaire quotes Poe approvingly: "celui-là seul est poëte qui est le maître de sa mémoire, le souverain des mots, le registre de

ses propres sentiments toujours prêt à se laisser feuilleter"
(*Poe*, p. 709).

At the time when Baudelaire was writing the "Peintre de
la vie moderne" the question of memory was fresh in his mind
for another reason—his work on the *English Opium-Eater*.
In the chapter "Tortures de l'opium" he comments on the
usurpation by memory of the place of the will in the Opium-
Eater: "de même que les étoiles voilées par la lumière du jour
reparaissent avec la nuit, de même aussi toutes les inscriptions
gravées sur la mémoire inconsciente reparurent comme par
l'effet d'une encre sympathique" (I, 363). And a little later:
"Le lecteur a déjà remarqué que depuis longtemps l'homme
n'évoque plus les images, mais que les images s'offrent à lui,
spontanément, despotiquement. Il ne peut pas les congédier;
car la volonté n'a plus de force et ne gouverne plus les facultés.
La mémoire poétique, jadis source infinie de jouissances, est
devenue un arsenal inépuisable d'instruments de supplice"
(I, 365). Then the passage on "Le Génie enfant" treats the
role of the memory in the work of art: "Tel petit chagrin,
telle petite jouissance de l'enfant, démesurément grossis par
une exquise sensibilité, deviennent plus tard dans l'homme
adulte, même à son insu, le principe d'une œuvre d'art" (I,
380). And a few pages later: "Il revit tout l'univers de son
enfance, mais avec la richesse poétique qu'y ajoutait maintenant un esprit cultivé, déjà subtil, et habitué à tirer ses plus
grandes jouissances de la solitude et du souvenir" (I, 388).

All this leads up to the chapter on the palimpsest, to which
De Quincey compares the human mind. Baudelaire translates
certain passages very accurately, and summarizes others, evidently impressed by the whole chapter:

L'oubli n'est donc que momentané; et dans telles circonstances
solennelles, dans la mort peut-être, et généralement dans les excita-
tions intenses créées par l'opium, tout l'immense et compliqué
palimpseste de la mémoire se déroule d'un seul coup, avec toutes ses
couches superposées de sentiments défunts, mystérieusement embau-
més dans ce que nous appelons l'oubli (I, 389-90).

This last passage has an almost Proustian sound, and the parallel is worth pausing over.[44] Proust himself noted the analogy, while pointing out the differences, between himself and Baudelaire:

Chez Baudelaire enfin, ces réminiscences plus nombreuses encore, sont évidemment moins fortuites, et par conséquent à mon avis décisives. C'est le poète lui-même qui, avec plus de choix et de paresse recherche volontairement, dans l'odeur d'une femme par exemple, de sa chevelure et de son sein, les analogies inspiratrices qui lui évoqueront «l'azur du ciel immense et rond» et «un port remplis de flammes et de mâts» (*Le Temps retrouvé*, II, 82-83).

The essence of the difference between the Baudelairean and the Proustian role of memory is to be found in the word *volontairement*. For Proust the only significant memory is the *mémoire involontaire*, whereas with Baudelaire we have the constant recurrences of such expressions as "retrouvé à volonté." But the difference is not between *volontaire* and *involontaire* in the Proustian sense. Baudelaire's memory is by no means the impoverished, intellectualized instrument that the voluntary memory is for Proust. The workings of memory are the same in both cases; the past impression revived by an analogous sensation in the present. The difference is that for Proust the recall is, and must be, accidental; for Baudelaire it can be provoked.

When it comes to the role of memory in the work of art, the difference is more one of emphasis than anything else. For Proust the impression derived from so-called reality is transmuted by the memory into true reality, to be communicated by the taste of the madeleine, the feel of the starched napkin and the like. The task of the artist is to clear the ground, as it were, for these communications, and having received them to interpret them, to translate them.[45] For Baudelaire the original impression is conveyed to the memory, which makes a first draft for the artist, which can be evoked at will. But this material must be combined, fused by the creative imagination, and translated to the best of the artist's

ability.[46] Memory chooses, imagination arranges.[47] But for
Proust the involuntary memory has the predominant role that
the creative imagination has for Baudelaire.[48]

It is this memory, "resurrectionniste, évocatrice, une
mémoire qui dit à chaque chose: 'Lazare, lève-toi!' " which
Baudelaire finds in Guys, combined with an amazing swift-
ness of execution and the mysterious talent of the colorist. In
the succeeding chapters he discusses the various types of Guys's
work, evoking each group, each sketch, with unerring sureness. First comes the Crimean War series, then the Turkish
one. In "Le Militaire" Baudelaire points out that not only does
each country have its particular beauty, but also each profes-
sion, as here the soldier.

The next chapter takes up a subject dear to Baudelaire,
"Le Dandy." The type was in many ways his ideal; "j'étais
donc un dandy précoce" (II, 636), he says in "Fusées," and
the testimonies of his friends to his youthful *dandysme* are
numerous.[49] In the "Salon de 1846" *le dandysme* is praised as
"une chose moderne et qui tient à des causes tout-à-fait nouvelles" (II, 134). Both "Fusées" and "Mon Cœur mis à nu"
show a constant preoccupation with the dandy: "Le Dandy
doit aspirer à être sublime, sans interruption. Il doit vivre et
dormir devant un miroir"; "Eternelle supériorité du Dandy"
(II, 643, 646). In the "Notes nouvelles sur Edgar Poe" he
writes of the savage: "Il a le dandy, suprême incarnation de
l'idée du beau transportée dans la vie matérielle, celui qui
dicte la forme et règle les manières" (*Poe*, p. 704). And *le
dandysme* is one of the qualities Baudelaire finds and admires
in Delacroix: "E. Delacroix, quoiqu'il fût un homme de
génie, ou parce qu'il était un homme de génie complet, participait beaucoup du dandy" (II, 312).

It seems that Baudelaire had planned an article on the
dandy. On February 4, 1860, he writes to Poulet-Malassis:
"J'ai profité d'une invitation de *La Presse* pour lui livrer . . .
Le Dandysme littéraire ou la Grandeur sans conviction"
(*Corr.* I, 293). In June the cover of the *Paradis artificiels*

announces as "sous presse" *Réflexions sur quelques-uns de mes contemporains*, and includes in the table of contents, "La Famille des Dandies, ou Chateaubriand, de Custine, Paul de Molènes et Barbey d'Aurevilly." Later in the year Baudelaire writes to Calonne: "Je veux, pendant votre absence, livrer à la revue *L'Art philosophique* et *Le Dandysme littéraire*" (*Corr.* I, 343). But on December 3 he says: "Je vous consacrerai une enfilade de journées. . . . Le premier morceau, ce sera les *peintres*. Le deuxième, ce sera *le Dandysme*. Le livre de Sainte-Beuve me fournit, ce me semble, une occasion pour prendre Chateaubriand à un point de vue nouveau, le père du Dandysme" (*Corr.* I, 363). But in 1865 he writes to Sainte-Beuve, of the *Réflexions sur mes contemporains*: "Je dois avouer qu'il manque trois fragments importants . . . un dernier: *Chateaubriand et sa famille*. Vous savez que ma passion pour ce vieux *dandy* est incorrigible. En somme, peu de travail: dix jours peut-être. Je suis riche de notes" (*Lettres*, p. 429). It seems that at this point the article was to be centered on Chateaubriand, who was one of Baudelaire's lasting enthusiasms.

It seems likely that, as in other cases we have seen, Baudelaire borrowed a certain number of pages from an article unfinished and unlikely to be finished for an article he had well in hand. Here the marked break between the beginning of "Le Dandy" and the preceding chapter, and the fact that Guys is not mentioned until the next to the last paragraph seem to confirm this. Baudelaire begins this paragraph somewhat apologetically: "Ce qui a pu paraître au lecteur une digression n'en est pas une, en vérité. Les considérations et les rêveries morales qui surgissent des dessins d'un artiste sont, dans beaucoup de cas, la meilleure traduction que le critique en puisse faire; les suggestions font partie d'une idée mère, et, en les montrant successivement, on peut la faire deviner" (II, 352). One wonders, however, just when the addition was made. In February, 1860, when the Guys article was delivered to *La Presse*, Baudelaire was supposedly giving it the "Dandies" as well. The addition may have been made at some later date, when, in the course of its various peregrinations, the manuscript passed through Baudelaire's hands again. He had perhaps modified his original plan in the meantime, deciding to make the *dandy* article into an article on Chateaubriand, and so had parts of it available.

Baudelaire emphasizes the fact that the dandy is no modern type, but has an ancient and honorable history: Caesar and Catiline belong to it, and Chateaubriand found it among the Indians of the New World. And, slowly working towards a definition, in the way that has become so familiar to us, he finally finds that "c'est avant tout le besoin ardent de se faire une originalité, contenu dans les limites extérieures des convenances." Opposed to vulgarity and triviality, it is essentially aristocratic, "le dernier éclat d'héroïsme dans les décadences . . . un soleil couchant," soon to be engulfed by the rising tide of democracy. Then Baudelaire, suddenly remembering that he is writing about Guys, points out how the artist has expressed the dandy perfectly: "Le caractère de beauté du dandy consiste surtout dans l'air froid qui vient de l'inébranlable résolution de ne pas être ému; on dirait un feu latent qui se fait deviner, qui pourrait mais qui ne veut pas rayonner" (II, 352).

This chapter is followed by one on the being who, to Baudelaire's mind, is the very antithesis of the dandy—"La Femme." Woman, according to Joseph de Maistre, says Baudelaire, who evidently agrees with him, is *un bel animal.* "C'est une espèce d'idole, stupide peut-être, mais éblouissante, enchanteresse, qui tient les destinées et les volontés suspendues à ses regards"—a sentence which recalls the "Hymne à la Beauté," first published in *L'Artiste* of October 15, 1860:

Le Destin charmé suit tes jupons comme un chien.

It is not so much woman herself as the *mundus muliebris*[50] surrounding her that gives her her charm:

La femme est sans doute une lumière, un regard, une invitation au bonheur, une parole quelquefois; mais elle est surtout une harmonie générale, non-seulement dans son allure et le mouvement de ses membres, mais aussi dans les mousselines, les gazes, les vastes et chatoyantes nuées d'étoffes dont elle s'enveloppe, et qui sont comme les attributs et le piédestal de sa divinité; dans le métal et le minéral qui serpentent autour de ses bras et de son cou, qui ajoutent leurs étincelles au feu de ses regards, ou qui jasent doucement à ses oreilles (II, 353).[51]

The passage recalls a whole series of visions from the *Fleurs du Mal*—"Le Beau Navire," "Chanson d'après-midi," "Le Serpent qui danse," "Un Fantôme," and a dozen others.

All through the chapter Baudelaire's fundamental scorn of women, that comes out so brutally again and again in the *Journaux intimes*, is but slightly veiled. Few could have misunderstood the meaning of the chapter, but apparently Madame Aupick did, for Baudelaire writes to her in December, 1863: "Je suis désolé de t'arracher tes illusions, sur le passage où tu as cru voir l'éloge de ce fameux sexe. Tu l'as compris tout de travers. Je crois qu'il n'a jamais été rien dit de si dur que ce que j'ai dit dans le *Delacroix* et dans le *Figaro*. Mais cela ne concerne pas la *femme-mère*" (D.L.M., p. 178).

The next chapter, "Eloge du maquillage," begins with Baudelaire's most violent attack against the false conception of nature prevalent in the eighteenth century, a conception due largely to the denial of original sin: "La nature fut prise dans ce temps-là comme base, source et type de tout bien et de tout beau possible." Whereupon Baudelaire marshals a host of facts to show that nature and every natural impulse are wholly and entirely bad, that virtue is completely artificial and supernatural. He then transfers this from the moral order to the aesthetic: "La mode doit donc être considérée comme un symptôme du goût de l'idéal surnageant dans le cerveau humain au-dessus de tout ce que la vie naturelle y accumule de grossier, de terrestre et d'immonde, comme une déformation sublime de la nature, ou plutôt comme un essai permanent et successif de réformation de la nature" (II, 355).

Each new fashion is a reaching after beauty, "une approximation quelconque d'un idéal dont le désir titille sans cesse
l'esprit humain non satisfait." As for make-up, its aim is not
to imitate nature, but to correct and surpass her: "Qui oserait
assigner à l'art la fonction stérile d'imiter la nature? Le maquillage n'a pas à se cacher, à éviter de se laisser deviner; il peut,
au contraire, s'étaler, sinon avec affectation, au moins avec une
espèce de candeur" (II, 357).

The chapter is at first sight a *reductio ad absurdum* of
Baudelaire's aesthetics and theology alike, and the justification
of make-up by the doctrine of original sin leaves one a little
breathless. If one takes what Baudelaire says at its face value,
one might well criticize the leap from the moral to the
aesthetic, and, going deeper than that, question the orthodoxy
of his theology, which at this point seems to be a Manicheism
with Nature in the role of the Evil One. But I suspect that
the chapter is strongly flavored with Baudelaire's delight in
shocking the bourgeois, and it is perhaps wisest to say as
Asselineau did in reply to Baudelaire's repeated "Vous êtes
étonné?" "Une fois compris que c'était un système, il aurait
pu me montrer l'hippogriffe ou l'oiseau Rock que je leur
aurais dit: 'Bonjour, monsieur' " (*Crépet*, p. 283).

Nevertheless, there is no doubt that one of the important
aspects of Baudelaire's conception of nature is to be found
here, and this is perhaps the best place to consider that conception. At first Baudelaire's use of the word nature seems
puzzling, and at times contradictory. If one puts side by
side the three statements: "la nature est un temple"; "la
nature est un dictionnaire"; "la nature ne peut conseiller que
le crime"; one cannot but feel a certain bewilderment. Let
us see how Baudelaire's use of the word develops.

In the "Salon de 1845" the word seems to have a rather
vague and shifting meaning, with little importance attached
to it. So far as it is fixed, it suggests the romantic conception,
with the implication that the artist should imitate nature, not
follow in the footsteps of other artists. Baudelaire says of

Corot, "cet artiste aime sincèrement la nature" (II, 44), and of Français, that he has *"l'amour de la nature"* (II, 45). There are such expressions as "le caractère de la nature" and the like, but the only striking use of the word is in the section on sculpture, where Baudelaire says of David's statue of a boy "c'est bête comme la nature" (II, 52).

In the "Salon de 1846" the word becomes more important. The opening section has the definition, "un beau tableau étant la nature réfléchie par un artiste" (II, 64), and, later, "l'étude de la nature conduit souvent à un résultat tout différent de la nature" (II, 70). All this leads up to Delacroix's often repeated axiom "la nature est un vaste dictionnaire" (II, 78), an idea which is fundamental for Baudelaire, and is to play a large part in his conception of the imagination. Nature—here plainly the external world perceived by the senses—is assigned a definitely inferior role in relation to the artist; "les chefs-d'œuvre ne sont jamais que des extraits divers de la nature" (II, 79). This is put more strongly later on: "la première affaire d'un artiste est de substituer l'homme à la nature et de protester contre elle" (II, 115). So Baudelaire's first deliberate thought about nature puts it in a secondary place, as a "source" for the artist and the poet.

This idea encounters two others which attract Baudelaire; on the one hand the doctrine of correspondences, which gives to nature a seemingly more important role, and on the other hand the diatribes of De Maistre against nature. Here, however, *nature* is more than the outward and visible world; it has a philosophical and theological connotation. This is expressed in the well-known letter to Desnoyers of 1855:

Vous savez bien que je suis incapable de m'attendrir sur les végétaux, et que mon âme est rebelle à cette singulière religion nouvelle qui aura toujours, ce me semble, pour tout être *spirituel*, je ne sais quoi de *shocking*. Je ne croirai jamais que *l'âme des Dieux habite dans les plantes*, et, quand même elle y habiterait, je m'en soucierais médiocrement et considérerais la mienne comme d'un bien plus haut prix que celle des légumes sanctifiés. J'ai même toujours pensé qu'il y avait dans *la nature* florissante et rajeunie quelque chose d'affligeant, de dur, de cruel, — un je ne sais quoi qui frise l'impudence (*Corr.* I, 111).

And it is to this conception that the violent attack on nature in the "Peintre de la vie moderne" belongs: "la nature n'enseigne rien . . . elle pousse l'homme à tuer son semblable . . . la nature ne peut conseiller que le crime. . . . Le mal se fait sans effort, *naturellement,* par fatalité; le bien est toujours le produit d'un art" (II, 354-55). But the conception is far from being unrelated to Baudelaire's original one; this same chapter closes with the question: "Qui oserait assigner à l'art la fonction stérile d'imiter la nature?" (II, 357.) De Maistre himself had made the application:

Il semble que *l'imitation de la nature* offre un principe certain; malheureusement, il n'en est rien, car c'est précisément cette imitation qui fait naître les plus grandes questions. Il n'est pas vrai, en général, que dans les arts d'imitation il s'agisse d'*imiter la nature;* il faut l'imiter jusqu'à un certain point et d'une certaine manière. Si l'on passe ces bornes, on s'éloigne du beau en s'approchant de la nature (*Lettres et opuscules,* II, 137).

Baudelaire has found a moral and theological justification of his aesthetic subjugation of nature.

The "Salon de 1859" is rooted in this opposition to the imitation of nature. It attacks those who maintain that art is, and can only be, the exact reproduction of nature—an attitude developed in part by modern progress, so alien to poetry, with the invention of photography. To those who say "Copiez la nature, ne copiez que la nature," one might reply:

'Je trouve inutile et fastidieux de représenter ce qui est, parce que rien de ce qui est ne me satisfait. La nature est laide, et je préfère les monstres de ma fantaisie à la trivialité positive.' Cependant il eût été plus philosophique de demander aux doctrinaires en question, d'abord s'ils sont bien certains de l'existence de la nature extérieure, ou, si cette question eût paru trop bien faite pour réjouir leur causticité, s'ils sont bien sûrs de connaître *toute la nature,* tout ce qui est contenu dans la nature (II, 225-26).

Later in the article, writing of Fromentin, Baudelaire uses

a phrase which reconciles the seeming contradiction: "une faculté . . . qu'il possède à un degré éminent, est de saisir les parcelles du beau égarées sur la terre, de suivre le beau à la piste partout où il a pu se glisser à travers les trivialités de la nature déchue" (II, 255). Later he refers to "ce culte niais de la nature, non épurée, non expliquée par l'imagination" (II, 265). These last phrases suggest how nature should be treated. Nature in her superficial aspects, nature considered as sacred in herself, is not to be imitated; nature considered as an outward and visible sign is to be penetrated, interpreted. So we come back to the idea of correspondences. As Baudelaire says a little later in the Hugo article: "La nature qui pose devant nous, de quelque côté que nous nous tournions, et qui nous enveloppe comme un mystère, se présente sous plusieurs états simultanés dont chacun, selon qu'il est plus intelligible, plus sensible pour nous, se reflète plus vivement dans nos cœurs" (II, 520). Hence the role of the poet as the translator, the decipherer of nature, the seeker of analogies and metaphors.

I do not wish to create a false coherence; it is impossible to know how aware Baudelaire was of the apparent contradictions in his use of the word *nature*, and of their fundamental coherence. It is plain that for him nature is sometimes merely the world of the senses, sometimes the nature of the philosophers and theologians. But the relationship is plain; De Maistre had indicated it in his *Essai sur le principe générateur*: "Rien dans la nature n'étant ce qu'il doit être, le véritable artiste, celui qui peut dire: EST DEUS IN NOBIS, a le pouvoir mystérieux de discerner les traits les moins altérés, et de les assembler pour en former des touts qui n'existent que dans son entendement" (*Œuvres*, I, 53-54). And in 1856 Baudelaire writes to Toussenel: "*L'homme raisonnable* n'a pas attendu que Fourier vînt sur la terre pour comprendre que la nature est un *verbe*, une allégorie, un moule, un *repoussé*, si vous voulez. Nous savons cela, et ce n'est pas par Fourier que nous le savons, — nous les savons par nous-mêmes, et par les poëtes." And immediately afterwards: "la *nature* entière participe du péché original" (*Corr.* I, 131).

The unifying principle seems to me to be found in the often repeated "la Nature est un dictionnaire." A dictionary—therefore not a work of art, not a perfect thing, not sacred in itself, not to be imitated slavishly—but still a dictionary of meanings as well as of words. He who copies nature exactly might as well take the words of the dictionary as they come, with no regard for their meaning or relation; the true artist, the true poet, just as he chooses words from the dictionary with a careful regard for their meaning and connotation, chooses and arranges the aspects of nature, of which he has deciphered the inner meaning.

This leads to the question of the significance of the word *art* for Baudelaire—a word which appears constantly in these discussions of nature, and always in opposition to it. Never could anyone say less than Baudelaire, "Nature I loved, and next to Nature, Art." For him art is incomparably higher than nature. His first attempt at a definition of art, or rather of the function of art, occurs in the preface to the "Salon de 1846": "Or, vous avez besoin d'art. L'art est un bien infiniment précieux, un breuvage rafraîchissant et réchauffant, qui rétablit l'estomac et l'esprit dans l'équilibre naturel de l'idéal" (II, 62). *Idéal*—the key word of this "Salon," it will be remembered. The chapter on color begins to develop a more precise conception. There is the role of choice: "l'art n'étant qu'une abstraction et un sacrifice du détail à l'ensemble" (II, 69), and "il n'y a pas de hasard dans l'art, non plus qu'en mécanique" (II, 77). The chapter "De l'idéal et du modèle" brings the definition, "l'art est une mnémotechnie du beau: or, l'imitation exacte gâte le souvenir" (II, 99), reaffirmed later: "la première affaire de l'artiste est de substituer l'homme à la nature et de protester contre elle" (II, 115). The opposition of art to nature, asserted here, is reëchoed throughout the critical work. It will be reinforced by Poe, who wrote in "Marginalia": "Were I called on to define, *very* briefly, the term 'Art,' I should call it 'the reproduction of what the senses perceive in Nature through the veil of the soul.' The mere imitation, however accurate, of what *is* in Nature, entitles no man to the sacred name of 'Artist' " (Virginia ed., XVI, 164).

The Gautier article fixes "la condition génératrice des œuvres d'art, c'est-à-dire l'amour exclusif du Beau, *l'Idée fixe*" (II, 465). And the "Salon de 1859" protests against the diminution of this idea, the increasing servility of contemporary art, whereas "l'artiste, le vrai artiste, le vrai poëte, ne doit peindre que selon qu'il voit et qu'il sent" (II, 226). The "Peintre de la vie moderne" defends art against tradition as well as against nature, and makes it supreme in the realm of morality as well: "le bien est toujours le produit d'un art" (II, 355). Finally the unfinished article on "L'Art philosophique" brings Baudelaire's quintessential definition: "Qu'est-ce que l'art pur suivant la conception moderne? C'est créer une magie suggestive contenant à la fois l'objet et le sujet, le monde extérieur à l'artiste et l'artiste lui-même" (II, 367).

But we have strayed far from the "Peintre de la vie moderne." The two final chapters, "Les Femmes et les filles" and "Les Voitures" take us back to Guys and his representations of those ever-changing fashions of which Baudelaire has just been speaking. Women high and low are evoked for us—society women, young girls, courtesans, actresses—a world of women, translated by Guys, and retranslated by Baudelaire with a skill which contradicts his comment: "Ce qui fait la beauté particulière de ces images, c'est leur fécondité morale. Elles sont grosses de suggestions, mais de suggestions cruelles, âpres, que ma plume, bien qu'accoutumée à lutter contre les représentations plastiques, n'a peut-être traduites qu'insuffisamment." Then there are the horses and carriages, and all that constitutes "ces paysages familiers et intimes qui font la parure circulaire d'une grande ville." And Baudelaire's final tribute to Guys is: "Il a cherché partout la beauté passagère, fugace, de la vie présente, le caractère de ce que le lecteur nous a permis d'appeler la *modernité*. Souvent bizarre, violent, excessif, mais toujours poétique, il a su concentrer dans ses dessins la saveur amère ou capiteuse du vin de la Vie" (II, 363).

I am inclined to find the "Peintre de la vie moderne" my favorite of all Baudelaire's critical articles. When the "inevitable, terrible why" presents itself, my reasons are many. First of all, it is one of the richest in general ideas, ideas that go far beyond the particular subject. The stimulating and suggestive quality of what Baudelaire says of beauty, of art, of the parallel between genius and childhood, of the role of memory in art, have led me far afield in the preceding pages. Then in the "Peintre de la vie moderne," more than in any other work of his maturity, Baudelaire seems to have recaptured the freshness of his youthful enthusiasm, while adding to it the riches of thought and experience he has since acquired. The "Salon de 1859" is as suggestive and perhaps more synthesized; but as aesthetic experience it represents a series of disappointments; the pictures illustrate Baudelaire's thought negatively, not positively. And the *Ouf!* of relief with which he approaches the word FIN (II, 285) has suggested itself many pages before. But the last page of the "Peintre de la vie moderne" is as vigorous, as enthusiastic as the first; Baudelaire's delight in the discovery of the painter for whom he has been waiting so long makes itself felt throughout.

Critics have sometimes questioned the integral value of this enthusiasm, and regretted that Baudelaire did not live to know the group of *peintres de la vie moderne* of a few years later.[52] Manet's early work he knew and admired, but Degas, Renoir, Toulouse-Lautrec all came too late. It is perhaps true that Guys is clothed with the mantle of those greater than he, but his work has stood the test of time well, and the exhibition of his work in Paris in 1937 showed that seventy-five years after Baudelaire wrote an admiring public still found in Guys's work the same charm of transitory beauty which had delighted him. My own difficulty is that I always see Guys through Baudelaire; I had not seen a single example of his work until I had read Baudelaire, and a detached and impartial judgment is nearly impossible for me.

Moreover, Baudelaire found in Guys an artist who in practice as well as in theory was extraordinarily congenial to him, whose subjects again and again were his own. The poet and the critic are side by side here, and the pages of the "Peintre de la vie moderne" again and again echo the *Fleurs du Mal* and the *Petits poëmes en prose*. This, and Baudelaire's long practice in translating pictures into words give us on every page visions, suggestions, glimpses that make us almost forget that only a printed page is before us. Baudelaire is completely at his ease, completely sure of himself, and the result is a supreme piece of criticism.

"Richard Wagner et Tannhäuser à Paris,"[53] which I have placed with the "Salon de 1859" and the "Peintre de la vie moderne" at the height of Baudelaire's critical work, is very different from the other two articles. In them Baudelaire was dealing with the plastic arts, he was writing not only as an enthusiast but as a critic of long experience in the field. But the Wagner article is his only excursion into the field of musical criticism.

There has been little mention even of music in the previous criticism, though one has an impression of a critic sensitive to music. There is the use of musical terms in the criticism of painting, as we have seen, and in 1855 Baudelaire, writing of Delacroix, says: "Puis ces admirables accords de sa couleur font souvent rêver d'harmonie et de mélodie, et l'impression qu'on emporte de ses tableaux est souvent quasi musicale" (II, 162). Later Baudelaire added to the article at this point the stanza from "Les Phares":

> Delacroix, lac de sang hanté des mauvais anges,
> Ombragé par un bois de sapins toujours vert,

Où, sous un ciel chagrin, des fanfares étranges
Passent, comme un soupir étouffé de Weber.

At the end of the "Exposition de 1855," as in many other
passages, part of the *fêtes du cerveau* which are likened to
opium dreams is that "les sons tintent musicalement." But
the *Fleurs du Mal* are our best witness that there was no
insensibility to music in Baudelaire:

La musique souvent me prend comme une mer!

The only musicians mentioned by name before the Wagner
article are Weber and Beethoven. In the "Salon de 1845," as
in "Les Phares," the painting of Delacroix suggests Weber's
music: "Cette haute et sérieuse mélancolie . . . plaintive et
profonde comme une mélodie de Weber" (II, 85). For
Beethoven the comparison is a literary one; the Gautier article
speaks of "la prodigieuse symphonie qui s'appelle *Ténèbres*,"
and adds, "Je dis symphonie, parce que ce poëme me fait
quelquefois penser à Beethoven" (II, 478-79). In the Wagner
article itself, Weber and Beethoven appear again: "Dans ce
que j'avais éprouvé, il entrait sans doute beaucoup de ce que
Weber et Beethoven m'avaient déjà fait connaître" (II, 488).

Baudelaire's knowledge of music appears to have been
negligible, and his experience was confined to a general sensitivity to beauty of sound, until Wagner gave it shape and
form for him. On February 17, 1860, soon after the
three Wagner concerts at the Salle Ventadour, Baudelaire
wrote Wagner a long letter; this is a spontaneous first draft of
the article,[54] characterized by the enthusiasm which is Baudelaire's most endearing trait. He apologizes for the shameful
treatment Wagner has received from the critics, and then
says: "Avant tout, je veux vous dire que je vous dois *la plus
grande jouissance musicale que j'aie jamais éprouvée.*" Then
he describes the first time he had heard Wagner's music:

Ce que j'ai éprouvé est indescriptible, et si vous daignez ne pas rire,

j'essaierai de vous le traduire. D'abord il m'a semblé que je connaissais cette musique, et plus tard, en y réfléchissant, j'ai compris d'où
venait ce mirage; il me semblait que cette musique était *la mienne*,
et je la reconnaissais comme tout homme reconnaît les choses qu'il
est destiné à aimer. Pour tout autre que pour un homme d'esprit,
cette phrase serait immensément ridicule, surtout écrite par quelqu'un
qui, comme moi, *ne sait pas la musique*, et dont toute l'éducation se
borne à avoir entendu (avec grand plaisir, il est vrai) quelques beaux
morceaux de Weber et de Beethoven.

Baudelaire then proceeds to the translation of his impressions,
in a passage which prefigures the one on the overture to
Lohengrin in the article. At the end he says: "Depuis le jour
où j'ai entendu votre musique, je me dis sans cesse, surtout
dans les mauvaises heures: *Si, au moins, je pouvais entendre ce
soir un peu de Wagner!* . . . Une fois encore, Monsieur, je
vous remercie; vous m'avez rappelé à moi-même et au grand,
dans de mauvaises heures." And he adds a postscript: "Je
n'ajoute pas mon adresse, parce que vous croiriez peut-être
que j'ai quelque chose à vous demander." Wagner, however,
sought him out, divining in him "un esprit extraordinaire qui
poursuivait avec une fougueuse énergie et jusque dans leurs
dernières conséquences les impressions qu'il avait reçues de
ma musique."[55] On February 28 Baudelaire writes to Champfleury: "J'écris immédiatement à M. Wagner pour le remercier de tout mon cœur. J'irai le voir, mais pas tout de suite.
Des affaires assez tristes me prennent tout mon temps. Si vous
le voyez avant moi, dites-lui que ce sera pour moi un grand
honneur de serrer la main d'un homme de génie, insulté par
toute la populace des esprits frivoles" (*Corr.* I, 306). Shortly
after this he writes to Madame Sabatier: "Je suis si malheureux, et si ennuyé, que je fuis toute distraction. J'ai même,
tout récemment, malgré l'envie que j'ai de le connaître, refusé
une charmante invitation de Wagner" (*Corr.* I, 187).[56] The
relations between them seem to have been friendly from this
time on; a few days after the publication of the article
Wagner wrote to Baudelaire:

Mon cher monsieur Baudelaire, j'étais plusieurs fois chez vous sans
vous trouver. . . . Ne me serait-il pas possible de vous dire bientôt,
à haute voix, comment je m'ai [*sic*] senti enivré en lisant ces belles
pages qui me racontaient — comme le fait le meilleur poëme — les
impressions que je me dois vanter d'avoir produites sur une organisa-
tion si supérieure que la vôtre? (*Crépet*, pp. 451-52.)

All the letters that have been preserved indicate a mutual
esteem. Wagner's letter indeed, as well as what he says in the
Histoire de ma vie ("Baudelaire se distingua par une brochure
spirituelle et mordante écrite en ma faveur"), suggests that
perhaps—like Delacroix—he was unaware of the value of
Baudelaire's criticism, but the tone—unlike Delacroix's—is
exceedingly friendly.[57]

Indeed Wagner had reason to be grateful to Baudelaire, for
up to the time of his article the French press had given Wagner
a cold welcome indeed. The history of Wagner criticism in
France has been treated fully elsewhere,[58] and I shall recall
only a few points here. The first work of Wagner performed
in France was the overture to *Tannhäuser*, played at the
Concert de Sainte-Cécile on November 25, 1850. There was
little comment on it in the press, and that superficial. However, one of those most interested in Wagner was Gérard de
Nerval, who in this same year had been present at the first
performance of *Lohengrin* in Germany, and it may well have
been through Gérard that Baudelaire became interested in
Wagner. In 1852 the publication of Wagner's *Oper und
Drama* opened the way for a violent attack by the composer
and critic Fétis, in a series of articles in the *Revue Musicale*,
to which Baudelaire refers. Five years later a group of French
journalists, Gautier among them, was present at a performance of *Tannhäuser* at Wiesbaden. The accounts varied very
much in their tone, but there seems to have been little or no
real appreciation of Wagnerian music. In 1858 the *Tannhäuser* overture was performed again at the Concert de Paris,
but no other Wagnerian music was performed until Wagner's
arrival in Paris at the end of 1859. A group of friends and

admirers soon gathered around him, but even before his concerts a storm of malevolent criticism was let loose. The three concerts were given at the Théâtre Italien on January 25, and February 1 and 8, 1860. A week after the last one Baudelaire writes to Poulet-Malassis:

Riez un peu, mais gardez-moi le secret: notre bon, notre admirable Asselineau m'a dit, comme je lui reprochais, à lui qui sait la musique, de n'être pas allé aux concerts Wagner: 1° *que c'était si loin, si loin de chez lui* (salle des Italiens)! 2° *qu'on lui avait dit, d'ailleurs, que Wagner était* REPUBLICAIN! Je lui ai répondu que j'y serais allé, quand même c'eût été un royaliste, que cela n'empêchait ni la sottise, ni le génie. — Je n'ose plus parler de Wagner; on s'est trop foutu de moi. Ç'a été, cette musique, une des grandes jouissances de ma vie; il y a bien quinze ans que je n'ai senti pareil enlèvement (*Corr.* I, 297).

The concerts were greeted with a combination of enthusiasm and opposition that, as one critic suggested, recalled the great days of *Hernani*. But the press was almost without exception unfavorable, Scudo, whom we shall find pilloried in Baudelaire's pages, being the leader. There were indeed exceptions to the hue and cry, and some not without perception. For example, Emile Perrin writes of *Lohengrin*, in the *Revue Européenne*, in terms which suggest what Baudelaire is to say later: "Qu'elle est heureuse cette phrase mélodique qui semble venir comme un chœur céleste des profondeurs de l'infini, s'approche, grandit, éclate en gerbe lumineuse, puis s'éloigne, s'éteint et se perd, laissant dans l'air l'invisible nuage d'un murmure qu'on écoute alors qu'on ne l'entend plus."[59] But the great champion of Wagner, aside from Baudelaire, was Champfleury. He too had little musical knowledge, but replaced it by an enthusiasm which won Wagner's gratitude.

In the year which intervened between the concerts and the performance of *Tannhäuser* Wagner wrote and published the *Lettre sur la musique*. Meanwhile *Tannhäuser*, not without difficulty, had been accepted at the Opera, and rehearsals began in September, followed by one difficulty after another.

Finally the first performance took place on March 13, 1861, amid a confusion of applause and of hisses, the latter, alas, predominating. The following performances were even more riotous, and caricatures and parodies gave the opera an unenviable glory, the press following suit with almost complete unanimity of prejudice and misunderstanding.

A little over a fortnight after the *première*, when the failure of *Tannhäuser* was settled, Baudelaire's article, on which he had been at work for some time, appeared. His first idea had been to write poems inspired by Wagner; he says in his letter to him: "J'avais commencé à écrire quelques méditations sur les morceaux de *Tannhäuser* et de *Lohengrin* que nous avons entendus; mais j'ai reconnu l'impossibilité de tout dire" (*Corr.* I, 301). The *Revue Anecdotique* for the second half of February, 1860, notes that "Le poète Charles Baudelaire prépare quelques morceaux de poésie en l'honneur de l'auteur de *Lohengrin.*" The first actual mention of the article is in May of this year, when Baudelaire writes to Poulet-Malassis: "Le *Wagner* s'augmente tant que je serai obligé de le détacher du volume des *Contemporains*" (*Corr.* I, 331). In July he says: "je travaillerai au *Wagner* et à mon drame, chez ma mère" (*Corr.* I, 337), and in October, to Grandguillot, director of the *Constitutionnel*, "Je ne retournerais en tout cas à Honfleur qu'après vous avoir livré votre Wagner, ce qui serait à la fin du mois" (*Corr.* I, 360). Apparently there were difficulties here, for Baudelaire writes to Poulet-Malassis on December 5: "Wagner m'ayant envoyé son livre (j'ignore s'il est mis en vente), cela va me contraindre à rentrer tout de suite en relation avec Grandguillot" (*Corr.* I, 364). On March 25, 1861, he writes once more to Poulet-Malassis: "Le jour de ma rencontre avec De Broise, je sortais d'une imprimerie où on me détenait depuis trois jours, depuis 10 h. du matin jusqu'à 10 h. du soir, pour en finir avec le *Wagner*, qui va enfin paraître à l'*Européenne*" (*Corr.* I, 382). And on March 29, to his mother: "Un gros travail de moi sur Richard Wagner va paraître le 31. Faut-il te l'envoyer?" (*L.M.*, p. 216). On

April 1 he writes again to her: "Enfin, l'idée fixe a disparu, chassée par une occupation violente et inévitable, l'article Wagner, improvisé en trois jours dans une imprimerie: sans l'obsession de l'imprimerie, je n'aurais jamais eu la force de le faire" (*L.M.*, pp. 218-19). The last statement is obviously an exaggeration of what Baudelaire had written to Poulet-Malassis. That letter shows that the article, dated March 18, was completed only on March 22, just over a week after the *première* of *Tannhäuser*. But in the *Revue Européenne* text there is no reference, except vaguely in the last two paragraphs, to the performance as having taken place, and the article must have been practically completed before then.

Baudelaire's article is interesting in itself as his only excursion into musical criticism, and for the example it furnishes of the validity of his critical method in unfamiliar regions. It is also exceedingly interesting as showing the skeleton, as it were, of that method more clearly than any of the other articles. What I mean is this; I said at the beginning that the *transformation de la volupté en connaissance* seems to me the essence of Baudelaire's criticism; at the heart of it is the direct experience of the work of art, then the fortifying, and perhaps modifying of that experience by knowledge, information, illumination from all possible sources. In the art and literature criticism the two are more or less coexistent. The critic's experience is that of one already at home in the subject; *volupté* already has a foundation of *connaissance*. But with music the case is different; here we have first the experience, then the acquisition of the necessary knowledge and finally the return to the experience, strengthened and enriched by the knowledge acquired. The reader will see that the first three of the four parts into which the article is divided (the last is a general conclusion) represent these three steps.

At the beginning Baudelaire puts his criticism on a very personal basis: "Qu'il me soit permis, dans cette appréciation, de parler souvent en mon nom personnel. Ce *Je*, accusé justement d'impertinence dans beaucoup de cas, implique cependant une grande modestie; il enferme l'écrivain dans les limites les plus strictes de la sincérité" (II, 482). He then recalls the history of the preceding thirteen months; Wagner's return to Paris, the Fétis articles, "une diatribe affligeante," the announcement of the concerts, the ill will of the critics. He points out that the program showed Wagner's courage; it was composed entirely of orchestral music, unrelieved by solos of any kind. But the audience was enthusiastic over the overtures to *Tannhäuser* and *Lohengrin,* and although parts seemed obscure, impartial critics were willing to wait to hear them in their proper setting. "En attendant, il restait avéré que, comme symphoniste, comme artiste traduisant par les mille combinaisons du son les tumultes de l'âme humaine, Richard Wagner était à la hauteur de ce qu'il y a de plus élevé, aussi grand, certes, que les plus grands" (II, 484). Here is Baudelaire's favorite expression of *translator* for the artist, and he proceeds to enlarge on it. The statement that music cannot translate anything with the sureness of words or painting, is, says Baudelaire, only partly true: "Elle traduit à sa manière, et par les moyens qui lui sont propres. Dans la musique, comme dans la peinture et même dans la parole écrite, qui est cependant le plus positif des arts, il y a toujours une lacune complétée par l'imagination de l'auditeur" (II, 485).[60] Here, as elsewhere in the article, Baudelaire is thinking of the imagination stimulated by the work of art, not the imagination which created it originally; the imagination which re-creates, thus making something of its own.

Even without the help of the other arts, as in opera, music can convey its own message. Baudelaire shows this by a comparison of three different interpretations of the overture to *Lohengrin;* Wagner's own, printed in the concert program, that of Liszt in his *Lohengrin et Tannhäuser,* and Baudelaire's own, already suggested in his letter to Wagner. In speaking of the last two, Baudelaire uses the word imagination: "la page où l'imagination de l'illustre pianiste (qui est un artiste et un philosophe) traduit à sa manière le même morceau," and "la traduction inévitable que mon imagination fit du même morceau, lorsque je l'entendis pour la première fois, les yeux fermés, et que je me sentis pour ainsi dire enlevé de terre." And here the doctrine of correspondences is brought in:

Le lecteur sait quel but nous poursuivons: démontrer que la véritable musique suggère des idées analogues dans des cerveaux différents. D'ailleurs, il ne serait pas ridicule ici de raisonner *a priori*, sans analyse et sans comparaisons; car ce qui serait vraiment surprenant, c'est que le son *ne pût pas* suggérer la couleur, que les couleurs *ne pussent pas* donner l'idée d'une mélodie, et que le son et la couleur fussent impropres à traduire des idées; les choses s'étant toujours exprimées par une analogie réciproque, depuis le jour où Dieu a proféré le monde comme une complexe et indivisible totalité (II, 486-87).

Here Baudelaire quotes the two quatrains of the "Correspondances" sonnet. He then describes his own impressions (before he had read the program); his sense of freedom and happiness, of space and of light, increasing with extraordinary speed and intensity, "*ce surcroît toujours renaissant d'ardeur et de blancheur*." And he concludes: "Alors je conçus pleinement l'idée d'une âme se mouvant dans un milieu lumineux, d'une extase *faite de volupté et de connaissance*, et planant au-dessus et bien loin du monde naturel" (II, 487).[61]

As Baudelaire says, there are obvious differences among the three translations, but the resemblances are far more striking; in all three there is the sense of happiness, of isolation; of extraordinary greatness and beauty; of intense light that is a delight to the eyes; and of space reaching out to its uttermost limits. In his own words:

Aucun musicien n'excelle, comme Wagner, à *peindre* l'espace et la profondeur, matériels et spirituels. C'est une remarque que plusieurs esprits, et des meilleurs, n'ont pu s'empêcher de faire en plusieurs occasions. Il possède l'art de traduire, par des gradations subtiles, tout ce qu'il y a d'excessif, d'immense, d'ambitieux, dans l'homme spirituel et naturel. Il semble parfois, en écoutant cette musique ardente et despotique, qu'on retrouve, peintes sur le fond des ténèbres, déchiré par la rêverie, les vertigineuses conceptions de l'opium (II, 488).

Many a critic would stop here, more than content to have translated his own experience with such sureness. But not so Baudelaire, and here is one of the essential qualities of his criticism.

A partir de ce moment, c'est-à-dire du premier concert, je fus possédé du désir d'entrer plus avant dans l'intelligence de ces œuvres singulières. J'avais subi (du moins cela m'apparaissait ainsi) une opération spirituelle, une révélation. Ma volupté avait été si forte et si terrible, que je ne pouvais m'empêcher d'y vouloir retourner sans cesse. Dans ce que j'avais éprouvé, il entrait sans doute beaucoup de ce que Weber et Beethoven m'avaient déjà fait connaître, mais aussi quelque chose de nouveau que j'étais impuissant à définir, et cette impuissance me causait une colère et une curiosité mêlée d'un bizarre délice (II, 488).

For a long time his one desire was to hear Wagner played, on his friends' pianos, at popular concerts; an undated letter to Poulet-Malassis notes: "Hier soir mardi on a repris les *Noces de Lohengrin* au casino" (*Corr.* I, 291).

Then comes the further step: "Cependant, des répétitions fréquentes des mêmes phrases mélodiques, dans des morceaux tirés du même opéra, impliquaient des intentions mystérieuses et une méthode qui m'étaient inconnues. Je résolus de m'informer du pourquoi et de transformer ma volupté en connaissance avant qu'une représentation scénique vînt me fournir une élucidation parfaite" (II, 489). Here, as I said at the beginning, is the fundamental movement of Baudelaire's criticism, from an intense experience to a knowledge of what lies behind that experience, imagination calling upon intelligence. So Baudelaire read all he could lay his hands on, "l'indigeste et abominable pamphlet de M. Fétis," Liszt's *Lohengrin et Tannhäuser*, the English translation of Wagner's *Oper und Drama* and, when it appeared early in December, 1860, the *Lettre sur la musique*.[62] The second section of the article is largely devoted to what he acquired from this reading, what he found significant and illuminating there. He makes no attempt, however, to acquire technical musical knowledge all at once; there is nothing resembling the hotchpotch of musical terms hastily acquired for the occasion which we find in Gautier's musical articles. What Baudelaire does is to extract from his reading what is significant for his own experience. There is a good deal of direct quotation from Wagner, and much more outside quotation marks that is borrowed from him and from Liszt; indeed not since the early "Salons" have we met pages that are so frankly borrowings. The reason is obvious; this reading was fresh in his mind, there had been little time for it to soak in the "deep well of unconscious cerebration," and these pages, almost alone in Baudelaire's later criticism, have an air of patchwork about them. Their great interest is that they allow us to see Baudelaire at work, gathering from scattered pages the ideas that supply the answer to his insistent *why*: "Parmi ces documents fort connus aujourd'hui, je ne veux extraire que ceux qui me paraissent plus propres à éclairer et à définir la nature et le caractère du maître" (II, 489-90). First of all, he seeks an explanation of Wagner's revolutionary opinions in "cette facilité à souffrir, commune à tous les artistes et d'autant plus grande que leur instinct du juste et du beau est plus prononcé." Here Baudelaire may well be thinking of the Baudelaire of 1848 even more than of the Wagner of 1860. He then notes Wagner's early love of the theatre, as well as of music, so that a double way of thinking, poetical and musical, early became an ingrained habit with him. In this connection Baudelaire recalls, "comme par un phénomène d'écho mnémonique, différents passages de Diderot qui affirment que la vraie critique musicale ne peut pas être autre chose que le cri ou le soupir de la passion noté et rhythmé" (II, 491). He also notes Wagner's preoccupation with Greek drama, and quotes his letter to Berlioz, as well as the *Lettre sur la musique*. He sums up:

Ce goût absolu, despotique, d'un idéal dramatique, où tout, depuis une déclamation notée et soulignée par la musique avec tant de soin qu'il est impossible au chanteur de s'en écarter en aucune syllabe, véritable arabesque de sons dessinée par la passion, jusqu'aux soins les plus minutieux relatifs aux décors et à la mise en scène, où tous les détails, dis-je, doivent sans cesse concourir à une totalité d'effet, a fait la destinée de Wagner (II, 492-93).

Baudelaire notes the combination of classic and romantic in Wagner, the classic beauty of structure and the legendary and mediaeval subjects. He quotes at length from the *Lettre sur la musique* what Wagner says of myth and legend as the ideal subject matter for the poet, and concludes: "Comment Wagner ne comprendrait-il pas admirablement le caractère sacré, divin du mythe, lui qui est à la fois poëte et critique?"

This leads Baudelaire to the great page which is his final word on criticism and the critic. On the one hand, he says, Wagner's great critical intelligence has made some people mistrust his musical genius, thus despoiling genius of its rational quality and turning it into something merely instinctive, and on the other hand people have accused him of writing his operas to prove his theories, *a posteriori*. Not only is the chronology false in this particular case, says Baudelaire, but the thing itself is impossible. Then comes the statement of his critical creed which I have already quoted, but which may well be replaced in its context here:

Ce serait un événement tout nouveau dans l'histoire des arts qu'un critique se faisant poëte, un renversement de toutes les lois psychiques, une monstruosité; au contraire, tous les grands poëtes deviennent naturellement, fatalement, critiques. Je plains les poëtes que guide le seul instinct; je les crois incomplets. Dans la vie spirituelle des premiers, une crise se fait infailliblement, où ils veulent raisonner leur art, découvrir les lois obscures en vertu desquelles ils ont produit, et tirer de cette·étude une série de préceptes dont le but divin est l'infaillibilité dans la production poétique. Il serait prodigieux qu'un critique devînt poëte, et il est impossible qu'un poëte ne contienne pas un critique. Le lecteur ne sera donc pas étonné que je considère le poëte comme le meilleur de tous les critiques (II, 495-96).

The idea may have been suggested to Baudelaire by a passage in Poe's "Letter to B——,"[63] which ends "A poet, who is indeed a poet, could not, I think, fail of making a just critique," but Baudelaire carries it far beyond. At the root of the passage is the idea we have met so often that imagination is incomplete without intelligence, that genius is not merely instinctive and that thus the complete poet must contain the critic. But intelligence can exist divorced from imagination, hence the critic does not contain the poet. However with the poet the poetic experience must come first, and only afterwards does he feel the need of inquiring into how the experience happened, how poetry was produced. This is the function of the critic; and inevitably, according to Baudelaire, the poet, who knows the processes of poetic production firsthand, will be the best of critics.

Through all this, by *poet* Baudelaire means maker, creator in any of the arts, as the examples he adduces in addition to Wagner show—Da Vinci, Hogarth, Reynolds, Delacroix, Diderot, Goethe, Shakespeare. And what he says is true in a still wider sense; even for the pure critic the experience of whatever he is criticizing should precede the acquiring of information about it. Here in this very article Baudelaire gives us the example; he has not read up on Wagner's theories and then listened to his music. The experience of the music is the only valid stimulus for the quest for knowledge. For poet-critic or simple critic, the order *volupté-connaissance* is the only right one. So I hope that no one of my readers has reached this point without having long since turned from my pages to those of Baudelaire.

In the third part of the article Baudelaire, having translated his experience, having learned all he can about what lies behind it, turns back to Wagner's music. He studies successively three of the operas, *Tannhäuser, Lohengrin,* and *The Flying Dutchman,* selections from which, with the prelude to *Tristan,* had made up the program of the concerts. But this return to experience is only partial; Baudelaire had seen none of the operas on the stage, and hence his direct experience is confined to the librettos and the selections played at the concerts. So it is not surprising that here, as in the second part, we find many echoes of Liszt. The *pattern* for the perfect critical experience is here; only practical difficulties stood in the way of its complete working out.

The first sentence on *Tannhäuser* shows the closeness of the theme to Baudelaire's own preoccupations: "*Tannhäuser* représente la lutte des deux principes qui ont choisi le cœur humain pour principal champ de bataille, c'est-à-dire de la chair avec l'esprit, de l'enfer avec le ciel, de Satan avec Dieu." As with the overture of *Lohengrin*, Baudelaire gives his own impression, for, though much has already been written about it, "c'est le propre des œuvres vraiment artistiques d'être une source inépuisable de suggestions." Here the impression left by the overture is more definite; Baudelaire knows the opera and its theme, and the translation is therefore in more precise terms of the struggle between the two opposing principles. Still it is above all of his personal impressions that he writes: "Tout cerveau bien conformé porte en lui deux infinis, le ciel et l'enfer, et dans toute image de l'un de ces infinis il reconnaît subitement la moitié de lui-même." Baudelaire's analysis is not of the music itself; he says that a technical review, by a competent hand, will appear later. His analysis is of what is translated by the music, "l'homme général, universel, vivant morganatiquement avec l'idéal absolu de la volupté." The overture, he maintains, is perfectly comprehensible without the libretto. Then he touches on other parts of *Tannhäuser* which had been played at the concerts—with a certain amount of help from Liszt on the perfect accord of words and music.

For *Lohengrin*, Baudelaire tells the story with a good deal of detail, and draws a parallel between it and the stories of Psyche and of Eve. This leads him into a digression on myths and legends.

Le mythe est un arbre qui croît partout, en tout climat, sous tout soleil, spontanément et sans boutures. Les religions et les poésies des quatre parties du monde nous fournissent sur ce sujet des preuves surabondantes. Comme le péché est partout, la rédemption est partout, le mythe partout. Rien de plus cosmopolite que l'Eternel (II, 502).

Returning to *Lohengrin*, Baudelaire notes, characteristically, the "aristocratic" restraint in the wedding music, unlike the turbulènce of a common crowd. Then he picks up the idea of the *leit-motiv*, which he calls "ce système mnémonique," thus attaching it to what has been in his mind about memory. Here he quotes a long page from Liszt, explaining the *leit-motiv*. He notes in conclusion that without poetry Wagner's music would still be a poetic work, having all the essential qualities of poetry, "tant toutes choses y sont . . . prudemment *concaténées*."

The Flying Dutchman is also analyzed in detail, but Baudelaire obviously knows it only through the libretto and the overture, "lugubre et profonde comme l'Océan, le vent et les ténèbres." He then leaves the individual works, and sets about finding the particular quality of Wagner: "Un artiste, un homme vraiment digne de ce grand nom, doit posséder quelque chose d'essentiellement *sui generis*, par la grâce de quoi il est *lui* et non un autre" (II, 508). What he finds in Wagner above all is "l'intensité nerveuse, la violence dans la passion et dans la volonté . . . si, par le choix de ses sujets et sa méthode dramatique, Wagner se rapproche de l'antiquité, par l'énergie passionnée de son expression il est actuellement le représentant le plus vrai de la nature moderne." Here Wagner, like Delacroix, is attached to the idea of the *beau moderne* not by his subjects, but by his temperament. Baudelaire finds in this intensity, this concentration, this passion the chief characteristics of genius. As for Wagner's future success, he recalls the early resistance to Hugo's plays and Delacroix's painting, and insists that the failure of *Tannhäuser* would prove nothing: "Dans quelle histoire a-t-on jamais lu que les grandes causes se perdaient en une seule partie?" (II, 510.) It seems that these two concluding paragraphs, unlike the rest of the article, may well have been written after the performances of *Tannhäuser*; very likely this is what Baudelaire was driven to write under the eye of the waiting printer.

In the *Revue Européenne* the article ended here, but when it appeared in pamphlet form a postscript was added, "Encore quelques mots," dated April 8, in which Baudelaire discusses the failure of the performance, and warns those who are shouting that the "music of the future" is dead and buried not to rejoice too soon. In a sentence reminiscent of De Maistre he says: "Ils ignorent aussi de quelle patience et de quelle opiniâtreté la Providence a toujours doué ceux qu'elle investit d'une fonction" (II, 511). As for the reasons for the failure, they are many: the audience, unused to serious opera; many weaknesses in staging, orchestra, and singing; and finally the timidity of the press. "Le *Tannhäuser* n'avait même pas été entendu." Baudelaire's whole tone is one of profound discouragement, the discouragement he has felt about Delacroix, about Poe, but he concludes: "Enfin l'idée est lancée, la trouée est faite, c'est l'important."

So ends Baudelaire's one venture into musical criticism. It is not without its weaknesses, chief among them Baudelaire's lack of technical knowledge of music. But there is no attempt to disguise this under a veneer of technical terms; Baudelaire's position is entirely sincere. As M. Suarès says: "En musique, il n'a point de connaissances précises, et sa culture est médiocre. . . . La critique de Baudelaire . . . touche le fond, même quand elle se trompe sur le détail. Sans doute, si on la prend du côté musical, la critique de Baudelaire est pleine de confusion et de naïvetés qui font sourire; mais où le musicien est en défaut, il n'arrive jamais à l'artiste de l'être."[64] Then too Baudelaire's criticism of the three operas seems curiously literary; this is inevitable, since his experience of them was only through the librettos and the fragments heard at the concerts. But when all this has been said, the fact remains that Baudelaire was almost alone in recognizing the genius of Wagner. His infallible taste, his poetic sensitiveness judged more surely than the information and experience of the professional musical critics. The article is the shining proof of the validity of Baudelaire's critical method. To quote M. Suarès once more:

Plus on va, plus on admire la supériorité de Baudelaire dans la critique d'art. Pour mieux dire, il n'est pas critique: Baudelaire est un grand esprit qui s'applique aux œuvres de l'art, et qui discerne du premier coup en quoi les unes sont de l'ordre le plus élevé, en quoi les autres ne pourront jamais l'être. Il est le bien voyant, le vrai poète qui pense sur la poésie.

The article has the peculiar interest, as I have said, of showing the *transformation de la volupté en connaissance* in action. Moreover, it represents a special functioning of the imagination, not so much in the creator as in those whom he addresses. In the art and literary criticism Baudelaire is thinking particularly of the imagination as it creates the work of art; here it is the imagination of the listener as he deciphers the translation and thus makes his own version.

In these three articles of the years 1859 to 1861 we have, I believe, the peak of Baudelaire's critical work. His power of translating an aesthetic experience is at its height, and he is at the point where, as he says in the Wagner article, the poet pauses to reflect on his art and conclude from his experience. The "Salon de 1859," where the fortuitous assembly of pictures in a Salon are all brought to bear on the great question of the imagination; the "Peintre de la vie moderne," where Baudelaire rejoices in the advent of his long-awaited modern painter and evokes the varied aspects of his art; the Wagner article, where all the resources of the poet and critic are brought to bear on an unfamiliar art: here are three shining facets of Baudelaire's criticism.

Chapter Four

THE LAST YEARS

Une pensée unique et systématique.—Letter of February 23, 1865.

THE CURVE of Baudelaire's critical work of the last years is significant. The poet's life has become increasingly difficult and full of disappointments, and in spite of heroic efforts to make a fresh start there is a decided lessening of literary activity, culminating in the tragedy of the last sad years in Belgium. The year 1861 is still a productive one, yielding the long series of articles on contemporary poets, as well as the account of the Delacroix murals in Saint-Sulpice; in 1862 there is a visible lessening of critical activity; in 1863 comes the great last tribute to Delacroix; and after that only brief notes and unfinished articles. Moreover, from the Wagner article on, Baudelaire's criticism is more and more an application of the principles he had already established. There are no new lines of thought, and Baudelaire seems to have read little that finds an echo in his articles.[1] For this reason I have felt justified in abandoning in this chapter the strict chronological order which has seemed of primary importance up to this point. There are a large number of articles, and it has seemed to me more interesting to relate those that have some connection with each other than to keep to a chrono-logical order that at this point has no great significance. Then too, it is impossible to date with any certainty some of the articles which were not published until after Baudelaire's death.

The series of articles grouped in *L'Art romantique* under the head of "Réflexions sur mes contemporains" were written (with the possible exception of the one on Banville) for Eugène Crépet's anthology, *Les Poëtes français* (1862), and first published in the *Revue Fantaisiste* between June 15 and August 15, 1861. One might be tempted to find in these articles a parallel to the great articles of art and music criticism, and to set up a triptych of which the central panel should be the "Salon de 1859" and the "Peintre de la vie moderne," with the Wagner article and the "Réflexions" the side wings. But such an arrangement, alluring in its symmetry, seems to me to give to the "Réflexions" an importance which is not theirs by right.

The first of the "Réflexions" is the article on Victor Hugo. Its sincerity, like that of the Gautier article of 1859, has been questioned, and, one may well think, with reason. For Baudelaire's frequent previous mentions of Hugo, both in his published work and in his correspondence, are in general far from favorable.[2] His personal acquaintance with Hugo was only slight. Writing to him in 1859, he says: "vous, que je n'ai vu que deux fois, et il y a de cela presque vingt ans" (*Corr.* I, 273). Prarond says: "Lui, qui récitait beaucoup, disait peu de vers d'Hugo. Il s'était fait introduire cependant à la place Royale. . . . Baudelaire allait, mais fort rarement, je crois, visiter Victor Hugo, de 1842 à 1846."[3] And Baudelaire says at the beginning of his article: "je le rencontrai quelquefois dans la compagnie d'Edouard Ourliac, par qui je connus aussi Pétrus Borel et Gérard de Nerval" (II, 518).

Baudelaire's first published mention of Hugo, in the "Salon de 1845," is disparaging: "c'est M. Victor Hugo qui a perdu M. Boulanger" (II, 28). The following year he denounces the conventional parallel between Hugo and Delacroix, qualifying Hugo as "un ouvrier beaucoup plus adroit qu'inventif, un travailleur bien plus correct que créateur." A long passage damns him in no uncertain terms:

M. Victor Hugo laisse voir dans tous ses tableaux, lyriques et
dramatiques, un système d'alignement et de contrastes uniformes.
L'excentricité elle-même prend chez lui des formes symétriques. Il
possède à fond et emploie froidement tous les tons de la rime, toutes
les ressources de l'antithèse, toutes les tricheries de l'apposition. C'est
un compositeur de décadence et de transition, qui se sert de ses outils
avec une dextérité véritablement admirable et curieuse. M. Hugo
était naturellement académicien avant de naître, et si nous étions
encore au temps des merveilles fabuleuses, je croirais volontiers que
les lions verts de l'Institut, quand il passait devant le sanctuaire
courroucé, lui ont souvent murmuré d'une voix prophétique: 'Tu
seras de l'Académie!' (II, 76).[4]

Here it is above all the artificiality, the conscious symmetry
and antitheses of Hugo's work that Baudelaire finds so dis-
pleasing. Later his political and social opinions, so diametri-
cally opposed to those Baudelaire had been absorbing from
Poe and De Maistre, could not but widen the breach. "Fusées"
has a bitter note on "Hugo-Sacerdoce . . . si peu élégiaque,
si peu éthéré, qu'il ferait horreur même à un notaire" (II,
639). However there is an appearance at least of friendly relations in the late 1850's: Hugo's somewhat pompous acknowl-
edgement of the *Fleurs du Mal*,[5] Baudelaire's disavowal of the
remark attributed to him in an article in the *Figaro*, "Hugo!
qui ça, Hugo? Est-ce qu'on connaît ça . . . Hugo?" (*Corr.*
I, 211.)

It is in connection with the Gautier article of 1859 that
Baudelaire most definitely changes his position. The article
itself, as well as the "Salon de 1859," contains several flattering references to Hugo. And between the publication of the
article in *L'Artiste* on March 19, and its separate publication
in the autumn, Baudelaire made a great effort to obtain a
letter-preface from Hugo: "Une lettre de vous, Monsieur,
qu'aucun de nous n'a vu depuis si longtemps, de vous, que je
n'ai vu que deux fois, et il y a de cela presque vingt ans, —
est une chose si agréable est précieuse!" There is a near apology
for the divergence of his views from Hugo's:

J'ai donc maintenant quelques explications à vous donner. Je sais

vos ouvrages par cœur, et vos préfaces me montrent que j'ai dépassé
la théorie généralement exposée par vous sur l'alliance de la morale
et de la poésie. Mais en un temps où le monde s'éloigne de l'art avec
une telle horreur, où les hommes se laissent abrutir par l'idée exclusive
d'utilité, je crois qu'il n'y a pas grand mal à exagérer un peu dans
le sens contraire. J'ai peut-être réclamé trop. C'était pour obtenir
assez (*Corr.* I, 273-74).

The apologetic, almost fawning tone is a strange and disturbing contrast to the defiant affirmations of the Gautier
article itself and the conclusion of the "Notes nouvelles sur
Edgar Poe": "Victor Hugo serait moins admiré s'il était
parfait . . . il n'a pu se faire pardonner tout son génie
lyrique qu'en introduisant de force et brutalement dans sa
poésie ce qu'Edgar Poe considérait comme l'hérésie moderne
capitale, — *l'enseignement*" (*Poe*, p. 713). But the letter
achieved its end, for Hugo's reply (II, 766-67), with the
famous "Vous créez un frisson nouveau," was the speedy
answer. However the preface emphasizes fundamental differences between the two: "Vous ne vous trompez pas en
prévoyant quelque dissidence entre vous et moi. Je comprends
toute votre philosophie (car, comme tout poëte, vous con-
tenez un philosophe): je fais plus que la comprendre, je
l'admets: mais je garde la mienne. Je n'ai jamais dit: l'Art
pour l'Art: j'ai toujours dit: l'Art pour le Progrès."

Such is the history, up to 1861, of Baudelaire's relations with
Hugo and his attitude towards him; first outspoken criticism,
then silence, and then a somewhat disquieting flattery. When
it comes to the writing of the 1861 article Baudelaire does not
seem entirely at his ease; he writes to the director of the
Revue Fantaisiste, where the article was to appear: "Je tâcherai
de dire en 10 pages maximum ce que je pense de raisonnable
sur Hugo" (*Corr.* I, 383). The article itself, especially in its
opening and closing pages, confirms one's suspicions; there
are too many sentences, whole paragraphs even, of the kind of
vague and conventional praise that Baudelaire had meted out
to Gautier two years before. "Du fond de son exil, vers lequel

noȿ regards et nos oreilles sont tendus, le poëte chéri et vénéré nous annonce de nouveaux poëmes" (II, 529); it is hard to believe that the sentence is Baudelaire's. But happily there are better things, when Baudelaire embarks on qualities in Hugo that he sincerely admires; "cette faculté d'absorption de la vie extérieure, unique par son ampleur, et . . . cette autre faculté puissante de méditation" (II, 522), the universality of Hugo (a passage recalling the earlier one on Delacroix), the "atmosphère morale" of his poetry. In this last case the reader may well question Baudelaire's sincerity again, and find that "un sourire et une larme dans le visage d'un colosse" (II, 524) is one of his less happy formulas.

But where Baudelaire's admiration for Hugo needs no goad is in his discussion of Hugo as the poet of the mystery of life, in close contact with the cosmic forces, "disposé à prendre sans cesse un bain de nature" (II, 520). Not only the external aspect of nature but its inward meaning are translated into words by Hugo's poetry. And this leads Baudelaire to a page which goes deep into his own conception of poetry, in one at least of its most significant aspects. After recalling Fourier, Lavater, Swedenborg, and his cherished doctrine of correspondences—"tout, forme, mouvement, nombre, couleur, parfum, dans le *spirituel* comme dans le *naturel*, est significatif, réciproque, converse, *correspondant*" (II, 521),—he goes on to find in the poet above all the diviner of correspondences:

Si nous étendons la démonstration (non-seulement nous en avons le droit, mais il nous serait infiniment difficile de faire autrement), nous arrivons à cette vérité que tout est hiéroglyphique, et nous savons que les symboles ne sont obscurs que d'une manière relative, c'est-à-dire selon la pureté, la bonne volonté ou la clairvoyance native des âmes. Or, qu'est-ce qu'un poëte (je prends le mot dans son acception la plus large), si ce n'est un traducteur, un déchiffreur? Chez les excellents poëtes, il n'y a pas de métaphore, de comparaison ou d'épithète qui ne soit d'une adaptation mathématiquement exacte dans la circonstance actuelle, parce que ces comparaisons, ces métaphores et ces épithètes sont puisées dans l'inépuisable fonds de l'*universelle analogie*, et qu'elles ne peuvent être puisées ailleurs (II, 521).

Baudelaire then turns back to Hugo, asking whether in the history of poetry many poets can be found who are such magnificent repertories of human and divine analogies. But the splendid passage ends with the parallel already sadly familiar to us from the Gautier article:[6] Germany had Goethe, England had Shakespeare and Byron, it is right that France should now have Victor Hugo.

But later Baudelaire comes back to the aspect of Hugo which had appealed so much to him, the metaphysical poet, Œdipus obsessed by one Sphinx after another. It is the emphasis on this (suggested many years earlier by the "Pente de la rêverie") that seems to have attracted Baudelaire in all honesty to the later Hugo. The recurrence of the great metaphysical questions (occurring so often in the pages of the *Journaux intimes*), the contemplation of the sky, with its mysterious attraction, stimulates Baudelaire's own imagination to a page that echoes the turgid magnificence of the more obscure *Contemplations*:

Que des systèmes et des groupes nouveaux, affectant des formes inattendues, adoptant des combinaisons imprévues, subissant des lois non enregistrées, imitant tous les caprices providentiels d'une géométrie trop vaste et trop compliquée pour le compas humain, puissent jaillir des limbes de l'avenir, qu'y aurait-il dans cette pensée de si *exorbitant*, de si monstrueux, et qui sortît des limites légitimes de la conjecture poétique? (II, 526.)

Baudelaire points out how the word *conjecture* defines the nonscientific character of poetry, and saves it from the danger of didacticism. To give himself up to the reveries suggested by the spectacle of life on the earth and in the skies, to translate the eternal conjectures of human curiosity is the proper function of the poet.

The article ends with a page or so on the *Légende des siècles* (1859), which Baudelaire admires whole-heartedly. On October 1, 1859, he had written to Poulet-Malassis: "*La Légende des siècles* a décidément un meilleur air de livre que *Les Contemplations*, sauf encore quelques petites folies modernes" (*Corr.* I, 277). And on October 10, to his mother: "As-tu reçu la *Légende des siècles*, un beau livre qui vient de paraître? Ce Victor Hugo est infatigable" (*L.M.*, p. 177). Later in the month he writes to her:

Je suis très étonné de ce que tu me dis de la *Légende des siècles*. Il est possible que le vers souvent haché, brisé, aussi souvent épique que lyrique, te fatigue. Mais jamais Hugo n'a été si pittoresque ni si étonnant que dans le commencement de *Rathbert* (le Concile d'Ancône), *Zim-Zizimi, le Mariage de Roland, la Rose de l'Infante*; il y a là des facultés éblouissantes que lui seul possède (*D.L.M.*, p. 115).

This very real enthusiasm is reflected in the article, which, more than any other contemporary criticism of the *Légende*,[7] goes to the root of the matter in its discussion of the epic in modern times; the necessity of brevity, and above all of subjects taken from myth, legend, and fable, the rightful domain of poetry. Hugo, according to Baudelaire, has risen above national and temporal distinctions, and looks down on humanity from a philosophic height.

The article is indeed a curious patchwork of forced commonplaces of praise and flashes of sincere and penetrating criticism. There is no doubt that certain sides of Hugo, his sense of the mystery of life, as well as the magnificent evocations of the *Légende*, appealed greatly to Baudelaire. But we know that much of Hugo's philosophy, many of his works, were entirely uncongenial to him, and the ignoring of these, the veiling of them in purple platitudes, is profoundly disturbing to the reader.

In this connection we may depart from chronology slightly, and consider Baudelaire's only other article on Hugo, the review of *Les Misérables*, published in *Le Boulevard* on April 2, 1862. It begins with a long quotation from the previous article, on the implicit morality of parts of the *Légende*: "La morale n'entre pas dans cet art *à titre de but*." But in

Les Misérables "la morale entre directement *à titre de but,* ainsi qu'il ressort d'ailleurs de l'aveu même du poëte" (II, 578). The problem of wealth and poverty cannot fail to move any writer: "l'unique divergence c'est de savoir si l'œuvre d'art doit n'avoir d'autre but que *l'art,* si l'art ne doit exprimer d'adoration que pour *lui-même,* ou si un but, plus noble ou moins noble, inférieur ou supérieur, peut lui être imposé" (II, 579). Baudelaire leaves the question unanswered; we know very well what his own answer was. He goes on to discuss the method of the book, "un livre de charité, c'est-à-dire un livre fait pour exciter, pour provoquer l'esprit de charité" (II, 579). It is a poem rather than a novel, the characters living abstractions raised to epic heights: "C'est un roman construit en manière de poëme, et où chaque personnage n'est *exception* que par la manière hyperbolique dont il représente une *généralité*" (II, 580). Baudelaire's admiration for the chapter "Tempête sous un crâne" seems exaggerated beyond the limits of possible sincerity: "le chapitre . . . contient des pages qui peuvent enorgueillir à jamais non-seulement la littérature française, mais même la littérature de l'Humanité pensante" (II, 582). But his conclusion is sadly evasive: "Malgré tout ce qu'il peut y avoir de tricherie volontaire ou d'inconsciente partialité dans la manière dont, aux yeux de la stricte philosophie, les termes du problème sont posés, nous pensons, exactement comme l'auteur, que *des livres de cette nature ne sont jamais inutiles*" (II, 583). Even for those who find in orthodoxy, in Catholic doctrine, an explanation, comprehensive at least, if not complete, of the mysteries of life, the book should be welcome. But Baudelaire's last word, harking back to De Maistre, is: "Hélas! du Péché Originel, même après tant de progrès depuis si longtemps promis, il restera toujours bien assez de traces pour en constater l'immémoriale réalité!" (II, 584.)

The article is even more disquieting, in its sense of all that is left unsaid, all its half-truths, than the previous one. And Baudelaire's correspondence confirms this impression. On

May 24 he writes to his mother: "Quant aux nouveaux *Misérables*, je crains fort de n'avoir pas le courage de les demander. La famille Hugo et les disciples me font horreur" (*L.M.*, p. 270). A few months later he writes again to his mother about the book, which he had sent her, together with his article: "Ce livre est immonde et inepte. J'ai montré, à ce sujet, que je possédais l'art de mentir. Il m'a écrit pour me remercier une lettre absolument ridicule. Cela prouve qu'un grand homme peut être un sot" (*L.M.*, p. 274).[8] And Asselineau, referring to Baudelaire's rage at *Les Misérables*, says: "Il a tenu même, pour répondre à certaines perfidies, à faire dans un journal un compte rendu de ces mêmes *Misérables* dans lequel il a montré toute sa dextérité; car, au fond, le livre, avec ses énormités morales, ses paradoxes de plomb, l'agaçait profondément" (*Crépet*, p. 301).

The previous article, in spite of its reserves, seems to mark the point at which Baudelaire could praise Hugo with most sincerity, and from this time on there is an increasing exasperation. The letter to the *Figaro* on the Shakespeare anniversary, in 1864, has a bitter passage on Hugo (II, 765), and in 1865 Baudelaire writes to Ancelle about Hugo, who was arriving in Brussels: "Il paraît que lui et l'Océan se sont brouillés. Ou il n'a pas eu la force de supporter l'Océan, ou l'Océan *lui-même* s'est ennuyé de lui" (*Lettres*, p. 409).[9] The same letter refers to *Les Misérables* as "le déshonneur de Hugo." The notes for an article on *Les Travailleurs de la mer* (II, 614) are too fragmentary to suggest a judgment, except in the last phrase "Le Dénouement fait de la peine (critique flatteuse)," but one can hardly think that it would have been judged very differently from *Les Misérables*. Finally, in the letter to Ancelle of February 18, 1866, Hugo is not excepted from the "racaille moderne"—indeed he seems one of them: "toute la racaille moderne me fait horreur. Vos académiciens, horreur. Vos libéraux, horreur. La vertu, horreur. Le vice, horreur. Le style coulant, horreur. Le progrès, horreur" (*Lettres*, p. 523). In a word, Baudelaire's opinion of Hugo, at first unfavorable, seems to have risen somewhat, thanks to the *Contemplations* and the *Légende*, towards 1860, and then to have crashed down again, chiefly because of *Les Misérables*. Yet with all this shifting from unjust disparagement to unworthy praise, Baudelaire succeeded as no critic had yet done in perceiving and defining the real greatness of Hugo.

To go back to the *Poëtes français* series; Baudelaire begins his second article with an answer to what is likely to be the thought of the reader on seeing the title, "Marceline Desbordes-Valmore," that here is a poet completely uncongenial to Baudelaire. He notes how a friend, when told of one's likings or tastes, will point out how inconsistent they are, and one can only answer: "C'est possible, mais c'est ainsi. J'aime cela; je l'aime, probablement à cause même de la violente contradiction qu'y trouve tout mon être" (II, 533). Such, he says, is his situation with Madame Desbordes-Valmore. Here, again, one might be tempted to question his sincerity. There are only two other mentions of her in his published work (II, 557, 608), both favorable, but slight. And the correspondence gives us only a brief note, on the question of copyright, to Hippolyte Desbordes-Valmore, the son of the poet. In it Baudelaire says: "C'est moi que ai été chargé de rendre justice à votre admirable mère, et je crois que je l'ai fait dans de bons termes" (*Corr.* I, 381).

On actually reading the article one feels that Baudelaire, undertaking the article almost as a wager, has in spite of himself been impressed by this poetry, notwithstanding its flaws, its carelessness. "Jamais aucun poëte ne fut plus naturel; aucun ne fut jamais moins artificiel. Personne n'a pu imiter ce charme, parce qu'il est tout original et natif" (II, 534). But unquestionably there is a less worthy motive in the following paragraphs, which emphasize the characteristically feminine quality of this poetry; Baudelaire avails himself of the opportunity to compare the poet with other female authors, "pastiches de l'esprit mâle," in a vehement passage where only

the name of George Sand (which many a passage of the
Journaux intimes supplies) is lacking. But Baudelaire's praise
of Desbordes-Valmore is certainly sincere in part, and he finds
for her some of the happy phrases that fix the particular
quality of an author. "Elle a les grandes et vigoureuses
qualités qui s'imposent à la mémoire, les trouées profondes
faites à l'improviste dans le cœur, les explosions magiques de
la passion. Aucun auteur ne cueille plus facilement la formule
unique du sentiment, le sublime qui s'ignore" (II, 535).

Baudelaire ends with a paragraph which begins: "Je me suis
toujours plu à chercher dans la nature extérieure et visible des
exemples et des métaphores qui me servissent à caractériser
les jouissances et les impressions d'un ordre spirituel" (II,
536). Again the idea of correspondences; but what seems to
me important is the use of the word *chercher*, that implies
a conscious effort, a deliberate choice. The conception of the
imagination, as I have said, was enlarged and enriched by the
doctrine of correspondences; it is equally true that the fundamental idea of the imagination as an active agent, as held by
Delacroix and Baudelaire, controls the discovery of the correspondences, prevents the poet from accepting them passively.
"La nature est un dictionnaire"—a dictionary where the
words have fixed meanings, it is true, but where alternative
meanings are given for almost every word. It is for the user
of the dictionary, the poet, to choose the meanings and relate
them. So Baudelaire, here, finds a parallel for the poetry of
Madame Desbordes-Valmore in an English garden,[10] delight-
fully described. The passage, like the whole article, has a
freshness, a spontaneity, which the conjunction of author and
subject would hardly lead one to expect.

In the next article, on Auguste Barbier, Baudelaire makes
up for the restraint he had imposed on himself in the Hugo
article. With an immense sigh of relief, as it were, he takes up
"cette fastidieuse question de l'alliance du Bien avec le Beau,
qui n'est devenue obscure et douteuse que par l'affaiblissement
des esprits" (II, 529). He recalls his own long-standing

admiration for Barbier, expressed in the 1851 Pierre Dupont
article (II, 404-5), but insists on the fact that "l'origine de
cette gloire n'est pas *pure*; car elle est née de l'occasion. La
poésie se suffit à elle-même" (II, 530). The article is a reiteration of Baudelaire's well-known principles: "Tel poëme est
beau et honnête; mais il n'est pas beau *parce qu'*il est honnête"; a pointing out of the neglect of form that is the
inevitable consequence of the overemphasis on content and
idea. The rest of the article is a demonstration of the effect of
this in Barbier, his neglect of form and also "une certaine
solennité plate ou une certaine platitude solennelle." Baudelaire's conclusion is categoric: "*Auguste Barbier est un
grand poëte, et justement il passera toujours pour tel. Mais il
a été un grand poëte malgré lui, pour ainsi dire; il a essayé de
gâter par une idée fausse de la poésie de superbes facultés
poétiques; très-heureusement ces facultés étaient assez fortes
pour résister même au poëte qui les voulait diminuer*" (II,
533). The outspoken judgment has been fully ratified by
posterity, but it was plain speaking of a living poet, and
Eugène Crépet refused to accept the article for the *Poëtes
français*.

The fourth article, on Gautier, who in his turn wrote the
article on Baudelaire for the *Poëtes français*, is notable chiefly
for Baudelaire's emphasis on the fact that Gautier, as well as
being the perfect artist, has the quality often denied him by
his critics, sentiment. The rest of the article is in the somewhat
painfully adulatory tone of the 1859 article:

Heureux homme! homme digne d'envie! il n'a aimé que le Beau; il
n'a cherché que le Beau; et quand un objet grotesque ou hideux s'est
offert à ses yeux, il a su encore en extraire une mystérieuse et sym-
bolique beauté! Homme doué d'une faculté unique, puissante comme
la Fatalité, il a exprimé, sans fatigue, sans effort, toutes les attitudes,
tous les regards, toutes les couleurs qu'adopte la nature, ainsi que le
sens intime contenu dans tous les objets qui s'offrent à la contemplation de l'œil humain (II, 539).

All the mentions of Gautier at this period show the same

apparent admiration. The Wagner article refers to Gautier's "certitude plastique qui donne un charme irrésistible à tous ses écrits" (II, 483), and the articles on Leconte de Lisle and Hégésippe Moreau both have flattering references to him. And in 1862 Baudelaire writes to his mother: "Th. Gautier seul peut me comprendre quand je parle peinture" (*L.M.*, p. 274). But in the last of the great articles, that on Delacroix in 1863, there is a return to the earlier attitude: "comme a dit autrefois Théophile Gautier, dans une crise d'indépendance" (II, 318). However the final phrase is deleted in the 1868 edition.

The next article takes Baudelaire back to one of his early acquaintances and enthusiasms, Pétrus Borel, one of the stars of the somber romantic sky for him. Baudelaire notes—and ascribes to his fatal *guignon*—the contrast between the talent Pétrus Borel showed in *Madame Putiphar* for example, and the strange weaknesses elsewhere. But the *Lycanthrope* played an important part in literary history:

Cet esprit à la fois littéraire et républicain, à l'inverse de la passion démocratique et bourgeoise qui nous a plus tard si cruellement opprimés, était agité à la fois par une haine aristocratique sans limites, sans restrictions, sans pitié, contre les rois et contre la bourgeoisie, et d'une sympathie générale pour tout ce qui en art représentait l'excès dans la couleur et dans la forme, pour tout ce qui était à la fois intense, pessimiste et byronien (II, 542).

And Baudelaire admits the attraction Borel has for him: "il a, en somme, une couleur à lui, une saveur *sui generis*" (II, 543). Again it is the particular individual quality, so well defined in this brief article, that attracts Baudelaire. The article, though accepted, never appeared in the *Poëtes français*, as the Pétrus Borel section, for reasons unknown to us, was omitted.

The one-page article on Gustave Le Vavasseur, one of the friends of Baudelaire's early years, is almost entirely devoted to personal recollections. The poetry has only two or three sentences: "Il est *naïvement compliqué. . . . Vire et les Virois* sont un petit chef-d'œuvre et le plus parfait échantillon de

cet esprit précieux, rappelant les ruses compliquées de l'es-
crime, mais n'excluant pas, comme aucuns le pourraient croire,
on le voit, la rêverie et le balancement de la mélodie" (II,
544). Baudelaire seems to be saying all he can in favor of a
friend's poetry, and, for friendship's sake, leaving the rest
unsaid.

The next article, one of the longest and most substantial
of the series, deals with another friend of Baudelaire's youth,
Banville.[11] The two had known each other well in the Hôtel
Pimodan days, and one of the earliest of the *Fleurs du Mal*
is "A Théodore de Banville" (I, 200), first published in the
1868 edition, and there dated 1842. In it Baudelaire writes of

> des constructions dont l'audace correcte
> Fait voir quelle sera votre maturité.

Later on the relations between the two became less friendly,
in part no doubt because of Baudelaire's vehement attack on
"L'Ecole païenne" in 1852. Banville is not mentioned by
name, but is obviously alluded to; the notes for *Le Hibou
philosophe* have "*l'Ecole païenne* (Banville)." Another reason for the cooling of the friendship was Marie Daubrun, the
actress.[12] But the separation was not permanent and, to judge
by a letter from Banville to Baudelaire, published by Crépet,[13]
the old affection was reëstablished. A note in "Fusées" (possibly
in view of the article) reads: "Théodore de Banville n'est pas
précisément matérialiste; il est lumineux. Sa poésie représente
les heures heureuses" (II, 631). The last phrase recalls Shelley's
definition in the *Defense of Poetry*: "Poetry is the record of
the best and happiest moments of the happiest and best
minds."

The article itself begins by recalling the impression made
by Banville's first volume, the *Cariatides*, although the various influences which were obvious in it obscured what was
to be Banville's great originality, "sa marque de fabrique . . .
la certitude dans l'expression lyrique" (II, 545). But in the
Stalactites the light is clearer, the outlines sharper, and many

of the shorter poems recall the elegance of antique vases. Still it is not until later that "le poëte, réunissant dans un accord parfait l'exubérance de sa nature primitive et l'expérience de sa maturité, produira, l'une servant l'autre, des poëmes d'une habileté consommée et d'un charme *sui generis*" (II, 546). Baudelaire then attempts to define this charm, and notes the frequent use of the word *lyre*, which seems to characterize Banville's talent: "La *lyre* exprime en effet cet état presque surnaturel, cette intensité de vie où l'âme *chante*, où elle est *contrainte de chanter*, comme l'arbre, l'oiseau et la mer . . . le talent de Banville est essentiellement, décidément et volontairement lyrique" (II, 547). And Baudelaire goes on, in one of the passages all too rare in this group of articles, in which he presses a definition closer and closer: "La lyre fuit volontiers tous les détails dont le roman se régale. L'âme lyrique fait des enjambées vastes comme des synthèses; l'esprit du romancier se délecte dans l'analyse." Hence the poet's delight in mythology and allegory: "la mythologie est un dictionnaire d'hiéroglyphes vivants, hiéroglyphes connus de tout le monde" (II, 547). Baudelaire adds that "tout poëte lyrique, en vertu de sa nature, opère fatalement un retour vers l'Eden perdu. Tout, hommes, paysages, palais, dans le monde lyrique, est pour ainsi dire *apothéosé*" (II, 548). Even such poetry can wear modern dress now and then, but Banville is the pure lyric poet, free from the Satanic tendency of modern art: "un original de la nature la plus courageuse. En pleine atmosphère satanique ou romantique, au milieu d'un concert d'imprécations, il a l'audace de chanter la bonté des dieux et d'être un parfait *classique*" (II, 551). All in all, the article is one of the most satisfying, largely because one of the most sincere, of this series. Though Baudelaire may have had his reservations about Banville's poetry, there is much in it that he admires, and that leads him into the penetrating criticism, the increasingly precise definitions that are his at his best.

There can be little doubt that the next article, on Pierre

Dupont, must have been far from easy for Baudelaire to write. In his earlier article on Dupont, ten years before, he had proclaimed his faith in the utility of art, condemned "la puérile utopie de l'école de *l'art pour l'art.*" Since then, as we have seen, his opinions had been very different, as the Barbier article shows, and we might expect the same sort of volte-face here. But Baudelaire seems still under the spell of those early years: "heureuses flâneries d'un temps, où nous n'écrivions pas encore, l'œil fixé sur une pendule, délices d'une jeunesse prodigue, ô mon cher Pierre, vous en souvenez-vous?" (II, 553.) He maintains his admiration, though on different grounds: "Je sais que les ouvrages de Pierre Dupont ne sont pas d'un goût fini et parfait; mais il a l'instinct, sinon le sentiment raisonné, de la beauté parfaite" (II, 554). Baudelaire claims that Dupont's revolutionary activity, happily, did not lead him entirely astray from his instinct: "La contemplation de l'immortelle beauté des choses se mêle sans cesse, dans ses petits poëmes, au chagrin causé par la sottise et la pauvreté de l'homme. Il possède, sans s'en douter, un certain *turn of pensiveness* qui le rapproche des meilleurs poëtes didactiques anglais" (II, 555). Baudelaire maintains that in spite of his tendency to didacticism, in spite of his inconceivable carelessness of form, Dupont is and will remain one of France's most valued poets. The conclusion is not entirely convincing; one feels rather that Baudelaire has decided to maintain his admiration of Dupont at any price, on whatever grounds may seem possible. It is curious to note that this article is one of the few Baudelaire was ever willing to alter at the suggestion of an editor. He writes to Eugène Crépet: "Je ne puis m'occuper que des retouches de *Pierre Dupont,* puisque je considère les deux autres [*Barbier* and *Hégésippe Moreau*] comme excellentes. Votre aveuglement seul fait obstacle à ce que vous soyez de mon avis. Je vous en supplie, ne m'en parlez plus" (*Corr.* I, 388).

The subject of the next article is a major poet, Leconte de Lisle. After a page on the poet's origins and personality,

Baudelaire comes to his poetry, beginning "je cherche à
définir la place que tient dans notre siècle ce poëte tranquille
et vigoureux." The salient characteristic he finds in Leconte
is an intellectual aristocracy; the only contemporaries with
whom he can be compared are Gautier and Renan. The comparison is developed in one of the most admirable pages of
Baudelaire's literary criticism:

Le seul poëte auquel on pourrait, sans absurdité, comparer Leconte
de Lisle, est Théophile Gautier. Ces deux esprits se plaisent également
dans le voyage; ces deux imaginations sont naturellement cosmopolites. Tous deux ils aiment à changer d'atmosphère et à habiller
leur pensée des modes variables que le temps éparpille dans l'éternité.
Mais Théophile Gautier donne au détail un relief plus vif et une
couleur plus allumée, tandis que Leconte de Lisle s'attache surtout
à l'armature philosophique. Tous deux ils aiment l'Orient et le désert;
tous deux ils admirent le repos comme un principe de beauté. Tous
deux ils inondent leur poésie d'une lumière passionnée, plus pétillante
chez Théophile Gautier, plus reposée chez Leconte de Lisle. Tous
deux sont également indifférents à toutes les piperies humaines et
savent, sans effort, n'être jamais dupes. Il y a encore un autre homme,
mais dans un ordre différent, que l'on peut nommer à côté de Leconte
de Lisle, c'est Ernest Renan. Malgré la diversité qui les sépare, tous
les esprits clairvoyants sentiront cette comparaison. Dans le poëte
comme dans le philosophe, je trouve cette ardente, mais impartiale
curiosité des religions et ce même esprit d'amour universel, non pas
pour l'humanité prise en elle-même, mais pour les différentes formes
dont l'homme a, suivant les âges et les climats, revêtu la beauté et
la vérité. Chez l'un non plus que chez l'autre, jamais d'absurde
impiété. Peindre en beaux vers, d'une nature lumineuse et tranquille,
les manières diverses suivant lesquelles l'homme a, jusqu'à présent,
adoré Dieu et cherché le beau, tel a été, autant qu'on en peut juger
par son recueil le plus complet, le but que Leconte de Lisle a assigné
à sa poésie (II, 559-60).

The passage seems to me one of the best in all Baudelaire's
literary criticism, with its sure choice of parallels, its careful
discriminations and its precise and balanced phrases. One is
tempted to go on to quote the rest of the article, with its
characterization of Leconte's varied subjects, among which

Baudelaire, with a preference ratified by posterity, puts first of all the nature poems:

Des poëmes où, sans préoccupation de la religion et des formes successives de la pensée humaine, le poëte a décrit la beauté, telle qu'elle posait pour son œil original et individuel; les forces imposantes, écrasantes de la nature; la majesté de l'animal dans sa course ou dans son repos; la grâce de la femme dans les climats favorisés du soleil, enfin la divine sérénité du désert ou la redoubtable magnificence de l'Océan (II, 560).

Taken as a whole, the article is to me the most satisfying of the series; its subject is the poet who next to Hugo is the most distinguished of the group, and it is marred by neither the reticences nor the conventional praise of the Hugo article.

The final article, on Hégésippe Moreau, is of a very different nature; so violent in its criticism that it was refused by Eugène Crépet and published only after Baudelaire's death, in *L'Art romantique*. Baudelaire begins with a tribute to Gérard de Nerval and Poe, and by contrast damns the unfortunate Hégésippe, "presque le contraire d'un homme de lettres," (II, 562), "un poncif romantique collé, non pas amalgamé, à un poncif dramatique. Tout en lui n'est que poncifs réunis et voiturés ensemble" (II, 564). He is completely lacking in originality, except at rare moments, and he is but "l'idole des fainéants et le dieu des cabarets." These are hard sayings, but anyone who has had the misfortune to read Moreau will not think them exaggerated. One only regrets that Baudelaire should have spent his time on so unworthy a subject.

Looking back on the series of "Réflexions" one wonders how many of them would have been written of Baudelaire's free will, and which of his contemporaries he would have chosen to write on. The answer may perhaps be found in the letter to Ancelle of February 18, 1866 (*Lettres*, p. 523), in which the four poets who figure among the exceptions to the "racaille moderne" are Vigny, Banville, Gautier, and Leconte de Lisle. Since Baudelaire did the articles on three of the four, he may perhaps have had some say in the matter.

The articles seem very uneven in value; those on Leconte and Banville, and to a lesser extent the one on Desbordes-Valmore, penetrating and appreciative; the Hugo a curious hotchpotch of conventional verbiage and discriminating judgment; the Borel slight, but sure; the Barbier poised and just criticism; the Moreau damning to a degree; the Pierre Dupont somewhat overlaid with sentiment; the Gautier thin and sticky; and the Le Vavasseur so slight as to be hardly worth mentioning. Neither the series as a whole, nor any of the individual articles, in spite of their qualities, reach the great heights of Baudelaire's criticism; partly for reasons which touch all Baudelaire's literary criticism, and which I shall discuss later, and partly because in none of them is there the movement of a general idea developing in connection with a particular case that is so characteristic of the great art criticism. One might expect that from this series of articles on poets might emerge a synthesis of Baudelaire's conception of poetry. I do not think that this is the case; but this is perhaps the best place to pause and see how clear a conception of poetry has emerged from the criticism up to this point.

So much of modern poetic theory, as well as practice, looks back, avowedly or not, to Baudelaire, that one might expect to find a fully developed definition here in his critical work. But, in so far as the word is concerned, this is not the case. It is not only that Baudelaire's use of *poésie* hesitates, fluctuates; we have seen how such words as *imagination* are slow in reaching their full significance. But *poésie*, to my mind, never has for Baudelaire the weight and significance that other words attain. It is frequently used in the "Salons," early and late, in a completely nonliterary sense. At the beginning of the "Salon de 1845" Baudelaire writes of one of Delacroix's pictures: "Nul . . . ne peut imaginer ce que l'artiste a mis de poésie intime, mystérieuse et romantique dans cette simple tête" (II, 17). There are many other examples of this use of *poésie*.[14] It can be something in the artist's treatment, it can be inherent in the subject—the poetry of a model, a city, a costume, a battlefield. And it is poetry in this larger sense that Baudelaire seems to mean in the preface to the "Salon de 1846": "Vous pouvez vivre trois jours sans pain; — sans poésie, jamais" (II, 62). But in the "Conseils aux jeunes littérateurs," of the same year, where the statement is repeated, it seems to refer more explicitly to written poetry. In general however *poésie* seems to carry a somewhat vague significance of something beyond the visible and external, lying beneath the surface. It is fairly closely related to the idea of correspondences, I think; beneath the outward and visible sign an inward and spiritual poetry lies hidden.

At one point, in the 1851 Pierre Dupont preface, Baudelaire assigns a social role to poetry: "je préfère le poëte qui se met en communication permanente avec les hommes de son temps, et échange avec eux des pensées et des sentiments traduits dans un noble langage suffisament correct" (II, 404). And again:

C'est une grande destinée que celle de la poésie! Joyeuse ou lamentable, elle porte toujours en soi le divin caractère utopique. Elle contredit sans cesse le fait, à peine de ne plus être. Dans le cachot, elle se fait révolte; à la fenêtre de l'hôpital, elle est ardente espérance de guérison; dans la mansarde déchirée et malpropre, elle se pare comme une fée du luxe et de l'élégance; non-seulement elle constate, mais elle répare. Partout elle se fait négation de l'iniquité (II, 412).

But this conception is soon profoundly modified, largely by the influence of Poe. In 1855, in "L'Essence du rire," Baudelaire uses the phrase which was to become famous later: "la poésie pure . . . cette poésie, limpide et pure comme la nature" (II, 172). And "Fusées" has a note on "Régions de la Poésie pure" (II, 638). But it is in the "Notes nouvelles sur Edgar Poe" that Baudelaire shows most plainly just how his ideas have been modified and to what extent they have maintained themselves. I have already pointed out how in the long

passage from the "Poetic Principle" Baudelaire, after affirm-
ing with Poe that "la poésie n'a pas d'autre but qu'elle-
même," introduces a statement of his own: "Je ne veux pas
dire que la poésie n'ennoblisse pas les mœurs, — qu'on me comprenne bien, — que son résultat final ne soit pas d'élever
l'homme au-dessus du niveau des intérêts vulgaires; ce serait
évidemment une absurdité" (*Poe*, p. 710). The absolute isolation of poetry by Poe goes too far for Baudelaire. But poetry
—herè again through Poe, I think—has narrowed in meaning, as is plain in the following passage, again borrowed from
Poe: "C'est à la fois par la poésie et *à travers* la poésie, par et
à travers la musique, que l'âme entrevoit les splendeurs situées
derrière le tombeau" (*Poe*, p. 711). Here again poetry is related to correspondences[15] (mentioned just before), but now
it is the means, and not the end.

It is natural that Baudelaire should have been thinking particularly of *written* poetry at this time; he was preparing the
second edition of the *Fleurs du Mal*, and planning a preface
for it, of which only a series of notes remain (I, 580-83).
One of these proposes a series of questions which Baudelaire
intends to answer, among them being: "Qu'est-ce que la
poésie? Quel est son but?" But he is discouraged: "je me suis
arrêté devant l'épouvantable inutilité d'expliquer quoi que ce
soit à qui que ce soit." Another group of notes deals with a
series of questions connected with the writing of poetry
rather than with its essence.[16] It is evident that Baudelaire's
reading of Poe and his thinking about the *Fleurs du Mal* were
making his use of *poésie*, his thinking about it, more specific
than before. In the Gautier article the passage from the "Notes
nouvelles" is quoted at length, and then the "aesthetic error"
of the phrase, "la poésie du cœur," is attacked: "l'Imagination
seule contient la poésie" (II, 468). Again in the "Salon de
1859," in which poetry has been opposed to progress (II,
224) and to imitation (II, 225), Baudelaire says: "je réclame
sans cesse l'application de l'imagination, l'introduction de la
poésie dans toutes les fonctions de l'art" (II, 262). Here it is

evident that poetry is closely related to the imagination, is the handiwork and product of the imagination.

This may perhaps furnish the key to what seems to me the essential thing about Baudelaire's conception of poetry—that it is not something separate and apart, but of a piece with all art. Constantly in using the word *poet* he means it in its original sense of maker; "creative artist," one might almost translate. In the chapter on "La Reine des facultés" in the "Salon de 1859" for example: "L'artiste, le vrai artiste, le vrai poëte, ne doit peindre que selon qu'il voit et il sent" (II, 226). And I have noted how in the great passage on criticism in the Wagner article (II, 495-96) *poëte* is consistently used with this meaning, for painters as well as for writers. Again the Hugo article has: "qu'est-ce qu'un poëte (je prends le mot dans son acception la plus large), si ce n'est un traducteur, un déchiffreur?" (II, 521.)[17] And all that Baudelaire says of Banville as a pure lyric poet (II, 546-51) shows how much broader his own conception of poetry is.

All this explains somewhat why *poésie* is not one of the fundamental words in Baudelaire's vocabulary. It does not represent something occult, mysterious, remote; it is the work of the creative imagination, it is art, and all that Baudelaire says of imagination and of art bears upon it. So it seems to me that what modern theorists of poetry owe to Baudelaire is to be found in his ideas on art in general, on the workings of the imagination, not in any isolated theory of poetry *per se*. It seems to me too that it is just here that Baudelaire's strength lies, in the fact that he does not divorce poetry from art as a whole, but keeps it subject to the general conditions of art. If the advocates of *la poésie pure*, of the poetry-mysticism equivalence, had maintained the relation, they would have been less likely to go to the extremes they have, to propose theories applicable to poetry alone, making it an exception among the arts.

Besides the *Poëtes français* series, we have several other articles of literary criticism during this period. I have already discussed the review of *Les Misérables*; another review of a novel is that of *Les Martyrs ridicules*, by Léon Cladel, published in the *Revue Fantaisiste* at the end of 1861, and as the preface to the book in 1862. A letter from Poulet-Malassis to La Fizelière says: "*Les Martyrs ridicules* ont été entièrement *remaniés et refaits sur les indications de Baudelaire.* Je doute même que la collaboration n'ait pas été plus loin. L'impression de la préface en vers de *Madame Putiphar* en tête de la troisième partie du livre est bien du fait de Baudelaire, car le jeune Cladel n'avait jamais ouï parler de Borel à cette date de 1862" (*A.R.*, p. 569). (It will be remembered that Baudelaire had just been praising this passage in his article on Borel.) A collaboration with Baudelaire for another work is indicated by Cladel himself in a letter to Baudelaire of August 1, 1861: "Votre bonne lettre m'a rendu très heureux. 'Promettez-moi de venir avec vos épreuves non corrigées, nous les corrigerons ensemble.' Oui, oui, je vous le promets, et ce est [*sic*] un grand honneur, cher maître, que vous me faites" (*Crépet*, p. 344). The pages published by Cladel in the *Musée des Deux Mondes* on September 1, 1876, "Chez Feu mon maître," (*Crépet*, pp. 235-49) also describe this collaboration. Thus the novel has the double interest of having a preface by Baudelaire, and also of having been revised and corrected by him.

Baudelaire begins his article by saying that he had agreed to read the novel, at the request of Poulet-Malassis, only with reluctance, for the author was a young man, and he felt ill at ease with youth. The book describes "la jeunesse littéraire, la jeunesse *réaliste*, se livrant, au sortir de l'enfance, à l'art *réalistique* . . . elle a ses classiques, particulièrement Henri Murger et Alfred de Musset. . . . De son absolue confiance dans le génie et l'inspiration, elle tire le droit de ne se soumettre à aucune gymnastique" (II, 568). It is Cladel's satirical, penetrating description of this lamentable group that attracts Baudelaire: "un de ces livres *pince-sans-rire* dont le comique se fait d'autant mieux comprendre qu'il est toujours accompagné de l'emphase inséparable des passions" (II, 569). Baudelaire prizes above all Cladel's psychological gift: "la pénétration psychique de M. Cladel est très-grande, c'est là sa forte qualité; son art, minutieux et brutal, turbulent et enfiévré, se restreindra plus tard, sans nul doute, dans une forme plus sévère et plus froide, qui mettra ses qualités morales en plus vive lumière, plus à nu" (II, 570). Baudelaire's most serious reproach to Cladel is the too personal note of some passages: "Le poëte, sous son masque, se laisse encore voir. Le suprême de l'art eût consisté à rester glacial et fermé, et à laisser au lecteur tout le mérite de l'indignation" (II, 571). But his admiration for Cladel's "puissance sinistre-ment caricaturale" is great. Another word of high praise from him is: "quant à la moralité du livre, elle en jaillit naturelle-ment comme la chaleur de certains mélanges chimiques."

For the reader who sits down to *Les Martyrs ridicules* with a perspective of eighty years the book seems hardly worthy of Baudelaire's praise. The subject has its interest; a type of hero who in many ways bridges the gap between the romantic hero and the decadent one, between René and Des Esseintes. The best passages in the book are without doubt the analyses of the hero, his thoughts and actions. The other characters, except for the somewhat over sentimentalized Pipabs, are lifeless lay figures, obviously constructed as background for the hero. The plot is loose; it is difficult to put the opening passage in its proper chronological place, and the ending is abrupt and unsatisfactory. Most of the narrative, and all of the conversational parts are overeloquent and unconvincing. A good deal of the book is abominably written: "Après la gracieuse chanson des brises, les profondes harmonies de l'ouragan; après le vase de miel, la coupe pimentée."[18] Many of Maurthal's monologues are René gone to rot: "Monter, descendre, remonter tous les courants du désir, le torrent de mes aspirations, escalader les pics où plane le bonheur suprême,

avare, jaloux; plonger dans les gouffres où il se dissimule, je
le veux, je le veux! Que n'y parviendrai-je?"[19] There is an
amazing contrast between such passages and those where the
author analyzes the character of Maurthal with a devastating
ironic precision that makes him painfully alive for us.

It is not difficult to see what interested Baudelaire in the
book; the picture of a group, a way of life that was sadly
familiar to him, and the portrait of a hero whom he could
not have failed to compare to himself at such moments as:
"En vain, Maurthal voulut-il revenir au travail comme à un
moyen qui jadis lui avait donné quelques heures de repos; en
lui grondait bien encore le torrent des idées, mais entre la
conception et l'exécution s'élevait une barrière infranchis-
sable."[20] Maurthal's wretched existence, his nocturnal wan-
derings in Paris, his disappointments with his mistresses, his
ennui and regrets, his perpetual fresh starts, his aspirations
towards greatness, cannot have failed to strike a sympathetic
note. Baudelaire has harsh words for him indeed:

Alpinien, le principal *martyr*, ne se ménage pas; aussi prompt à
caresser ses vices qu'à les maudire, il offre, dans sa perpétuelle oscil-
lation, l'instructif spectacle de l'incurable maladie voilée sous le
repentir périodique. C'est un auto-confesseur qui s'absout, et se
glorifie des pénitences qu'il s'inflige, en attendant qu'il gagne, par
de nouvelles sottises, l'honneur et le droit de se condamner de nouveau (II, 570).

But his conclusion recalls some of his own exhortations to
himself in the *Journaux intimes*: "On peut espérer qu'à partir
de ce moment Alpinien est à moitié sauvé; il ne lui manque
plus que de devenir un homme d'action, un homme de devoir,
au jour le jour" (II, 572). There seems no doubt that the portrait of Alpinien Maurthal and his existence, the probing,
dispassionate way in which he is analyzed, gave the book its
interest for Baudelaire.

This leads the reader to wonder how large Baudelaire's own
part in the book was. Did he contribute not only the passage
from *Madame Putiphar*, but the quotation of the last three

stanzas of "Les Petites Vieilles" and the passage which introduces it:

Cécités, claudications, gibbosités, rabougrissements, déformations charnelles ou morales, tout, il eût voulu tout accaparer, tout résumer dans ses propres souffrances. Il suivait pendant des heures, des journées entières, des vieillards caducs qui lui paraissaient cacher les plus grandes infortunes sous leurs haillons, dans les rides de leur visage; des espérances invincibles dans leurs sourires pleins d'amertumes. A les suivre, à régler ses pas sur leurs pas, à contempler dans l'ombre ces abandonnés à qui il s'intéressait, que de fois ne se surprit-il pas chantant, solennel, des strophes profondes comme le gouffre des désespoirs, douloureuses comme les remords des damnés, et cependant portant l'espoir malgré l'anathème.[21]

Up to this point there is a distinctly Baudelairean quality in the passage; only the next sentence, which immediately introduces the quotation, seems of a different quality: "Tant il communiait avec la pensée du poète, Maurthal croyait dire le chant de sa piété et de son amour:

Mais moi, moi qui de loin tendrement vous surveille . . ."
Was the quotation included at Baudelaire's suggestion, or was it already there, and did he collaborate on the passage which precedes? Or did the poem itself lend a Baudelairean point to Cladel's pen? It seems impossible to tell, and impossible also to judge of the extent of Baudelaire's collaboration elsewhere. One is constantly struck, in reading the book, by the discrepancies in style, the terse firmness and precision of many of the analytical passages compared to the effusive banality of much of the rest, and it would seem likely that Baudelaire worked over these parts. At all events, the subject of the book, the treatment and Baudelaire's own collaboration combine to explain his certainly somewhat exaggerated praise of it. We may note that the only two books which Baudelaire praised to this extent, without the endorsement of posterity, are *La Double Vie* and *Les Martyrs ridicules*, in both of which he undoubtedly had a hand himself.

To about this period belongs the series of notes on "L'Esprit et le style de M. Villemain," found by Jacques Crépet among his father's papers, and first published in 1907. The notes are polemic rather than criticism—a violent attack on Villemain, largely inspired by his treatment of Baudelaire at the time of the latter's candidacy for the Academy. On December 25, 1861, Baudelaire writes to his mother: "M. Villemain est un cuistre et un sot, un singe solennel, à qui je ferai peut-être payer fort cher, si Dieu me prête vie, la manière dont il m'a reçu" (L.M., p. 252). Again on March 17, 1862: "Je n'ai de rancunes que contre M. Villemain à qui je vais le faire *publiquement* savoir" (L.M., p. 263). A later letter suggests that the article was finished, and about to be published.

One would hardly expect impartial criticism in such a case, and the article is a vicious attack on Villemain, whose works Baudelaire must have been reading with the express intention of finding—what is easy enough to find—all the stupidities, blunders, banalities and faults of style they contain. "Villemain représente l'inutilité affairée et hargneuse comme celle de Thersite" (II, 585). His mental habits, his judgment, his tone, his style—academic, incorrect, allusive—are vehemently attacked, with abundance of supporting evidence. Baudelaire is particularly violent on Villemain's judgment of Chateaubriand: "C'est bien la jugeote d'un pédagogue, incapable d'apprécier le grand gentilhomme des décadences, qui veut retourner à la vie sauvage" (II, 587). If one enjoys a sound literary drubbing, I know of no better example.

The "Lettre à Jules Janin"[22] is much the same type of polemic as the Villemain article, and, like it, was left by Baudelaire in the form of notes. It was inspired by an article by Janin in *L'Indépendance Belge* of February 11, 1865, entitled "Henri Heine et la jeunesse des poètes," in which he attacked Heine bitterly, and assigned Happiness to France as her Muse. As several of Baudelaire's letters show, he was infuriated by the article, and immediately drafted his reply, in the most violent terms: "Cher Monsieur, si je voulais pleinement soulager la colère que vous avez mise en moi, je vous écrirais cinquante pages au moins, et je vous prouverais que, contrairement à votre thèse, notre pauvre France n'a que fort peu de poëtes et qu'elle n'en a pas un seul à opposer à Henri Heine" (II, 605). He twits Janin with calling Béranger and Delphine Gay poets, and Musset, "croque-mort langoureux," a good poet. "Et Gautier? Et Valmore? et moi?" He reproaches Janin bitterly for his "dégoûtant amour de la joie," to which he opposes "Byron, Tennyson, Poe et Cie. Ciel mélancolique de la poésie moderne" (II, 609). The fragmentary and often repetitious notes, inspired, unlike the Villemain article, by entirely disinterested motives, have something of the fire of Baudelaire's youth in them, a last glow in the embers.

Then there are a few miscellaneous articles: the brief obituary notices of the military novelist Paul de Molènes (II, 602-4)[23] and of the actor Rouvière (II, 612-13) and two pieces of journalism, the first "Une Réforme à l'Académie," inspired by Sainte-Beuve's famous article, "Des prochaines elections à l'Académie," and the other a letter to the *Figaro* (published without signature on April 14, 1865), on the "Anniversaire de la naissance de Shakspeare." Baudelaire jeers at the make-up of the committee, noting that among others "M. Charles Baudelaire, dont le goût pour la littérature saxonne est bien connu, avait été oublié," and asserting that the object of the celebration was to "préparer et chauffer le succès du livre de V. Hugo sur Shakspeare, livre qui, comme tous ses livres, plein de beautés et de bêtises, va peut-être encore désoler ses plus sincères admirateurs" (II, 765).

But Baudelaire did not neglect art criticism during these years. In 1861 there is the brief article, "Peintures murales d'Eugène Delacroix à Saint-Sulpice,"[24] which gives the Biblical sources of the three frescoes, and describes them, with all Baudelaire's power of making his reader both see a picture and sense the impression it makes. Then he emphasizes the continued progress in the painter's art: "Jamais . . . Dela-

croix n'a étalé un coloris plus splendidement et plus savamment surnaturel; jamais un dessin plus *volontairement* épique"
(II, 304). And, criticizing those who make an arbitrary distinction between a materialistic and a spiritual art, he says:

Ces esprits superficiels ne songent pas que les deux facultés ne
peuvent jamais être tout à fait séparées, et qu'elles sont toutes deux
le résultat d'un germe primitif soigneusement cultivé. La nature
extérieure ne fournit à l'artiste qu'une occasion sans cesse renaissante
de cultiver ce germe; elle n'est qu'un amas incohérent de matériaux
que l'artiste est invité à associer et à mettre en ordre, un *incita-
mentum*, un réveil pour les facultés sommeillantes. Pour parler
exactement, il n'y a dans la nature ni ligne ni couleur. C'est l'homme
qui crée la ligne et la couleur. Ce sont deux abstractions qui tirent
leur égale noblesse d'une même origine (II, 305).

The article produced an appreciative letter from Delacroix:
"Je vous remercie bien sincèrement et de vos éloges, et des
réflexions qui les accompagnent et les confirment sur ces effets
mystérieux de la ligne et de la couleur, que ne sentent, hélas!
que peu d'adeptes."[25]

The next year brings the "Peintres et aqua-fortistes" (*Le
Boulevard*, September 14), of which "L'Eau-forte est à la
mode" (*Revue Anecdotique*, April 2) is an earlier and briefer
version. Baudelaire begins, as he had done in the "Salon de
1859," by regretting the degradation and prettyfication of the
arts, admitting that Courbet had at least contributed towards
reëstablishing a taste for freshness and simplicity, and a disinterested love of painting. He then calls attention to Legros
and Manet, pairing them: "MM. Manet et Legros unissent à
un goût décidé pour la réalité, la réalité moderne, — ce qui
est déjà un bon symptôme, — cette imagination vive et ample,
sensible, audacieuse, sans laquelle, il faut bien le dire, toutes
les meilleures facultés ne sont que des serviteurs sans maîtres,
des agents sans gouvernement" (II, 290). This is, I think, the
only important passage in the art criticism where Baudelaire's
judgment lacks its accustomed sureness. His pairing of Legros
with Manet is certainly due to an overestimate of Legros

(already highly praised in the "Salon de 1859") rather than
an underestimate of Manet, for whom the correspondence
gives further proof of admiration. In 1864 Baudelaire writes
to Thoré in defense of Manet's originality: "M. Manet, que
l'on croit fou et enragé, est simplement un homme très loyal,
très simple, faisant tout ce qu'il peut pour être raisonnable,
mais malheureusement marqué de romantisme depuis sa naissance. Le mot *pastiche* n'est pas juste. M. Manet n'a jamais vu
de *Goya*; M. Manet n'a jamais vu de *Greco*; M. Manet n'a
jamais vu la galerie Pourtalès. Cela vous paraît incroyable,
mais cela est vrai" (*Lettres*, pp. 361-62). And Baudelaire
cites his own so-called imitation of Poe. Then in 1865 he
writes to encourage Manet, depressed by his lack of success.
He quotes what a certain M. Chorner had said of Manet:
"ce qu'il m'a dit s'accorde avec ce que je sais de vous, et ce
que quelques gens d'esprit disent de vous: *Il y a des défauts,
des défaillances, un manque d'aplomb, mais il y a un charme
irrésistible*. Je sais tout cela; je suis un des premiers qui l'ont
compris" (*Lettres*, p. 436). A fortnight later he writes to
Madame Paul Meurice: "Manet a des facultés si brillantes et
si légères qu'il serait malheureux qu'il se décourageât. Jamais
il ne comblera absolument les lacunes de son tempérament.
Mais il a *un tempérament*, c'est l'important" (*Lettres*, p.
438). It must be remembered that at this time Baudelaire
had been able to see only a few of Manet's paintings. One may
well regret that he did not live to see the great flowering of
French painting in the years to come—Manet's later work,
Degas, who might well have been his ideal "peintre de la
vie moderne," Monet, Renoir, Cézanne. The critic and a
group of painters deserving of his best missed one another
by only a few years.

From painting Baudelaire turns to etching, so long neglected, but at last enjoying a return to popularity. He mentions some of the recent etchers, praising especially Whistler's
"série d'eaux-fortes, subtiles, éveillées comme l'improvisation
et l'inspiration, représentant les bords de la Tamise; merveil-

leux fouillis d'agrès, de vergues, de cordages; chaos de brumes, de fourneaux et de fumées tire-bouchonnées; poésie profonde et compliquée d'une vaste capitale" (II, 292). Then Legros, Bonvin, Yonkind, and finally Meryon, "le vrai type de l'aquafortiste achevé." But it is sadly characteristic of Baudelaire's wearied spirit at the time that his paragraph on Meryon is borrowed almost verbatim from the "Salon de 1859." Only a word is changed or added here and there; "une ville immense" becomes "une grande capitale," "une beauté si paradoxale," "une beauté arachnéenne et paradoxale" (II, 293). It seems as if Baudelaire were having more and more to draw on his previous resources, as if the former miraculous freshness of impression were fading. He ends with high praise for the art of etching: "C'est vraiment un genre trop *personnel*, et par conséquent trop *aristocratique*, pour enchanter d'autres personnes que celles qui sont naturellement artistes, très-amoureuses dès lors de toute personnalité vive. Non seulement l'eauforte sert à glorifier l'individualité de l'artiste, mais il serait même difficile à l'artiste de ne pas décrire sur la planche sa personnalité la plus intime" (II, 294).

In the way of art criticism there is also the page published in the *Figaro* in 1864, "Vente de la collection de M. E. Piot," and the "Catalogue de la collection de M. Crabbe," published in the *Œuvres posthumes*. One of Baudelaire's lectures in Belgium was given at the house of Crabbe, a Belgian collector. Many of the names we have met before in the art criticism reappear, and together with purely descriptive notes there are such comments as: "VERBOEKOVEN. — Etonnant, vitreux, désolant à rendre envieux Meissonier, Landseer, H. Vernet," and, on the other hand, "EUGENE DELACROIX. — Chasse au tigre. Delacroix alchimiste de la couleur. Miraculeux, profond, mystérieux, sensuel, terrible; couleur éclatante et obscure, harmonie pénétrante. Le geste de l'homme et le geste de la bête. La grimace de la bête, les reniflements de l'animalité. Vert, lilas, vert sombre, lilas tendre, vermillon, rouge sombre, bouquet sinistre" (II, 367).

This is perhaps the best point at which to consider an article which Baudelaire never completed and which was published only after his death, in *L'Art romantique*—"L'Art philosophique." He had been working on it for some years; in April, 1857, he writes to Poulet-Malassis that one of the articles still to be written for the *Curiosités esthétiques* is the "Peintres raisonneurs" (*Corr.* I, 168). The next year he writes to Calonne: "Vos peintres sont commencés. J'appellerai cela, si vous le voulez bien: *Les Peintres qui pensent;* il y aurait là un petit ton d'ironie qui serait la sauce du titre" (*Corr.* I, 218). In 1859 he summarizes for Calonne the thesis of what has now become "Les Peintres idéalistes":

Vous connaissez la thèse en avance. *Le siècle est fou et déraisonne en toutes choses, mais plus particulièrement en matière d'art,* à cause *de la confusion hérétique du bien avec le beau.* Tout chercheur d'idéalité pure est un hérétique aux yeux de la muse et de l'art. Je parlerai donc des *peintres idéalistes* comme de malades; quelquefois ils montrent du génie, mais un génie malade (*Corr.* I, 231).

This corresponds closely to what Baudelaire says in the early part of the article, which may well have been composed about this time; he mentions it several times in the course of the year, once as "Allemands." In 1860 it becomes "L'Art enseignant," "L'Art philosophique" and "Les Peintres philosophes," and in 1863, "La Peinture didactique." In 1865 it is mentioned as still unfinished, and in February, 1866, it appears in Baudelaire's table of contents of *Quelques-uns de mes contemporains* as "L'Art didactique, écoles allemande et lyonnaise." It seems probable, judging from the correspondence, that the introductory and concluding parts of the article were written about 1859, and the more fragmentary parts either noted down then or added little by little later on.

The article begins by pointing the contrast between two conceptions of art:

Qu'est-ce que l'art pur suivant la conception moderne? C'est créer une magie suggestive contenant à la fois l'objet et le sujet, le monde extérieur à l'artiste et l'artiste lui-même.

Qu'est-ce que l'art philosophique suivant la conception de Chenavard et de l'école allemande? C'est un art plastique qui a la prétention de remplacer le livre, c'est-à-dire de rivaliser avec l'imprimerie pour enseigner l'histoire, la morale et la philosophie (II, 368).

And Baudelaire notes how the arts, once separated, are infringing on each other's territory, how a kind of encyclopaedic philosophy penetrates the plastic arts: "Plus l'art voudra être philosophiquement clair, plus il se dégradera et remontera vers l'hiéroglyphe enfantin; plus au contraire l'art se détachera de l'enseignement et plus il montera vers la beauté pure et désintéressée" (II, 368). Baudelaire then discusses the two schools which have been most deeply affected by this error of philosophic art. First the German group, represented by Rethel and his "poems," as Baudelaire calls his pictures. Then the school of Lyons, represented by Chenavard[26] and Janmot (much of this part is in the form of notes). And Baudelaire concludes:

Tout esprit profondément sensible et bien doué pour les arts (il ne faut pas confondre la sensibilité de l'imagination avec celle du cœur) sentira comme moi que tout art doit se suffire à lui-même et en même temps rester dans les limites providentielles; cependant l'homme garde ce privilège de pouvoir toujours développer de grands talents dans un genre faux ou en violant la constitution naturelle de l'art (II, 374).

The article is plainly one which Baudelaire considered important, and there is no better statement of what art is and is not for him than the carefully worded opening paragraphs. The latter part, as always when Baudelaire's criticism is derogatory, is less interesting, with its discussion of artists who are at best mediocre. But the opening page is to my mind one of the most significant in Baudelaire's criticism.

Far and away the most interesting article of this period is "L'Œuvre et la vie d'Eugène Delacroix," Baudelaire's final tribute. Delacroix died on August 13, 1863, and the article appeared in three instalments in *L'Opinion Nationale*, September 2 and 14, and November 23. An undated letter of Baudelaire's to Poulet-Malassis asks for his help with the article:

> Vous m'avez tant tracassé aujourd'hui par vos voltiges (inutiles) que vous m'avez fait oublier deux choses importantes: l'une, le fameux programme du plafond d'Apollon, perdu par moi; l'autre, la liste (autant que vous vous souvenez) des travaux littéraires de Delacroix, dans la *Revue des Deux Mondes*, et de ceux, publiés précédement, sans doute dans *L'Artiste. Ricourt.*
> Ajoutez-y quelques réflexions de vous. Rapides et substantielles. Je les interpréterai et je les incolerai dans mes épreuves, si vous arrivez trop tard; vite, je vous prie (*Lettres*, p. 355).

Baudelaire begins by pointing out that his long-standing acquaintance with Delacroix qualifies him to write not only of the methods but of the personality of the artist. A detailed analysis of his work is impossible:

> Je crois, monsieur, que l'important ici est simplement de chercher la qualité caractéristique du génie de Delacroix et d'essayer de la définir; de chercher en quoi il diffère de ses plus illustres devanciers, tout en les égalant; de montrer enfin, autant que la parole écrite le permet, l'art magique grâce auquel il a pu traduire la *parole* par des images plastiques plus vives et plus appropriées que celles d'aucun créateur de même profession,—en un mot, de quelle *spécialité* la Providence avait chargé Eugène Delacroix dans le développement historique de la Peinture (II, 297).[27]

The paragraph describes admirably not only what Baudelaire does in this article, but the characteristic method of his criticism; the search for the particular quality of the artist he is discussing and the definition of it; the comparison of him with his predecessors; and the translation of his art.

Baudelaire classes Delacroix with the painters of "grandes *machines*," who are enumerated in a series of beautifully precise formulas:

> Quel est le plus grand de ces grands hommes si divers? Chacun peut décider la chose à son gré, suivant que son tempérament le pousse à préférer l'abondance prolifique, rayonnante, joviale presque, de Rubens, la douce majesté et l'ordre eurythmique de Raphaël, la

couleur paradisiaque et comme d'après-midi de Véronèse, la sévérité
austère et tendue de David, ou la faconde dramatique et quasi
littéraire de Lebrun (II, 297-98).

Then comes the question of Delacroix's contribution:

Mais enfin, monsieur, direz-vous sans doute, quel est donc ce je ne
sais quoi de mystérieux que Delacroix, pour la gloire de notre siècle,
a mieux traduit qu'aucun autre? C'est l'invisible, c'est l'impalpable,
c'est le rêve, c'est les nerfs, c'est *l'âme*; et il a fait cela,—observez-le
bien, monsieur,—sans autres moyens que le contour et la couleur.
. . . Delacroix est le plus *suggestif* de tous les peintres, celui dont
les œuvres, choisies même parmi les secondaires et les inférieures,
font le plus penser, et rappellent à la mémoire le plus de sentiments
et de pensées poétiques déjà connus, mais qu'on croyait enfouis pour
toujours dans la nuit du passé. L'œuvre de Delacroix m'apparaît
quelquefois comme une espèce de mnémotechnie de la grandeur et
de la passion native de l'homme universel (II, 298-99).

The hammered-out sentences condense and summarize all
that Baudelaire has said of Delacroix previously. He goes on
to speak of what he has often emphasized before, Delacroix's
universality, his culture, his wide reading. This leads him
to Delacroix's teaching:

Delacroix était passionnément amoureux de la passion, et froidement déterminé à chercher les moyens d'exprimer la passion de la
manière la plus visible. . . . Or, il disait sans cesse: 'Puisque je
considère l'impression transmise à l'artiste par la nature comme la
chose la plus importante à traduire, n'est-il pas nécessaire que
celui-ci soit armé à l'avance de tous les moyens de traduction les
plus rapides?' (II, 300.)

This brings up the question of the imagination, and Baudelaire introduces a long quotation from the "Salon de 1859"
on Delacroix's imagination (II, 301-4), followed by the
passage on color and line from his article on the Saint-
Sulpice frescoes (II, 304-6).

Baudelaire then turns from Delacroix the artist to Delacroix the man.[28] First his writings, in a style marked by
concision and intensity, "résultat habituel de la concentration
de toutes les forces spirituelles vers un point donné. *The hero*

is he who is immovably centred,' dit le moraliste d'outre-mer
Emerson" (II, 307). Then Baudelaire turns to the character
of Delacroix, "un curieux mélange de scepticisme, de poli-
tesse, de dandysme, de volonté ardente, de ruse, de despotisme,
et enfin d'une espèce de bonté particulière et de tendresse
modérée, qui accompagne toujours le génie" (II, 309). He
compares him to Stendhal and to Mérimée, and notes that he
"quoiqu'il fût un homme de génie, ou parce qu'il était un
homme de génie complet, participait beaucoup du dandy"
(II, 312). The portrait is completed by details and anecdotes,
such as that of Delacroix saying to a young painter: "Si vous
n'êtes pas assez habile pour faire le croquis d'un homme qui
se jette par la fenêtre, pendant le temps qu'il met à tomber
du quatrième étage sur le sol, vous ne pourrez jamais produire
de grandes machines" (II, 316). Then there are notes on
Delacroix's conversation, his opinions on his contemporaries,
his attitude towards women, his lack of tenderness for children, on which Baudelaire comments: "par le simple bon
sens, il faisait un retour vers l'idée catholique. Car on peut
dire que l'enfant, en général, est, relativement à l'homme, en
général, beaucoup plus rapproché du péché originel" (II,
320). Finally Baudelaire defends Delacroix against certain
criticisms that had been made, and concludes: "Je vous remercie de tout mon cœur, monsieur, d'avoir bien voulu me
laisser dire librement tout ce que me suggère le souvenir d'un
des rares génies de notre malheureux siècle, — si pauvre et si
riche à la fois, tantôt trop exigeant, tantôt trop indulgent, et
trop souvent injuste" (II, 322).[29]
    The article is representative of the best qualities of Bau-
delaire's criticism; his passionate and painstaking search for
the qualities in an artist that excite his admiration, his beautiful and precise definitions of them, his illuminating compari-
sons and contrasts, to which is added here a finished and life-
like portrait. No article could serve as a better epitome of
Baudelaire's criticism, and the only reason that I have not
grouped it with the greatest of the critical articles is that it

is their aftermath, profiting by all their wealth, but neither completing nor crystallizing his criticism as they do. It is fitting that Delacroix, who kindled the earliest gleams of Baudelaire's critical imagination, should be exalted in this magnificent sunset of his criticism.

Baudelaire, as has often been noted, judged his contemporaries with a sureness with which few critics have been blessed. Although his opinions, particularly on literature, have not, I think, the infallibility that has sometimes been attributed to them, the fact remains that he has left a body of the most difficult of all criticism, that of one's contemporaries, which sets him securely among the great masters of criticism. His method is of its very nature valid for all the arts, and I have, up to now, avoided separating it into criticism of art, of literature and of music. But at this point it is of interest to do this, to see whether the three groups, very unequal in extent, are of equal value and significance. To my mind the art criticism is without question the most interesting and important, both historically and intrinsically. As I have pointed out, it is chiefly through it that Baudelaire's ideas develop and take shape. But its intrinsic value also seems to me greater. Not only is it more completely disinterested, free from any but aesthetic motives, but also—and this is the crux of the matter—Baudelaire's experience of the plastic arts seems to have been more intense than that of the other arts. Finally, his art criticism has a completeness, both in the ground it covers and in the synthesis it makes, that is not found in the literary criticism.

I have noted that more than once the integrity of the literary criticism is vitiated by personal motives, some regrettable, some innocent enough. Unlike the art criticism, it presents no complete picture; it neglects significant figures and overemphasizes lesser ones. Moreover, in the later literary articles, one feels that for the first time Baudelaire is making *a priori* judgments, holding his authors up to a preëstablished standard. It seems to me too that Baudelaire's experience of literature is less intense, less coherent than his experience of art—perhaps because, in his own *métier*, an inevitable awareness of technique interferes with the unity of the impression. Perhaps too the task of reflecting, of re-creating in kind is bound to be a harder one; a sonnet may be an admirable criticism of a picture, but rarely of another poem. Even without going so far, it is evident that Baudelaire's type of criticism is in part a *transposition d'art*, and therefore somewhat handicapped in dealing with literature. But I believe that the question of personal experience is at the root of the matter, and that literature never gave to Baudelaire quite the *volupté* that painting did. Yet with all these strictures and reservations, the literary criticism has its wholly admirable moments. If one compares it with even the best of the literary criticism of the time, with Sainte-Beuve as well as the lesser lights, one finds a freshness, a vigor, a living and personal touch that is lacking in the criticism based on even the best of "methods."

It is, I think, somewhat misleading to qualify Baudelaire as a musical critic on the strength of the Wagner article. This article is to me unique not because it is on music, but because it is the article above all others in which Baudelaire is putting his method to the acid test, interpreting not a work of painting or literature, in which he has professional background and knowledge, but a work of music, an almost unknown realm to him. He establishes unquestionably the validity of the method; if one begins with the experience, then reflects and reasons on it, one need be no specialist. The article seems to me the final proof of Baudelaire's critical method, built on the firm foundation of the art criticism.

But, whatever hierarchy one may establish for the different categories, one is impressed above all by the fundamental unity of Baudelaire's criticism. The subject varies; the method remains constant. It is a method rooted and grounded in experience, and no small part of its value lies in the depth and intensity of that experience, and in Baudelaire's power of describing or rather of translating it. From the beginning he is endeavoring to perfect his translation, as it were; to find the exact words for the particular quality of the experience. A Delacroix painting, a Daumier caricature, a Flaubert novel, a Wagner overture; whichever it be, Baudelaire recalls and interprets his own experience for us. Thus far criticism is, as the "Salon de 1846" suggests, the reflection of the work of art in the mind of the critic. This aspect of Baudelaire's criticism is essentially poetic; many a passage of the critical work has the same relation to such poems as "Les Phares" or "Danse macabre" as certain of the *Petits Poëmes en prose* (such as "L'Invitation au voyage") have to their counterparts in the *Fleurs du Mal*. Neither in the *Petits poëmes* nor in the criticism does Baudelaire crystallize his experience into the perfect form of a finished poem; he gives us, rather, a more immediate and direct translation of his experience. But one need only compare such a passage as the description of Daumier's *Le Dernier bain* (II, 192-93) with such a poem as "Le Squelette laboureur" to realize that the former as well as the latter is the work of a poet. Such passages, with their delicate discriminations, their happy phrases and terse formulas, revive the experience of the reader who has shared it, and create it for the reader to whom it is unknown. The critic, translating his experience of the work of art, creates his own work of art, which in its turn is reflected in the mind of the reader, so that, as when one looks at one of Guys's pictures, "le spectateur est . . . le traducteur d'une traduction toujours claire et vibrante" (II, 338). "Comme de longs échos qui de loin se confondent," the correspondences between the work of art and the critic, then between the critic and his reader echo one another.

It is this experience, constantly enriched, this reflection of the work of art, that is the center of Baudelaire's criticism. But he does not stop here. Even in 1846 he evolves a criterium out of experience, and fifteen years later, at the peak of the critical work, his aim is to "transformer la volupté en con-

naissance." "Il est impossible qu'un poëte ne contienne pas
un critique"; infallibly from the poetic experience the intelligence will attempt to deduce general principles, the laws of
art. For Baudelaire, not only at the beginning, but all through
his critical career, experience comes first, then generalization.
His criticism is based not on hypothesis, but on immediate
experience. In the "Exposition de 1855" he makes this plain:

J'ai essayé plus d'une fois, comme tous mes amis, de m'enfermer
dans un système pour y prêcher à mon aise. Mais un système est une
espèce de damnation qui nous pousse à une abjuration perpétuelle;
il en faut toujours inventer un autre, et cette fatigue est un cruel
châtiment. Et toujours mon système était beau, vaste, spacieux,
commode, propre et lisse surtout; du moins il me paraissait tel.
Et toujours un produit spontané, inattendu, de la vitalité universelle
venait donner un démenti à ma science enfantine et vieillotte, fille
déplorable de l'utopie. J'avais beau déplacer ou étendre le criterium,
il était toujours en retard sur l'homme universel, et courait sans
cesse après le beau multiforme et versicolore, qui se meut dans les
spirales infinies de la vie (II, 145).

In so far as Baudelaire may be said to have a critical system,
it is experimental to the highest degree, akin to that of the
scientist, with all conclusions constantly referred back to experience. It is not the application of a system, it is the search
for a system.

This explains, I think, the sometimes disconcerting variations in vocabulary which I have noted. With each experience, or set of experiences, Baudelaire tries afresh to formu-
late his conclusions, to put into words the significance of the
experience. The vocabulary, like the whole method, is experimental; a word, a set of words, is tried, found adequate for
the moment (at times almost made so, it seems), but with a
new experience a new set of words comes into play. The
most striking example is, I think, the way in which Baudelaire,
from the beginning of his criticism, is feeling for the inclu-
sive word that will crystallize his entire thought; he tries
originalité, naïveté, idéal, correspondances, which, with his

conceptions of beauty and of art, are gradually absorbed into the quintessential and all-embracing *imagination*.

It is hardly necessary to reiterate that Baudelaire's thought, based on the immediate experience, is nevertheless constantly modified and enriched by other elements. A purely individualistic criticism, based on even a Baudelaire's perception and intelligence, might be somewhat thin; Baudelaire's has the complexity, the density, that come from the absorption of many elements. The preceding pages have shown how many and varied his debts were. Of them all, that to Delacroix seems to me the heaviest. It is the earliest in date, and the most enduring, as well as the most complex and pervasive. Delacroix affected the essentials of Baudelaire's thought as no one else did. Baudelaire's system could stand, indeed gain in strength, without the religious and political authoritarianism of De Maistre, without Poe's scorn of progress and democracy, his complete segregation of art and the artist. But what Baudelaire learned from Delacroix of the creative imagination and its workings is the very core of his thought. Yet the debt to Delacroix, like those to De Maistre, to Poe, to Stendhal, to say nothing of a host of minor borrowings, is finally fused in the white heat of Baudelaire's own thought.

I know of no criticism that has more to offer to the reader. There is first of all the poetic aspect; the wealth of admirable translations of works of art. The more congenial the subject, the more deeply Baudelaire penetrates into its inner mysteries, and illuminates them with his own poetic perception and subtle intelligence. All through these experiences Baudelaire is seeking for a system, thinking he has found one, then rejecting it as inadequate for some new form of beauty he has met. Only at the very end, looking back over his critical activity, does he realize that the clue to the labyrinth has been in his hand all the way, that the widely separated articles are held together by "une pensée unique et systématique." This system, wrought out of experience, is rich in suggestion for the reader, who will find much food for thought in the bounteous harvest of ideas that are gathered into the roomy storehouse of the Imagination. One may learn from Baudelaire a method of criticism that does not wither nor grow stale, a method that each one in his own measure may apply. We can indeed agree with him that, in his own case at least, the poet is the best of critics.

NOTES

CHAPTER ONE: THE DISCIPLE OF DELACROIX

1. Letter to J. Lemer, Feb. 23, 1865. *Lettres*, p. 415.
2. The full history of the *Curiosités esthétiques* and *L'Art romantique* is given in M. Crépet's edition of the two volumes (1923 and 1925). For the later publications see the volume *Juvenilia, Œuvres posthumes, Reliquiae*, ed. Jacques Crépet, I (Conard, 1939).
3. "Il y a quelques mois, j'ai découvert chez un marchand du passage des Panoramas, un tableau de mon père. . . . Mon père était un détestable artiste mais toutes ces vieilleries-là ont une valeur morale" (Dec. 30, 1857. *L.M.*, p. 153).
4. *Crépet*, p. 9.
5. "Des dessins à la plume que tu avais faits pour moi" (May 6, 1861. *L.M.*, p. 227).
6. "ENFANCE: Vieux mobilier Louis XVI, antiques, consulat, pastels, société dix-huitième siècle" (II, 697).
7. May 6, 1861. *L.M.*, p. 228.
8. E. Prarond, *Du Louvre au Panthéon* (1881), pp. 96-97. Quoted by A. Ferran, *L'Esthétique de Baudelaire* (1933), p. 579.
9. C. Asselineau, *Charles Baudelaire, sa vie et son œuvre* (1869), p. 8; T. de Banville, *Mes Souvenirs* (1883), p. 80; *Crépet*, pp. 36-37.
10. Prarond, quoted in *Crépet*, pp. 70-71. See also Asselineau, *Charles Baudelaire*, p. 12; Champfleury, *Souvenirs et portraits de jeunesse* (1872), p. 132; C. Dornier, "Un Témoin de la Bohème littéraire," *Revue de France*, II (1925), No. 5, pp. 68-89.
11. Banville, *Mes Souvenirs*, pp. 79-80, 94; Champfleury, *Souvenirs et portraits*, p. 134.
12. Asselineau, *Charles Baudelaire*, p. 12.
13. Ferran, *Esthétique de Baudelaire*, pp. 35-36; Champfleury, *Souvenirs et portraits*, p. 188.
14. "L'Œuvre et la vie d'Eugène Delacroix," *L'Opinion Nationale*, Sept. 2 and 14, Nov. 22, 1863; II, 296-322.
15. "J'ai eu le bonheur d'être lié très-jeune (dès 1845, autant que je peux me souvenir) avec l'illustre défunt, et dans cette liaison,

d'où le respect de ma part et l'indulgence de la sienne n'excluaient pas la confiance et la familiarité réciproques, j'ai pu à loisir puiser les notions les plus exactes, non seulement sur sa méthode, mais aussi sur les qualités les plus intimes de sa grande âme" (II, 296).

André Joubin's edition of Delacroix's *Correspondance* dates Delacroix's first letter to Baudelaire "ce 24 [avril 1845]": *Correspondance générale de Eugène Delacroix,* II (1936), 214. But the letter is reprinted, dated "ce 24 [décembre 1859]," in *Correspondance,* IV (1938), 140, with the following note: "Cette lettre, sans adresse, sans date, a déjà été publiée au t. II, p. 214 et attribuée à l'année 1845. Mais c'est une erreur; Baudelaire a connu Malassis vers 1847. De plus, les relations entre Delacroix et Baudelaire paraissent aussi plus tardives."

16. "M. Baudelaire continuait: Voyez-vous, Vitu, les créanciers sont comme les femmes. On ne saurait les aimer. Eugène Delacroix me disait hier" (Anon., "Les Boutiques de journaux: *Corsaire-Satan,*" *La Silhouette,* May 10 and 24, 1846). And years later a letter of Baudelaire to Sainte-Beuve has: "Il y a bien des années, je disais à E. Delacroix avec qui j'avais tout mon franc-parler. . . ." (March 30, 1865. *Lettres,* p. 429).

17. Eugène Delacroix, *Journal,* ed. André Joubin (3 vols., 1932), I, 258.

18. Asselineau, *Charles Baudelaire,* p. 16.

19. These various suggestions are summed up by Jacques Crépet in his preface to *La Vie et l'œuvre d'Eugène Delacroix* (1928). See also *A.R.,* pp. 444-45.

20. These articles, first republished by Piron in 1865, are collected in E. Delacroix, *Œuvres littéraires* (2 vols., 1923). Up to the time that Baudelaire wrote his first "Salons," Delacroix had published about half of these articles: "Des critiques en matière d'art," *Revue de Paris,* 1829; "Thomas Lawrence. Portrait de Pie VII," *Revue de Paris,* 1829; "Raphaël," *Revue de Paris,* 1830; "Michel-Ange," *Revue de Paris,* 1830; "Sur le *Jugement dernier,*" *Revue des Deux Mondes,* 1837; "Puget," *Plutarque français,* 1845.

21. George Sand, *Impressions et souvenirs,* new ed. (1896), pp. 72-90. (First published in 1873.)

22. For Balzac's debt to Delacroix, see F. Fosca, "Les Artistes dans les romans de Balzac," *Revue Critique,* March, 1922, and see also Mary Wingfield Scott, "Art and Artists in Balzac's *Comédie humaine*" (unpublished dissertation, University of Chicago, 1936).

23. "Salon de 1845"; II 15. But the notes for *Le Hibou philosophe,* dating from 1852, include: "Articles à faire . . . *Gustave Planche,*

éreintement radical, nullité et cruauté de l'impuissance, style d'im-
bécile et de magistrat" (II, 425).

24. "De la critique en matière d'art," *L'Artiste*, Series 2, I
(1839), 7. Quoted in Ferran, *Esthétique de Baudelaire*, p. 125.

25. Champfleury, *Souvenirs et portraits*, pp. 132-33.

26. See A. Ferran, "Baudelaire juge de Baudelaire," *Revue d'Histoire Littéraire de la France* (1929), pp. 447-57.

27. Champfleury, *Souvenirs et portraits*, p. 134.

28. This list is compiled from Baudelaire's own references to authors in his early works and correspondence, and from mentions by
his contemporaries of works and authors read by him. A sentence
from the article on Leconte de Lisle (1861) indicates his constant
preference of Latin authors to Greek: "Ma prédilection naturelle
pour Rome m'empêche de sentir tout ce que je devrais goûter dans la
lecture de ses poésies grecques" (II, 560).

29. See also *L.M.*, pp. 15, 17-18, and *D.L.M.*, pp. 21, 26.

30. Baudelaire et ***, *Mystères galans des théâtres de Paris*, ed.
Jacques Crépet (1938).

31. La Font de Saint-Yenne, *Réflexions sur quelques causes de
l'état présent de la peinture en France*. See André Fontaine, *Les
Doctrines d'art en France; peintres, amateurs, critiques, de Poussin
à Diderot* (1909), Chapter IX.

32. André Fontaine, *op. cit.*, p. 265, n. 5.

33. For an admirable discussion of Diderot as an art critic, see
Jean Thomas, *L'Humanisme de Diderot* (1934), Chapter IV,
"L'Humanisme et l'art."

34. *Ibid.*, p. 131.

35. The Introduction to *Le Salon de 1845 de Charles Baudelaire*,
ed. André Ferran (Toulouse, 1933), gives an excellent account of
the state of contemporary criticism, as well as a description of the
Salon of 1845, an analysis of the principal criticisms of it and a
comparison of Baudelaire's "Salon" with them.

36. J. Crépet, "A propos d'une toile célébrée par Baudelaire,"
Figaro, Nov. 15, 1924.

37. To this same period belongs the malicious article, with its
thinly veiled attack on Balzac, "Comment on paie ses dettes quand
on a du génie." The article is not critical in any strict sense, but it is
curious to find it very close in time to Baudelaire's many admiring
references to Balzac.

38. For Baudelaire's relations with Louis Ménard, see Henri
Peyre, *Louis Ménard (1822-1901)* (New Haven, 1932), especially
pp. 18-19, 24-25, and 46-48. M. Peyre says of this article of Baude-

laire's: "L'article tout entier est fort curieux; c'est un des premiers spécimens de la critique littéraire de Baudelaire, et l'on y trouve déjà son étonnante acuité, et sa sévérité pour tout ce qui n'a pas atteint un point de perfection ou de maturité suffisante" (p. 48).

39. La Fizelière and Decaux, in their bibliography of Baudelaire, give also a review of the *Romans, contes et voyages* of Arsène Houssaye, *Corsaire-Satan*, Jan., 1846, signed C. B. M. Crépet finally unearthed this article in the *Corsaire-Satan* for *July* 7, 1846, signed *A. B.* (See J. Crépet, "Une Page retrouvée de Baudelaire?" *Mercure de France*, May 1, 1937, p. 628.) M. Crépet—quite rightly, to my mind—considers the attribution so doubtful that he has not included the article among the *Juvenilia* of his edition.

40. See the curious letter to Monsieur R***, of 1845 (*Corr.* I, 21-22), in which "ultra-libéral" is qualified as "le plus beau titre que puisse porter un citoyen."

41. This is evidently a reminiscence of Casimir Périer's famous "A quoi un poëte est-il bon?" It is amusing to note that Poe had also been struck by the phrase; he mentions this "pert little query" in his review of *Undine* (*Burton's Gentleman's Magazine*, Sept., 1839; *Complete Works* of Edgar Allan Poe, ed. James A. Harrison (Virginia edition, 16 vols., New York, 1902), X, 30).

42. Here is a more significant *avant la lettre* parallel with Poe, who, reviewing *The Quacks of Helicon* in *Graham's Magazine*, Aug., 1841, wrote: "True criticism is the reflection of the thing criticized upon the spirit of the critic" (Virginia ed., X, 193).

43. In Saint-Denis du Saint-Sacrement, not, as Baudelaire says, in Saint-Louis au Marais.

44. See J. Giraud, "George Catlin, le 'cornac des sauvages,' et Charles Baudelaire," *Mercure de France*, Feb. 6, 1914.

45. The Fontanarès in the list of Balzac heroes, who had puzzled editors, has been identified as the hero of Balzac's play, *Les Ressources de Quinola*, played at the Odéon on March 19, 1842; see Georges Batault, "Fontanarès? (A propos de Baudelaire et de Balzac.)," *Mercure de France*, April 1, 1931. There is a mention of the play in Baudelaire's first article on Poe: "Balzac, en assistant aux répétitions des *Ressources de Quinola*, les dirigeait et jouait lui-même tous les rôles, corrigeait des épreuves de ses livres" (*Poe*, p. 666).

46. Prarond, *De quelques écrivains nouveaux*, p. 7, quoted by Ferran, *Esthétique de Baudelaire*, p. 599; Banville, *Galerie contemporaine*, Series 1, no. 5, quoted by Crépet, *C.E.*, pp. 474-75.

47. E. Delacroix, "Raphaël," *Revue de Paris*, XI (1830), 138; *Œuvres littéraires*, II, 12.

48. Baudelaire, in the "Salon de 1846," points out the errors of the popular parallel between Delacroix and Hugo. Even at the risk of falling into the same sort of error, I cannot refrain from pointing out what seems to me the much closer parallel between Delacroix and Chateaubriand. Delacroix would perhaps have relished the comparison as little as that with Hugo; he has an occasional hard word for Chateaubriand, such as: "Je commence à prendre furieusement en grippe les Schubert, les rêveurs, les Chateaubriand (il y a longtemps que j'avais commencé), les Lamartine, etc. Pourquoi tout cela passera-t-il? Parce que ce n'est point vrai" (Feb. 14, 1850. *Journal*, I, 340). But in 1860 he copies into the *Journal* some dozen pages from the *Mémoires d'outre-tombe*, evidently chosen because of Delacroix's sympathy with the ideas expressed in them (*Journal*, III, 240-47). Certainly there seems to be a marked resemblance between the two, especially in their later years; two melancholy, disillusioned, aristocratic figures, regretting the errors of the new generation, commenting sardonically on popular theories of progress; isolated, self-centered geniuses, proud of having been innovators in their time, yet with a classic tendency which asserts itself more and more. There are many differences between them, to be sure; yet one can hardly read the *Mémoires d'outre-tombe* and the *Journal* without perceiving an air of kinship between the two.

49. See also II, 18-19, 71-72; *Journal*, I, 459, II, 11, and the letter to Peisse already quoted.

50. See the chapter "Baudelaire critique d'art" in Camille Mauclair, *Le Génie de Baudelaire* (1933).

51. For Diderot's influence on Baudelaire, see the articles by J. Pommier, "Les *Salons* de Diderot et leur influence au XIXe siècle: Baudelaire et le *Salon de 1846*," *Revue des Cours et Conférences*, Series 2 (1936), pp. 289-306, 437-52, and H. Brugmans, "Quelques remarques sur Diderot et l'esthétique baudelairienne," *Neophilologus*, XXIII (1938), 284-90.

52. Diderot, *Œuvres complètes*, ed. J. Assézat and M. Tourneux (20 vols., 1875-77), X, 93, 97, 100.

53. It is worth noting that the "Salon de 1759," Diderot's first "Salon," was published in the March 9, 1845, number of *L'Artiste*, of which Baudelaire was a constant reader, so that he almost certainly had this particular "Salon" fresh in his mind.

54. M. Pommier remarks elsewhere: "Toute cette théorie de la couleur me donne d'ailleurs l'impression d'un plagiat" (*La Mystique de Baudelaire*, 1932, p. 162).

55. Sainte-Beuve, *Lundis*, III, 299.

56. *Ibid.*, III, 306.

57. For a more detailed study see my article, "Baudelaire and Stendhal," *PMLA*, March, 1939, and J. Pommier, "Un Plagiat de Baudelaire," *Bulletin de la Faculté des Lettres de Strasbourg*, May-June, 1937.

58. Champfleury, *Souvenirs et portraits*, p. 137.

59. Compare for example: "Chaque artiste devrait voir la nature à sa manière" (*Histoire de la peinture en Italie*, I, 168) and: "Le beau est partout et . . . chaque homme non seulement le voit, mais doit absolument le rendre à sa manière" (*Journal*, II, 395). Delacroix was an enthusiastic reader of the *Histoire de la peinture en Italie*, as a note in the article on the *Last Judgment* shows (*Œuvres littéraires*, II, 222).

60. Stendhal, *Histoire de la peinture en Italie*, ed. Paul Arbelet (2 vols., 1924), II, 155-57.

61. *Ibid.*, II, 75, 149. Many of Stendhal's ideas were far from being original with him (here the debt to Cabanis is evident), but it seems unquestionable that it was from Stendhal that Baudelaire got them.

62. Another Poe parallel: "The Apollo, too!—is a copy—there can be no doubt of it—blind fool that I am, who cannot behold the boasted inspiration of the Apollo! I cannot help—pity me!—I cannot help preferring the Antinous" ("The Assignation," *Southern Literary Messenger*, July, 1835; Virginia ed., II, 118-19).

63. The claims of Randolph Hughes in his article, "Baudelaire et Balzac," *Mercure de France*, Nov. 1, 1934, are obviously exaggerated. (Cf. *Mercure de France*, Nov. 15 and Dec. 1, 1934, and Jan. 1, 1935.) But Baudelaire certainly had Balzac at his fingertips.

64. Balzac, *Massimilla Doni, Œuvres complètes*, ed. M. Bouteron and H. Longnon (Conard) XXVII (1925), p. 435.

65. One wonders whether a sentence of *Massimilla Doni*—"Le hautbois n'a-t-il pas sur tous les esprits le pouvoir d'éveiller des images champêtres, ainsi que presque tous les instruments à vent?" (*ibid.*, p. 456)—may not have contributed to the lines of the *Correspondances* sonnet:

> "Il est des parfums frais comme des chairs d'enfants,
> Doux comme les hautbois, verts comme les prairies."

66. See R. Michaud, "Baudelaire, Balzac et les correspondances," *Romanic Review*, Oct., 1938.

67. See G. T. Clapton, "Lavater, Gall et Baudelaire," *Revue de Littérature Comparée* (1933), pp. 259-98, 429-56. It seems to me that Mr. Clapton exaggerates, not Baudelaire's great interest in

Lavater, nor the undeniable influence of Lavater on him, but the unique debt to Lavater of many passages which seem to me to be either the result of a very complex set of influences, or for which the immediate source might have been one of many.

68. See M. Ferran's edition of the "Salon de 1845," pp. 105-8. Heine's "Salon de 1831" was published in French in his *De la France*, 1833 (from which I quote) and reviewed by Sainte-Beuve (*Premiers lundis*, II, 248), who quotes the same passage as Baudelaire.

CHAPTER TWO: THE SHADOW
OF POE AND DE MAISTRE

1. The *Causeries* published in *Le Tintamarre* in 1846-47, in which Baudelaire had a hand, are too ephemeral in interest to demand consideration here. The same is true of the two numbers of the *Salut public*.

2. See especially J. Pommier, *La Mystique de Baudelaire* (1932); R. Vivier, *L'Originalité de Charles Baudelaire* (n.d.), pp. 149-54; Ferran, *L'Esthétique de Baudelaire*. For the doctrine of correspondences in general, see M. A. Chaix, *La Correspondance des arts dans la poésie contemporaine* (1919), and G. Maurevert, "Des Sons, des goûts et des couleurs," *Mercure de France*, June 15, 1939.

3. See R. Michaud, "Baudelaire, Balzac et les correspondances," *Romanic Review*, Oct., 1938, and the very controversial article by R. Hughes, "Vers la contrée du rêve: Balzac, Gautier et Baudelaire, disciples de Quincey," *Mercure de France*, Aug. 1, 1939, with the ensuing correspondence in the *Mercure*, Sept. 15-Oct. 1, and Nov 1, 1939, and April 1, 1940.

For Balzac's debt to Swedenborg see F. Baldensperger, *Orientations étrangères chez Honoré de Balzac* (1927), and J. Van der Elst, "Autour du *Livre mystique*: Balzac et Swedenborg," *Revue de Littérature Comparée* (Jan.-March, 1930), pp. 88-123; and for his debt to De Quincey, see G.-A. Astre, "H. de Balzac et 'L'Anglais mangeur d'opium,' " *Revue de Littérature Comparée* (Oct.-Dec., 1935), pp. 755-72.

4. Gérard de Nerval, *Aurélia*, ed. Henri Clouard (1928), p. 97.

5. The most recent edition of the *Journaux intimes*, based on the manuscript, is that of Jacques Crépet (1938). M. Crépet's notes discuss fully both the manuscript and previous editions. My references are, as for the rest of Baudelaire's work, to the Pléiade edition, noting any changes and variants supplied by M. Crépet's edition.

6. In a note to the sentence "On dit que j'ai trente ans; mais si

j'ai vécu trois minutes en une . . . , n'ai-je pas quatre-vingt-dix ans" (II, 637), Ad. Van Bever, in his edition of the *Journaux intimes* (1919), suggests that this indicates that "Fusées" was at least begun in 1851, when Baudelaire was thirty. (So M. Le Dantec, *Œuvres diverses*, p. 532.) M. Crépet, however, dates "Fusées" as of 1855 to 1862, and "Mon Cœur mis à nu," 1859 to 1866. He refuses to accept the 1851 hypothesis on the grounds that: 1) Baudelaire's opinions in 1851 were democratic and popular (as the Pierre Dupont preface shows), the very opposite of most of those expressed in "Fusées"; 2) the passage follows immediately, and on the same page of the manuscript, a passage used by Baudelaire in the "Notes nouvelles sur Edgar Poe" in 1857; 3) the idea Baudelaire expresses is a commonplace, and the number thirty has no chronological significance.

For my own part, I am not entirely convinced by M. Crépet. As we shall see, Baudelaire's ideas, from 1850 on, were in a state of confusion and change, and it seems to me that the pages of "Fusées" may well represent the progress of that change, and belong, if not to 1851 precisely, to the years immediately following. As for the vicinity of this passage to the one used in 1857, it seems to me no evidence; Baudelaire, economical of every idea, may well have turned back in 1857 to notes set down some years earlier. And finally, for the *trente*, it seems to me likely that Baudelaire would have taken the round number *nearest* his own age; that is, that he is more likely to have written "on dit que j'ai trente ans" when he was thirty-one or thirty-two, than when he was thirty-five or thirty-six. Moreover, a letter to his mother of Dec. 9, 1851, says: "Je vais avoir 30 *ans* dans trois mois juste. Ceci me suscite beaucoup de réflexions qu'il est facile de deviner" (*L.M.*, p. 49), which indicates that he was thinking a good deal about his age at this time. I hold no particular brief for 1851 as an absolute date, but 1852 or 1853 seems to me in no way made impossible by what M. Crépet says.

7. For both the sources and the later transformations of the jottings, the *Eclaircissements* of M. Crépet's edition are invaluable.

8. Among the most valuable studies are: E. Seylaz, *Edgar Poe et les premiers symbolistes* (Lausanne, 1923); L. Lemonnier, *Les Traducteurs d'Edgar Poe* (1928), *Edgar Poe et la critique française* (1928), and *Edgar Poe et les poètes français* (1933); C. Mauclair, *Le Génie de Baudelaire* (1933); A. Ferran, *L'Esthétique de Baudelaire*, Part II, Chapter I, "Edgar Poe ou le principe poétique"; R. Michaud, "Baudelaire et Edgar A. Poë [*sic*]: une mise au point," *Revue de Littérature Comparée* (Oct.-Dec., 1938), pp. 666-83; and

the notes to the Poe volumes of the Crépet and Le Dantec editions of Baudelaire.

9. Asselineau, *Charles Baudelaire*, p. 39.

10. *Ibid.*, p. 41.

11. W. J. Stillman, *Autobiography of a Journalist* (2 vols., Boston, 1901), I, 116, 165.

12. For a complete list of Baudelaire's references to Poe, see the bibliography of L. Lemonnier's *Edgar Poe et la critique française*.

13. Andrew Lang, *Letters to Dead Authors* (London, 1886), p. 148.

14. De Maistre, *Lettres et opuscules inédits* (2 vols., 1851).

15. Sainte-Beuve had also written an article on De Maistre in 1843 (*Portraits littéraires*, II, 387-466), but at that time Baudelaire's interests were not such that De Maistre would have made the same appeal to him as in 1851.

16. The quotation is from the *Soirées de Saint-Pétersbourg*, Entretien 6, *Œuvres posthumes*, I, 369. All the references to De Maistre, except for the *Lettres et opuscules*, are to the edition of J. B. Pélagaud and Company, Lyons and Paris: *Œuvres* (4 vols., 1859-60), *Œuvres posthumes* (4 vols., 1854-60).

17. See also II, 433, 582, 587, 353, 658.

18. If Baudelaire read De Maistre with such enthusiasm in the 1850's, it seems strange that relatively few echoes of his interest should appear in "Fusées," whereas "Mon Cœur mis à nu" is crowded with them. Is it possible that "Mon Cœur mis à nu" overlaps "Fusées" chronologically more than has been thought?

19. One of my students, Mother Mary Alphonsus S.H.C.J., is preparing a dissertation on Baudelaire and De Maistre. To discussion with her I owe much for the pages which follow.

20. See also Flaubert's letter to Baudelaire and the latter's reply, *Paradis artificiels*, ed. Crépet, pp. 309-11. Flaubert's letter is there dated "Croisset, lundi," and Baudelaire's "26 juin 1860." The editors of Flaubert's correspondence have dated this letter "lundi 22 octobre 1860" (Gustave Flaubert, *Correspondance*, new enlarged ed., Conard, IV, 407), which is obviously impossible given the date of Baudelaire's reply.

21. See also *Soirées*, Entretien 2, *Œuvres posthumes*, I, 70-71, and Entretien 5, *Œuvres posthumes*, I, 334-35 ("hiéroglyphes parlants").

22. See the letter to Poulet-Malassis on the latter's eighteenth century catalogue: "Moi, qui suis un remarquable échantillon de crapule et d'ignorance, je vous aurais fait un catalogue éblouissant, rien

qu'avec les souvenirs de mes lectures, du temps que je lisais le XVIIIe siècle—soit en philosophes matérialistes, soit en curiosités de *sorcellerie* et de *sciences mystiques*, soit en *romanciers* et *voyageurs*" (Corr. I, 163).

23. See the numerous letters to Sainte-Beuve in the correspondence, and the article by L. Lemonnier, "Baudelaire et Sainte-Beuve," *Enquêtes sur Baudelaire* (1929), pp. 23-55.

24. There is a curious autobiographical parenthesis which shows how strongly Baudelaire was feeling towards his step-father at this time, and recalls the legend of his shouting in the streets in 1848: "Il faut fusiller le général Aupick!" "Il est bon que chacun de nous, une fois dans sa vie, ait éprouvé la pression d'une odieuse tyrannie; il apprend à la haïr. . . . Combien de natures révoltées ont pris vie auprès d'un cruel et ponctuel militaire de l'Empire!" (II, 406.)

25. These notes are interesting as showing something of what Baudelaire was reading at the time. Among the "articles à faire" are an "appréciation générale des ouvrages de Th. Gautier, de Sainte-Beuve . . . *Balzac, auteur dramatique*," and a number of *éreintages*, among them Gustave Planche, Jules Janin, A. Dumas, Eugène Sue, Paul Féval. Possible books to be reviewed are "le dernier volume des *Causeries du Lundi* . . . *Lettres et Mélanges* de Joseph de Maistre . . . La traduction d'Emerson" (II, 425-26).

26. A letter to Madame Aupick of July 9, 1851, speaks of "la nécessité de finir mon article," with a note by M. Crépet, "Nous ignorons de quel article il s'agit; les bibliographies baudelairiennes ne fournissent aucune indication pour le second semestre 1851" (*D.L.M.*, p. 31). But may this not be the "Drames et romans honnêtes"?

27. It should be noted that, if what Baudelaire himself says is correct, these articles were composed somewhat hurriedly. He writes to his mother on March 27, 1852, enclosing the "Drames et romans honnêtes" and the "Ecole païenne": "Et tous les jours s'envolent dans des foules de courses stériles, ou dans la confection d'articles maladifs faits à la hâte pour gagner quelque argent" (*L.M.*, p. 50).

28. The passage, as has been noted, is obviously inspired by the beginning of Pétrus Borel's *Madame Putiphar* (1839). But not till 1852 does Baudelaire find himself in agreement with it.

29. *Juvenilia*, p. 566.

30. Champfleury, *Contes d'automne* (1854), p. 296.

31. For illustrated editions see Charles Baudelaire, *De l'Essence du rire et généralement du comique dans les arts plastiques*, with a

preface by Jacques Crépet (1925), and C. Baudelaire, *Les Dessins de Daumier* (1924).

32. Baudelaire himself queries the source of his quotation, saying that he has a vague memory of having read it in Joseph de Maistre, but as a quotation, perhaps from Bossuet or Bourdaloue. I have pursued it in vain. Mr. Clapton in his article on "Lavater, Gall and Baudelaire," *Revue de Littérature Comparée* (1933), p. 444, suggests as a possible source a sentence of Lavater's in the *Souvenir pour des voyageurs chéris*, "Le Sage sourit souvent et rit rarement." He also points out other parallels between Baudelaire's ideas on laughter and Lavater's.

A little later Baudelaire notes that "le Sage par excellence, le Verbe Incarné, n'a jamais ri. Aux yeux de Celui qui sait tout et qui peut tout, le comique n'est pas" (II, 167). This may have been suggested by a phrase of De Maistre's in a letter to the king of Sardinia: "Ces reproches, Sire, feraient rire Dieu, si Dieu riait" (*Lettres et opuscules*, I, 182).

33. G. T. Clapton, "Balzac, Baudelaire and Maturin," *French Quarterly*, June and Sept., 1930. "One of the most suggestive ideas that Baudelaire borrowed from Maturin is the theory of laughter" (p. 97). Again the sources are certainly more complex than Mr. Clapton seems to think, although *Melmoth* is certainly one of the important ones.

For another indication of Baudelaire's recent reading of De Maistre compare: "Tous les mécréants de mélodrame, maudits, damnés, fatalement marqués d'un rictus qui court jusqu'aux oreilles, sont dans l'orthodoxie pure du rire" (II, 171), and: "Ce rictus épouvantable, courant d'une oreille à l'autre" (*Soirées*, Entretien 4, *Œuvres posthumes*, I, 241).

34. Stendhal, *Racine et Shakespeare*, ed. Pierre Martino (2 vols., 1925), I, 26.

35. H. Bergson, *Le Rire, essai sur la signification du comique* (1931), pp. 201-2. (*Le Rire* was first published in the *Revue de Paris* in 1899.)

36. I have discussed Baudelaire's appreciation of Goya in my article "Le Cosmopolitisme de Baudelaire et l'Espagne," *Revue de Littérature Comparée* (Jan.-March, 1936), pp. 91-97.

37. For Baudelaire's *cosmopolitisme* see the articles just cited.

38. Compare the note in "Fusées": "L'homme, c'est-à-dire chacun, est si *naturellement* dépravé qu'il souffre moins de l'abaissement universel que de l'établissement d'une hiérarchie raisonnable" (II, 639), and: "S'il était permis d'établir des degrés d'importance

parmi les choses d'intuition divine, je placerais la hiérarchie avant le dogme tant elle est indispensable au maintien de la foi" (*Lettres et opuscules*, II, 285).

39. The phrase recalls Poe's: "In the multiform of the tree, and in the multicolor of the flower he recognized the most direct and the most energetic efforts of Nature at physical loveliness" ("The Landscape Garden," *Snowden's Lady's Companion*, Oct., 1842: Virginia ed., IV, 265).

40. "Ligeia," Virginia ed., II, 250, and *passim*; *Poe*, p. 243.

41. It is to be noted that one whole page of this discussion (II, 148-49) did not appear in the article when it was first published. With two or three other passages it seems to have been added by Baudelaire in preparation for the inclusion of the article in the *Curiosités esthétiques*.

42. The passage occurs in the "Tale of the Ragged Mountain" (Virginia ed., V, 167: *Poe*, p. 226). It is quoted directly in the "Poëme du Haschisch" (I, 303).

43. *Juvenilia*, p. 579.

44. *Ibid.*, p. 298.

45. *Ibid.*, p. 299.

46. See *Histoires extraordinaires*, ed. Crépet, pp. 393-94.

47. For a study of a poetic text and the changes made in it, see E. M. Schenck and M. Gilman, "*Le Voyage* and *L'Albatros*: the First Text," *Romanic Review*, Oct., 1938.

48. See M. Crépet's notes in *Nouvelles histoires extraordinaires* (1933), pp. 319-32.

49. *Sartain's Union Magazine*, 1850 (Virginia ed., XIV, 266-92).

50. *Eureka, La Genèse d'un poëme*, ed. Jacques Crépet (1936), p. 153. (*La Genèse d'un poëme* is not included in the Poe volume of the Pléiade edition.)

51. See L. G. Miller, "Gustave Flaubert and Charles Baudelaire— Their Correspondence," *PMLA*, June, 1934.

52. March 18, 1857. Flaubert, *Correspondance*, IV, 164.

53. R. Descharmes, *Flaubert* (1909), p. 103, n. 3.

54. Flaubert, *Correspondance*, IV, 229.

55. A letter from Baudelaire to Ernest Feydeau of June 14, 1858 (*Amateur d'Autographes*, XLIII, 1910, 381) says that he is writing an article on *Fanny*: "voici certes un beau livre, compact, solide, dont tous les membres sont bien assemblés, et qui restera. . . . Vous disposez d'une étonnante puissance analytique. Et vous donnez à l'analyse un ton et un accent *lyrique*." The article never appeared; the reason is probably to be found in a letter from Baudelaire to his

mother of Dec. 11, 1858 (*L.M.*, p. 175), in which he says: "*Fanny,
immense succès*, livre répugnant, archi-répugnant."

56. The expression also occurs in Balzac's *Louis Lambert*, and in
a note to De Maistre's *Eclaircissement sur les sacrifices* (*Œuvres
posthumes* II, 332, n. 1): "Homo duplex in viis suis. Jac. I, 8."

57. I, 321, 360.

58. For a description of the proof sheets see Baudelaire, *Textes
inédits*, ed. Y.-G. Le Dantec (1934), pp. 50-51, and for the annotations see J. Crépet, "Un manifeste baudelairien," *Mercure de France*
(Sept. 1, 1936), pp. 396-411.

59. See especially E. Raynaud, "Baudelaire et Théophile Gautier,"
Mercure de France, Oct. 16, 1917 (reprinted in the author's *Charles
Baudelaire*, Garnier, 1922), and A. Ferran, *L'Esthétique de Baude-
laire*, pp. 535-44.

60. See, in addition to the above, H. Dérieux, "La Plasticité de
Baudelaire et ses rapports avec Théophile Gautier," *Mercure de
France*, Oct. 1, 1917, and E. Meyer, "Théophile Gautier et Baude-
laire," *Revue des Cours et Conférences*, April 15, 1926.

61. II, 466-68: cf. *Poe*, pp. 706, 710-11.

62. II, 468-69: cf. II, 413-15.

63. II, 476: cf. II, 215. I suspect that this passage belonged
originally to the unpublished and probably uncompleted section on
the English painters of the "Exposition de 1855."

64. Compare "Fusées": "De la langue et de l'écriture, prises
comme opérations magiques, sorcellerie évocatoire" (II, 634).

65. Compare André Gide's comment on this passage: "nous re-
fusons de nous prêter à ce jeu de parallèles, de comparaisons calami-
teuses, sur le modèle de cette populaire formule: le poireau, c'est
l'asperge du pauvre—formule qu'on ne sait pour qui elle est la plus
injurieuse: pour l'asperge, pour le pauvre ou pour le poireau. Oui,
Gautier occupe une place considérable; c'est seulement fâcheux
qu'il la remplisse si mal" (*Incidences*, 1924, p. 162).

66. Review of *The Damsel of Darien, Burton's Gentleman's
Magazine*, May-Nov., 1839 (Virginia ed., X, 53; see also XIII, 86—
"No work of art can embody within itself a proper *originality* with-
out giving the plainest manifestations of the creative spirit, or, in
more common parlance, of *genius* in its author"—and XIII, 143,
XIV, 73 and *passim*).

67. "Fifty Suggestions" (Virginia ed., XIV, 176-78).

68. Review of *Conti the Discarded, Southern Literary Messenger*,
Feb., 1836 (Virginia ed., VIII, 230).

69. "Marginalia" (Virginia ed., XVI, 137).

70. "The Purloined Letter," *The Gift*, 1845 (Virginia ed., VI, 46-47).

71. "W. C. Bryant," *Godey's Lady's Book*, April, 1846 (Virginia ed., XIII, 131).

72. Review of Hawthorne, *Godey's Lady's Book*, Nov., 1847 (Virginia ed., XIII, 148).

73. Review of *Barnaby Rudge*, *Graham's Magazine*, Feb., 1842 (Virginia ed., XI, 41).

74. *Unpublished Letters* of Samuel Taylor Coleridge, ed. Earl Leslie Griggs (2 vols., New Haven, 1933), II, 67, To an unknown correspondent [Dec. 1811]. See also what Poe himself says: "It appears to me that what seems to be the gross *inconsistency* of plagiarism as perpetrated by a poet, is very easily thus resolved:— the poetic sentiment (even without reference to the poetic power) implies a peculiarly, perhaps abnormally keen appreciation of the beautiful, with a longing for its assimilation, or absorption, into poetic identity. What the poet intensely admires, becomes thus, in very fact, although only partially, a portion of his own intellect. It has a secondary origination within his own soul—an origination altogether apart, although springing from its primary origination from without. The poet is thus possessed by another's thought, and cannot be said to take of it, possession. But, in either view, he thoroughly feels it as *his own* . . . in fact all literary history demonstrates that, for the most frequent and palpable plagiarisms, we must search the works of the most eminent poets" ("The Longfellow War," *Broadway Journal*, April 5, 1845: Virginia ed., XII, 105-6).

CHAPTER THREE: THE POET AS CRITIC

1. Poe, "Morella," Virginia ed., II, 27.

2. For a study of the history of the word *original*, see L. P. Smith, "Four Romantic Words," in *Words and Idioms* (Boston, 1925), pp. 66-134, which gives the history of *romantic, original, creative, genius,* and also suggests their relation to the idea of the imagination.

3. *Essais*, I, xxi, "De la force de l'imagination."

4. *Pensées*, ed. Brunschvig, II, 82.

5. Article "Imagination," *Dictionnaire philosophique*, ed. Garnier, XIX, 429.

6. For the introduction of the word *creative* see Smith, *op. cit.*

7. Vigny, *Stello*, ed. F. Baldensperger (1925), p. 261. See also Chapters XXXVIII and XXXIX.

8. The more exalted conception never seems to have really taken root in France. The last edition of the *Dictionnaire de l'Académie* defines: *"Imagination,* n. f. Faculté de se représenter quelque chose dans l'esprit. . . . Il se dit particulièrement, en termes de Littérature et de Beaux-Arts, de la Faculté d'inventer, de concevoir, jointe au talent de rendre vivement ses conceptions." Compare with this the *Oxford English Dictionary's* 4b: "The creative faculty of the mind in its highest aspect; the power of framing new and striking intellectual conceptions; poetic genius."

9. It is curious to find the doctrine of *imitation* salvaged by one of its chief modern exponents in the following terms: "If there is to be any recovery of humanistic or religious truth, at least along critical lines, it would appear desirable to associate the creative process once more, not with spontaneity, but with imitation, imitation of the type that implies *a supersensuous model imaginatively apprehended."* Irving Babbitt, *On Being Creative* (Boston, 1932), p. 132. The italics are mine.

10. Catherine Crowe, *The Night Side of Nature, or Ghosts and Ghost Seers,* London [1848].

11. Baudelaire's debt to Catherine Crowe has been treated in two articles: G. T. Clapton, "Baudelaire and Catherine Crowe," *Modern Language Review,* XXV (1930) 286-305, and Randolph Hughes, "Une Etape de l'esthétique de Baudelaire: Catherine Crowe," *Revue de Littérature Comparée* (Oct.-Dec., 1937), pp. 680-99. Both these articles tend, I think, to exaggerate the influence on Baudelaire of Mrs. Crowe's book, which he could only have read after his interests had already been oriented in this direction by Balzac, Swedenborg, and others. Neither articles cites close verbal parallels, and it seems probable that Baudelaire was attracted to *The Night Side of Nature* by ideas already familiar and congenial to him, such as "The whole of nature is one large book of symbols, which, because we have lost the key to it, we cannot decipher" (Chapter IV, p. 19), and that the passage which he quotes marks the limit of what he owes to "cette excellente Mme Crowe."

12. Randolph Hughes, *op. cit.,* p. 698.

13. See Floyd Stovall, "Poe's Debt to Coleridge," *University of Texas Studies in English,* No. 10, July 8, 1930.

14. "Fifty Suggestions," Virginia ed., XIV, 183.

15. Mr. Hughes, in the article cited above, seems to me to exaggerate greatly the importance of this idea to Baudelaire, as well as his debt to Mrs. Crowe, when he says: "Baudelaire a atteint le stade le plus important, sinon le dernier et le plus avancé, de sa philoso-

phie esthétique, lorsqu'il a établi une fois pour toutes une distinction entre la fantaisie et l'imagination; et lorsqu'il s'est finalement convaincu que l'exercice de l'imagination, chez l'artiste, est non point simplement un travail d'imitation ou de représentation, mais un acte essentiellement créateur, dans le sens le plus strict du term" (*op. cit.*, p. 680). Mr. Hughes considers that the "influence funeste" of Poe, "ce commis-voyageur de l'esthétique," is responsible for the difficulty and hesitation Baudelaire felt in accepting this conception. "Car dans tous les domaines, et surtout lorsqu'il s'agissait de questions d'ordre philosophique, il avait singulièrement peu d'originalité et d'indépendance. . . . Il ne pouvait faire fond sur lui-même; il lui fallait un soutien, et ce soutien, il l'a trouvé dans l'"excellente' Mrs. Crowe" (p. 698). This whole conclusion seems to me false; fundamentally so in regard to Baudelaire's originality, and also in its attitude on Poe and Mrs. Crowe.

Poe is indeed well damned by Mr. Hughes for his failure to accept the distinction between fancy and imagination. At times he refuses to admit that the distinction exists: "If so at all, it is one without a difference; without even a difference of *degree*." But later in the same article Poe says: "The truth is that the just distinction between the fancy and the imagination (and which is still but a distinction *of degree*) is involved in the consideration of the *mystic* . . . here employed in the sense of Augustus William Schlegel and of most other German critics. It is applied by them to that class of composition in which there lies beneath the transparent upper current of meaning an under or *suggestive* one. What we vaguely term the *moral* of any sentiment is its mystic or secondary expression. It has the vast force of an accompaniment in music. This vivifies the air; that spiritualizes the *fanciful* conception, and lifts it into the *ideal*" (Review of *Alciphron*, *Burton's Gentleman's Magazine*, Jan., 1849. Virginia ed., X, 61, 65).

My own inclination is to agree with Poe, and to take comfort in the company of such critics as the late Lascelles Abercrombie and Professor J. L. Lowes; the latter writes: "I have long had the feeling, which this study has matured to a conviction, that Fancy and Imagination are not two powers at all, but one. The valid distinction which exists between them lies, not in the materials with which they operate, but in the degree of intensity of the operant power itself. Working at high tension, the imaginative energy assimilates and transmutes; keyed low, the same energy aggregates and yokes together those images which, at its highest pitch, it merges indissolubly into one" (*The Road to Xanadu*, Boston, 1927, p. 103).

16. There is a passage in Sainte-Beuve's 1833 article on Heine which, although it does not use the word imagination, expresses its workings admirably: "Souvent, le soir, regardant quelque coin de ciel, des toits lointains, çà et là un rare feuillage, je me suis dit qu'un tableau qui retracerait exactement cette vue si simple serait divin; puis j'ai compris que cette fidélité entière était impossible à saisir directement; que mon émotion résultait du tableau en lui-même et de ma disposition sentimentale à le réfléchir; que, de l'observation directe de l'objet, et aussi de la réflexion modifiée de cet objet au sein du miroir intérieur, l'art devait tirer une troisième image *créée* qui n'était tout à fait ni la copie de la nature, ni la traduction aux yeux de l'impression insaisissable, mais qui avait d'autant plus de prix et de vérité, qu'elle participait davantage de l'une et de l'autre" (*Premiers lundis*, II, 257-58).

17. Review of *The Culprit Fay, Southern Literary Messenger*, April, 1836. Virginia ed., VIII, 283, n. 2.

18. "Marginalia," Virginia ed., XVI, 155-56. The passage is frequently used by Poe; see the articles on N. P. Willis, *Broadway Journal*, Jan. 18, 1845 (Virginia ed., XII, 37-40) and *Godey's Lady's Book*, 1846 (Virginia ed., XV, 13-14).

19. Review of *Literary Remains of the late William Hazlitt, Southern Literary Messenger*, Sept., 1836 (Virginia ed., IX, 145).

20. "The Opal," 1845 (Virginia ed., XIV, 187). See also the passage quoted in note 15 of this chapter.

21. Baudelaire mentions these two painters particularly in the letter to Nadar quoted above: "Entre autres choses vraiment distinguées qu'on ne remarquera pas, remarque, dans une grande salle carrée, au fond, à gauche, où l'on a entassé des paquets de choses religieuses impayables, deux petits tableaux, l'un (no. 1215) *Les Sœurs de charité*, par *Armand Gautier*, l'autre (no. 1894) *L'Angelus*, par *Alphonse Legros*. Ce n'est pas d'un style extrêmement élevé, mais c'est très-pénétrant" (*Corr.* I, 265).

22. The allusion to Hood's Cupid, and the possibility of this passage having originally belonged to the caricature articles, is discussed in my article, "Baudelaire and Thomas Hood," *Romantic Review* (July-Sept. 1935), pp. 241-44.

23. *Journal intime*, Oct. 31, 1852.

24. It is amusing to note how, as so often, Baudelaire makes a quotation which is in his mind do double service. This same quota-

tion is tucked into the *Mangeur d'opium*, on which Baudelaire was working at this same time, in a very different context (I, 334).

25. "Dans la sculpture, j'ai trouvé aussi (dans une des allées du jardin, pas très loin d'une issue) quelque chose qu'on pourrait appeler de la *sculpture vignette-romantique*, et qui est fort joli: une jeune fille et un squelette s'enlevant comme une Assomption. Le squelette embrasse la fille. Il est vrai que le squelette est esquissé en partie, et comme enveloppé d'un suaire sous lequel il se fait sentir. Croirais-tu que, *trois fois déjà, j'ai lu, ligne par ligne*, tout le catalogue de la sculpture, et qu'il m'est impossible de trouver quoi que ce soit qui ait rapport à cela? Il faut vraiment que l'animal qui a fait ce joli morceau l'ait intitulé: *Amour et Gibelotte*, ou tout autre titre à la *Compte-Calix*, pour qu'il me soit impossible de la trouver dans le livret. Tâche, je t'en prie, de savoir cela: le sujet et le nom de l'auteur" (*Corr.* I, 266).

26. "Danse macabre" was first published in the *Revue Contemporaine* on March 15, 1859; "Le Masque" in the same review on November 30, 1859.

27. Delécluze, "Salon de 1859," *Journal des Débats*, April 15, 27; May 5, 13, 18, 26; June 3, 16, 30, 1859.

28. Gautier, "Salon de 1859," *Moniteur Universel*, April 18, 23, 30; May 7, 21, 28; June 3, 11, 16, 18, 23, 25, 29; July 1, 6, 7, 13, 20, 29; August 3, 6, 15, 25; Sept. 4, 21; Oct. 10, 1859.

29. Castagnary, "Salon de 1859," *Salons, 1857-1870*, 1892 (first published in *L'Audience*).

30. A. Dumas, *L'Art et les artistes contemporains au Salon de 1859*, 1859.

31. Maurice Aubert, *Souvenirs du Salon de 1859*, 1859.

32. Published in *Le Figaro*, Nov. 26, 28, and Dec. 3, 1863. Baudelaire's letter to Jules Lemer of Feb. 23, 1865 (*Lettres*, p. 419) gives for the title *Le Peintre de la modernité*. The article was republished separately, with reproductions of Guys water colors, by R. Kieffer, 1923.

33. See *A.R.*, pp. 455-56.

34. For Guys, see Georges Grappe, *Constantin Guys* (n.d.) and Jean-Paul Dubray, *Constantin Guys*, (1930). See also the catalogue of the Guys exhibition at the Musée des Arts décoratifs in 1937, and the many articles inspired by the exhibition.

35. For further details on the connection between Baudelaire and Guys, see *A.R.*, 454-55.

36. See for example II, 416, 417, 422, 423, 166, 441, 444.

37. Virginia ed., XIV, 198.

38. It is difficult to understand M. Ferran's statement (*L'Esthé-tique de Baudelaire*, p. 240): "Delacroix est l'aède de cette épopée de la couleur. Il est apte à 'sentir' la vie moderne, à lui arracher son secret pour le livrer superbement dans l'œuvre révélatrice. Il saura, lui, voir dans les âmes et son art s'approfondira pour comprendre, sous les apparences, le tragique du présent." I have noted earlier Baudelaire's attempt to attach Delacroix to the modern by stating that the quality of his melancholy makes of him "le vrai peintre du XIXe siècle." But Baudelaire's conception of *le peintre de la vie moderne* goes far beyond that.

39. "An infinity of error makes its way into our Philosophy, through Man's habit of considering himself a citizen of a world solely—of an individual planet—instead of at least occasionally contemplating his position as cosmopolite proper—as a denizen of the universe" ("Marginalia," Virginia ed., XVI, 167).

40. De Quincey, *Confessions of an English Opium-Eater* and *Suspiria de Profundis* (Boston, 1859), p. 208. This edition reproduces the original editions of 1822 and 1845, those used by Baudelaire.

Mr. Clapton says: "Les remarques de Baudelaire sur l'enfance et le génie ne sont guère que la généralisation des idées que De Quincey a exprimées à ce sujet dans l'introduction aux *Suspiria* et dans *The Afflication* [*sic*] *of Childhood*" (*Baudelaire and De Quincey*, p. 82). But, unless I am mistaken, De Quincey nowhere expresses the idea of genius being "l'enfance retrouvée *à volonté*," which is the crux of the matter.

41. Compare what Proust says: "cette infaillible proportion de lumière et d'ombre, de relief et d'omission, de souvenir et d'oubli, que la mémoire ou l'observation conscientes ignoreront toujours" (*Le Temps retrouvé*, II, 25).

42. See also the section "Réalisme et idéalisme," *Œuvres litté-raires*, I, 57-58, and the passage already referred to, "De l'emploi du modèle," *Journal*, II, 85-88.

An admirable example of this unconscious artistic activity, it seems to me, is the fact that the early chapters of memoirs and autobiographies are almost invariably more interesting than the later ones. The memory has had time to do its work. The only exceptions, I think, are the autobiographies of writers whose imagination completes the unfinished work of the memory.

43. St. Augustine, *Confessions*, with an English translation by William Watts, 1631 (Loeb Classical Library, New York, 1912), X, viii and xiv.

44. Some of the points which follow are touched on in an article by Justin O'Brien, "La Mémoire involontaire avant Marcel Proust," *Revue de Littérature Comparée* (Jan.-March, 1939), pp. 19-36.

45. "Il fallait tâcher d'interpréter les sensations comme les signes d'autant de lois et d'idées, en essayant de penser, c'est-à-dire de faire sortir de la pénombre ce que j'avais senti, de le convertir en un équivalent spirituel. Or, ce moyen qui me paraissait le seul, qu'était-ce autre chose que faire une œuvre d'art?" (*Le Temps retrouvé*, II, 24.) "Ainsi j'étais déjà arrivé à cette conclusion que nous ne sommes nullement libres devant l'œuvre d'art, que nous ne le faisons pas à notre gré, mais que, préexistant à nous, nous devons, à la fois parce qu'elle est nécessaire et cachée, et comme nous ferions pour une loi de la nature, la découvrir" (*ibid.*, II, 27-28).

46. Both Baudelaire and Proust use the comparison of *translation* for the creation of a work of art. "Je m'apercevais que pour exprimer ces impressions pour écrire ce livre essentiel, le seul livre vrai, un grand écrivain n'a pas dans le sens courant à l'inventer puisque il existe déjà en chacun de nous, mais à le traduire. Le devoir et la tâche d'un écrivain sont ceux d'un traducteur" (*Le Temps retrouvé*, II, 41). And Baudelaire writes in his article on Hugo: "Or, qu'est-ce qu'un poëte (je prends le mot dans son acception la plus large), si ce n'est un traducteur, un déchiffreur?" (II, 521.) But Baudelaire's conception is much freer, as the passage on Guys shows (II, 338).

47. Baudelaire's method is that advised by Coleridge in *Table Talk*: "A poet ought not to pick nature's pocket: let him borrow, and so borrow as to repay by the very act of borrowing. Examine nature accurately, but write from recollection; and trust more to your imagination than to your memory."

48. Compare Benjamin Crémieux, *Du Côté de Marcel Proust* (1929), pp. 3-4: "Il semble qu'il faille en définitive tenir la mémoire pour sa faculté maîtresse et la considérer comme la génératrice, l'ordonnatrice de toutes ses autres facultés qui ne jouent que pour aider à l'exercice et à l'usage du souvenir. . . . L'acte créateur chez Proust n'est jamais (comme chez les imaginatifs), celui de projeter, de semer en avant de lui, et de pousser son 'idée' comme un cerceau ou plutôt comme une boule de neige qui grossit à mesure, ou mieux encore comme un germe qui se développe et prend forme, mais c'est celui de retenir, d'entasser, d'enchaîner ce qui voudrait fuir, de rappeler ce qui est resté en arrière, de le haler, de l'extraire, de le

fixer hors du temps. Il est tout entire tendu à revivifier, reformer ce qui fut et non pas à vivifier l'informe."

What is hard to discover with Proust, I think, is how far he has succeeded, in theory and in practice, in dethroning the imagination and setting up memory in her place. Does Proust use the word *imagination* except for the faculty of conceiving future experience (e.g. *Du Côté de chez Swann*, I, 82, 145; II, 160) or for the reproductive imagination that is practically equivalent to memory (e.g. *Le Temps retrouvé*, II, 15, where the use of the word is tantalizing to a degree)? To what extent does his memory perform functions that we are accustomed to associate only with the creative imagination? And to what extent is the action of the "creative memory" expressed or implied (*ibid.*, II, 56-69—especially p. 66)? These are problems I can only leave to Proust scholars.

49. See Asselineau, *Charles Baudelaire*, p. 45. For a detailed study see E. Raynaud, *Baudelaire et la religion du dandysme*, 1918.

50. Baudelaire uses the same expression in the *Mangeur d'opium* (the passage is his own, not De Quincey's): "je veux dire que le goût précoce du *monde* féminin, *mundi muliebris,* de tout cet appareil ondoyant, scintillant et parfumé, fait les génies supérieurs" (I, 382). A letter from Baudelaire to Poulet-Malassis rages over Calonne's correction to *mundi muliebri*, and then discusses the meaning of the expression (*Corr.* I, 320-22).

51. Compare Poe's passage in "Le Cottage Landor" (*Poe*, p. 648).

52. For example C. Mauclair, *Le Génie de Baudelaire*, pp. 172-73.

53. *Revue Européenne*, April 1, 1861, entitled "Richard Wagner." "Encore quelques mots" was added for the separate publication *Richard Wagner et Tannhäuser à Paris*, 1861.

54. *Corr.* I, 299-302. This letter, with a most interesting and valuable commentary, was first published by André Suarès, in the *Revue Musicale* of Nov. 1, 1922.

55. *Histoire de ma vie*, quoted by Crépet, *A.R.*, p. 511.

56. For the date of this letter (placed under 1857 in the *Correspondance*) see Albert Feuillerat, "Sur Deux Lettres de Baudelaire," *Modern Language Notes*, May, 1941, pp. 338-43.

57. For further details and letters, see *A.R.*, pp. 508-13.

58. See G. Servières, *Richard Wagner jugé en France*, 1887, and *Tannhäuser à l'Opéra en 1861*, 1895; the special number, *Wagner et la France*, of the *Revue Musicale*, Oct. 1, 1923; and the chapter, "Richard Wagner ou l'harmonie des correspondances," of André Ferran's *L'Esthétique de Baudelaire*, pp. 278-361.

59. Quoted by Ferran, p. 302.

60. Compare the passage in the *Mangeur d'opium* (Baudelaire is summarizing a long passage of De Quincey's): "Beaucoup de gens demandent quelles sont les idées positives contenues dans les sons; ils oublient, ou plutôt ils ignorent que la musique, de ce côté-là parente de la poésie, représente des sentiments plutôt que des idées; suggérant des idées, il est vrai, mais ne les contenant pas elle-même" (I, 347).

61. The letter to Wagner makes a closer analogy with color than is found here: "Par exemple, pour me servir des comparaisons empruntées à la peinture, je suppose devant mes yeux une vaste étendue d'un rouge sombre. Si ce rouge représente la passion, je le vois arriver graduellement, par toutes les transitions de rouge et de rose, à l'incandescence de la fournaise. Il semblerait difficile, impossible même d'arriver à quelque chose de plus ardent; et cependant une dernière fusée vient tracer un sillon plus blanc sur le blanc qui lui sert de fond. Ce sera, si vous voulez, le cri suprême de l'âme montée à son paroxysme" (*Corr.* I, 301).

62. Fétis, "Wagner, sa vie, son système de renovation de l'opéra, ses œuvres comme poète et comme musicien, son parti en Allemagne, appréciation de la valeur de ses idées," *Gazette musicale*, June 6, 13, 20, 27; July 11, 25; Aug. 8, 1852: F. Liszt, *Lohengrin et Tannhäuser de Richard Wagner*, Leipzig, 1851. For Wagner's works in French see R. Wagner, *Œuvres en prose*, trans. J.-G. Prod'homme and F. Caillé, 1910. The *Lettre sur la musique* is in Vol. VI, *Opéra et Drame* in Vols. IV and V.

63. *Southern Literary Messenger*, July, 1836 (originally preface to *Poems* of 1831). Virginia ed., VII, xxxvi-xxxvii.

64. A. Suarès, "La Première lettre de Baudelaire à Wagner," *Revue Musicale*, Nov. 1, 1922.

CHAPTER FOUR: THE LAST YEARS

1. In the 1861 articles there are still many traces of the *English Opium-Eater*. For example the quotation from Juvenal in the Barbier article, *Facit indignatio versum*, occurs in the last part of *Suspiria* (*Opium-Eater*, p. 263).

2. For a detailed study of Baudelaire's relations with Hugo see L. Barthou, *Autour de Baudelaire* (1917), pp. 33-59, and Ferran, *L'Esthétique de Baudelaire*, pp. 501-25.

3. *Crépet*, pp. 50-51, n. 2.

4. In 1855 Baudelaire's indignation against Hugo breaks out in connection with Delacroix: "Il lui est arrivé d'appeler les femmes de

Delacroix des grenouilles. Mais M. Victor Hugo est un grand poëte sculptural qui a l'œil fermé à la spiritualité" (II, 161).

5. Ferran, *L'Esthétique de Baudelaire*, p. 507.

6. "Nos voisins disent: Shakspeare et Goethe! nous pouvons leur répondre: Victor Hugo et Théophile Gautier!" (II, 478.) The Hugo article, it will be noticed, puts Byron side by side with Shakespeare, but removes Gautier, leaving Hugo in solitary poetic splendor.

7. See the collected "Jugements sur la *Légende des siècles*, première série, 1859," in Hugo, *La Légende des siècles*, ed. Paul Berret, I (1921), lxxxvii-cxxxvi.

8. For Hugo's letter, ending "Nous nous dévouons, vous et moi, au progrès par la Vérité," see II, 777.

9. See also *L.M.*, p. 355.

10. The passage is a tantalizing one to me; it is one of those which give one the impression that Baudelaire has borrowed it more or less directly. There a slight resemblance to a passage towards the end of *Suspiria*, not used by Baudelaire in the *Mangeur d'opium* (*English Opium-Eater*, pp. 285-86). But I have an uneasy feeling that there may be a closer parallel elsewhere. Baudelaire uses the English phrase "hysterical tears," which might furnish a clue. M. Crépet has a note to this, "Expression empruntée à Keats" (*A.R.*, p. 546), but I have been unable to find the phrase in Keats.

11. For an excellent and detailed study of Baudelaire and Banville, see J. Pommier, "Banville et Baudelaire," *Revue d'Histoire Littéraire de la France*, XXXVII (1930), 514-41.

12. See Albert Feuillerat, *Baudelaire et la Belle aux cheveux d'or*, New Haven, 1941.

13. *Crépet*, pp. 313-14. The letter is undated, and there are no letters to Banville in Baudelaire's published correspondence. But the reference to "des circonstances qui nous ont séparés" suggests the late 1850's.

14. See II, 94, 116, 130 ("Salon de 1846"); 236, 266, 271 ("Salon de 1859"); 325, 342 ("Peintre de la vie moderne"); 293 ("Peintres et aquafortistes").

15. Compare the words of a modern prose-writer who is an exquisite poet: "De grandes ressemblances balafrent le monde, et marquent ici et là leur lumière. Elles rapprochent, elles assortissent ce qui est et ce qui est immense. D'elles seules peut naître toute nostalgie, tout esprit, toute émotion. Poète, je dois l'être, elles seules me frappent" (J. Giraudoux, *L'Ecole des indifférents*).

16. See too the letter to Armand Fraisse of 1860 (*Corr.* I, 302).

17. See also the notes in "Mon Cœur mis à nu": "Il n'existe que

trois êtres respectables: le prêtre, le guerrier, le poëte. Savoir, tuer, et créer" (II, 648), and "Il n'y a de grand parmi les hommes que le poëte, le prêtre et le soldat" (II, 656).

18. Léon Cladel, Les *Martyrs ridicules*, with a preface by Charles Baudelaire (1862), p. 36.

19. *Ibid.*, pp. 37-38.

20. *Ibid.*, p. 102.

21. *Ibid.*, p. 217.

22. See *Juvenilia*, pp. 548-51.

23. Compare Baudelaire's letter to Paul de Molènes (*Corr.* I, 327-28) and *Juvenilia*, pp. 472-77.

24. The Pléiade edition, like the original edition of *L'Art romantique*, fails to indicate that its text for this article is incomplete, and must be supplemented by the long quotation which Baudelaire makes from the article in "L'Œuvre et la vie d'Eugène Delacroix" (II, 304-6). See M. Crépet's note in his edition of *L'Art romantique*, p. 447.

25. Delacroix, *Correspondance*, IV, 276.

26. For Chenavard, see what Baudelaire says in the "Salon de 1859" (II, 261) and the Delacroix article (II, 318).

27. This paragraph and the following section develop in detail what Baudelaire had suggested in the "Salon de 1859" (II, 242). The italicizing of the word *spécialité* in both passages suggests that Baudelaire is thinking of Swedenborg's and Balzac's use of it: "La Spécialité consiste à voir les choses du monde matériel aussi bien que celles du monde spirituel dans leurs ramifications originelles et conséquentielles. Les plus beaux génies humains sont ceux qui sont partis des ténèbres de l'Abstraction pour arriver aux lumières de la Spécialité. Spécialité, *species*, vue, spéculer, voir tout, et d'un seul coup; *Speculum*, miroir ou moyen d'apprécier une chose en la voyant tout entière. . . . La perfection de la vue intérieure enfante le don de Spécialité. La Spécialité emporte l'intuition" (*Louis Lambert*, ed. Conard, XXXI, 167).

28. I have already referred to much of this part of the article in discussing the relations between Baudelaire and Delacroix.

29. Baudelaire used the article as a lecture in Brussels in 1864; he supplemented it by a page which served as introduction to the lecture and which adds a few interesting details.

BIBLIOGRAPHY

CHRONOLOGICAL LIST OF BAUDELAIRE'S CRITICAL WORK

All of Baudelaire's critical work is here listed chronologically by date of publication or (in the case of posthumously published works) by date of composition, as closely as this can be determined. I have included not only the critical work in the strictest sense, but all articles which seem related to it.

I have listed the reprintings of each article during Baudelaire's lifetime (he died in 1867), together with the posthumous volume in which it is included—*Curiosités esthétiques* (*C.E.*), *L'Art romantique* (*A.R.*), *Œuvres posthumes*, edition of 1908 (*O.P.*).

An asterisk indicates a work of which Baudelaire was not sole author, but in which he undoubtedly had some share.

1844 *Mystères galans des théâtres de Paris. Cazal, 1844. (Ed. J. Crépet, 1938.)

1845 Salon de 1845. Jules Labitte, 1845. (*C.E.*)

"Les *Contes normands* et *Historiettes baguenaudières*." *Le Corsaire-Satan*, Nov. 4, 1845. (*O.P.*)

"Comment on paie ses dettes quand on a du génie." *Le Corsaire-Satan*, Nov. 24, 1845; *L'Echo*, Aug. 23, 1846. (*O.P.*)

1846 "Le Musée classique du Bazar Bonne-Nouvelle." *Le Corsaire-Satan*, Jan. 21, 1846. (*C.E.*)

"*Prométhée délivré*" and "*Le Siècle*." *Le Corsaire-Satan*, Feb. 3, 1846. (*O.P.*)

Salon de 1846. Michel-Lévy, 1846. (*C.E.*)

"Conseils aux jeunes littérateurs." *L'Esprit Public*, April 15, 1846. (*A.R.*)

*"Causeries." *Le Tintamarre*, Sept. 13, 1846; March 28, 1847. (*Œuvres en collaboration*, ed. J. Mouquet, 1932.)

1847 "Jules Janin et le *Gâteau des rois*." *Le Figaro*, March 31, 1934. (*Juvenilia*.)

1848 "Les *Contes* de Champfleury." *Le Corsaire-Satan*, Jan. 18, 1848. (*O.P.*)

*Le Salut Public, Feb. 27, March 1, 1848. (O.P.)
"Révélation magnétique." La Liberté de Penser, July 15, 1848. (O.P.)
1850 "Biographie des excentriques." La République du Peuple, 1850. (O.P.)
1851 "Pierre Dupont." Chants et chansons . . . de Pierre Dupont [1851]. (A.R.)
"Les Drames et les romans honnêtes." La Semaine Théâtrale, Nov. 27, 1851. (A.R.)
1852 "Le Hibou Philosophe." Le Figaro, Aug. 30, 1880. (O.P.)
"L'Ecole païenne." La Semaine Théâtrale, Jan. 22, 1852; La Revue de Poche, Dec. 25, 1866. (A.R.)
"Edgar Allan Poe, sa vie et ses ouvrages." Revue de Paris, March-April, 1852. (O.P.)
1853 "Morale du joujou." Le Monde Littéraire, April 17, 1853; Le Portefeuille, Aug. 19, 1855; Le Rabelais, June 13, 1857. (A.R.)
1854 "Dédicace des Histoires extraordinaires." Le Pays, July 25, 1854. (O.P.)
1855 "Note à Hans Pfaall." Le Pays, April 20, 1855. (O.P.)
"Exposition universelle—1855. Beaux-Arts." Part I, Le Pays, May 26, 1855; Part III, Le Pays, June 3, 1855; Part II, Le Portefeuille, Aug. 12, 1855. (C.E.)
"De l'essence du rire et généralement du comique dans les arts plastiques." Le Portefeuille, July 8, 1855; Le Présent, Sept. 1, 1857. (C.E.)
"Philibert Rouvière." Nouvelle Galerie des artistes dramatiques vivants [1855]; L'Artiste, Dec. 1, 1859. (A.R.)
"Histoire de Neuilly." Mercure de France, Sept. 15, 1935. (Juvenilia.)
"Puisque Réalisme il y a." Mesures, July 15, 1938. (Juvenilia.)
1856 "Edgar Poe, sa vie et ses œuvres." Histoires extraordinaires, 1856.
"Les Liaisons dangereuses." Choderlos de Laclos, De l'éducation des femmes, ed. E. Champion, 1903. (O.P.)
1857 "Quelque caricaturistes français." Le Présent, Oct. 1, 1857; L'Artiste, Oct. 24 and 31, 1858. (C.E.)
"Quelques caricaturistes étrangers." Le Présent, Oct. 15, 1857; L'Artiste, Sept. 1858. (C.E.)
"De la caricature." Œuvres posthumes, 1908.
"Une Estampe de Boilly." Œuvres posthumes, 1908.

"Madame Bovary." L'Artiste, Oct. 18, 1857. (A.R.)
"Notes nouvelles sur Edgar Poe." *Nouvelles histoires extra-ordinaires*, 1857.

1858 "Lettre au *Figaro." Le Figaro*, June 13, 1858. (O.P.)

1859 *"La Double Vie." L'Artiste*, Jan. 9, 1859. (A.R.)
"Théophile Gautier." *L'Artiste*, March 13, 1859; pamphlet, Poulet-Malassis, 1859. (A.R.)
"Salon de 1859." *Revue Française*, June 10 and 20, 1859. (C.E.)

1861 "Richard Wagner et Tannhäuser à Paris." *La Revue Euro-péenne*, April 1, 1861; *La Presse Théâtrale et Musicale*, April 14 and 21, May 5, 1861; pamphlet, E. Dentu, 1861. (A.R.)
"Victor Hugo." *Revue Fantaisiste*, June 15, 1861; *Les Poëtes français*, ed. E. Crépet, 1862. (A.R.)
"Marceline Desbordes-Valmore." *Revue Fantaisiste*, July 1, 1861; *Les Poëtes français*, 1862.
"Auguste Barbier." *Revue Fantaisiste*, July 15, 1861. (A.R.)
"Théophile Gautier." *Revue Fantaisiste*, July 15, 1861; *Les Poëtes français*, 1862. (A.R.)
"Pétrus Borel." *Revue Fantaisiste*, July 15, 1861. (A.R.)
"Gustave Le Vavasseur." *Revue Fantaisiste*, Aug. 1, 1861; *Les Poëtes français*, 1862. (A.R.)
"Théodore de Banville." *Revue Fantaisiste*, Aug. 1, 1861; *Les Poëtes français*, 1862. (A.R.)
"Pierre Dupont." *Revue Fantaisiste*, Aug. 15, 1861; *Les Poëtes français*, 1862. (A.R.)
"Leconte de Lisle." *Revue Fantaisiste*, Aug. 15, 1861; *Les Poëtes français*, 1862. (A.R.)
"Hégésippe Moreau." *L'Art romantique*, 1868.
"Peintures murales d'Eugène Delacroix à Saint-Sulpice." *Revue Fantaisiste*, Sept. 15, 1861. (A.R.)
"Les Martyrs ridicules." Revue Fantaisiste, Oct. 15, 1861; Preface to *Les Martyrs ridicules*, by Léon Cladel, 1862. (A.R.)

1862 "Une Réforme à l'Académie." *Revue Anecdotique*, Jan., 1862, No. 2. (O.P.)
"Paul de Molènes." *Revue Anecdotique*, March, 1862, No. 2. (O.P.)
"L'Eau-forte est à la mode." *Revue Anecdotique*, April 2, 1862. (O.P.)
"Les Misérables." Le Boulevard, April 20, 1862. (O.P.)

"Peintres et aquafortistes." *Le Boulevard,* Sept. 14, 1862.
(*A.R.*)

"L'Esprit et le style de M. Villemain." *Mercure de France,*
March 1, 1907. (*O.P.*)

1863 "L'Œuvre et la vie d'Eugène Delacroix." *L'Opinion Nationale,* Sept. 2 and 14, Nov. 22, 1863. (*A.R.*)

"Le Peintre de la vie moderne." *Le Figaro,* Nov. 26 and 28,
Dec. 3, 1863. (*A.R.*)

1864 "Anniversaire de la naissance de Shakspeare." *Le Figaro,* April
14, 1864. (*O.P.*)

"Vente de la collection de M. E. Piot." *Le Figaro,* April 24,
1864. (*A.R.*)

"Eugène Delacroix, ses œuvres, ses idées, ses mœurs." *L'Art,*
July, 1902. (*A.R.* ed. Crépet.)

1865 "Lettre à Jules Janin." *Œuvres posthumes,* 1887; *Bulletin
du Bibliophile,* Dec. 15, 1901. (*O.P.*)

"Le Comédien Rouvière." *La Petite Revue,* Oct. 28, 1865.

"Catalogue de la collection de M. Crabbe." *Le Gil Blas,*
June 14, 1890 (fragments); *L'Art et les artistes,* No. 26
(fragments). (*O.P.*)

"L'Art philosophique." *L'Art romantique,* 1868.

1866 *"Les Travailleurs de la mer." Œuvres posthumes,* 1908.

WORKS ON BAUDELAIRE'S CRITICISM

This list includes only books and articles which treat Baudelaire's criticism
at some length. Many of them are so general in character that I have not
referred to them specifically elsewhere. References to works on special aspects
of the criticism will be found in the notes.

Bernard, Emile. "Charles Baudelaire critique d'art et esthéticien."
Mercure de France, Oct. 16, 1919.

Bouyer, Raymond. "Baudelaire critique d'art." *Revue Bleue,* Nov. 8,
1902.

Ferran, André. L'Esthétique de Baudelaire. 1933.

Macchia, Giovanni. Baudelaire Critico. Florence, 1939.

Mauclair, Camille. "Baudelaire critique d'art et critique musical," in
Princes de l'esprit. 1931. (Reproduced, with slight changes, in
Le Génie de Baudelaire. 1933.)

Michelet, V.-E. "Charles Baudelaire ou le Divinateur douloureux," in
Figures d'évocateurs. 1913.

Reynold, Gonzague de. Charles Baudelaire. Geneva, 1920. (Chapter XII, "La Prose de Baudelaire: la critique et l'esthétique.")

Rhodes, S. A. The Cult of Beauty in Charles Baudelaire. New York, 1929. (Vol. II, Chapter VII, "The Art of Criticism.")

Suarès, André. "Baudelaire," in Sur la vie. 1912. (Vol. III.)

Vaudoyer, J. L. "Baudelaire critique d'art." *L'Opinion*, April 9, 1921.

Index

Allegory, 41, 112
American men of letters in Paris, 60
Amic, Henri, 69
Amiel, Henri F., quoted, 135
Analogies and correspondences, *see* Correspondences
Apuleius, 17
Art, Baudelaire's criticism of, 5, 68, 78, 221-26; his views and Poe's, about domain of, 111; role of memory in, 38, 136, 152-57; significance of the word, 165-67; philosophic art, 26, 216-17
"Art philosophique, L'," 166, 216-17
Art romantique, L', v, 3, 186
Asselineau, Charles, 12, 58, 61; quoted, 9, 59, 62, 161, 193; *La Double Vie,* 100-102, 210
Aubert's *Souvenirs du Salon de 1859,* 139
Aupick, Madame (Baudelaire's mother), 160
Aurélia (Gérard de Nerval), 56

Bacon, Lord Verulam, quoted, 87
Balzac, Honoré de, 14, 17, 26, 32, 52-53, 98, 104
Banville, Théodore de, 58, 99, 198-99, 202, 203; quoted, 33
Barbey d'Aurevilly, Jules, 57
Barbier, Auguste, 68, 99, 195, 203
Baudelaire, Charles, gradual realization of his significance as a critic, v; importance of chronology in study of criticism, v-vi, 185; originality developed slowly, vi, 34, 54, 114, 225; persons greatly influencing, vi, 52, 108, 225 (*see also* Delacroix; De Maistre; Poe; Stendhal); variations in vocabulary: significance of certain words,

vi, 23, 32, 33, 47, 67, 89, 107, 119, 122, 144, 150, 161, 203, 224 (*see entries under* Words); attitude toward own critical work, 3; volumes containing critical articles, 3; on function of criticism and position of the critic, 3-7, 28-29, 179-81; allies criticism to poetry, 4, 56, 86, 223; parallel development of his poetry and criticism, 5, 54, 115; art criticism his most important critical work, 5, 78, 221; experience always the point of departure for, 6, 7, 174, 177, 180, 223-25; earliest criticism that of art, 7; parents' talents and influence, 7; enthusiasm for art, 7-9; extensive readings, 14-17, 57-58, 115; literary enthusiasms, 16; his Samuel Cramer, 16, 51, 54; first critical articles, 17, 23-24; attitude toward the bourgeois, 19, 26, 27, 70, 110, 161; preference for color over line, 22, 29, 39, 213; first ventures into literary criticism, 24, 25, 26; sincerity questioned, 27, 102, 103, 106, 186; conception of beauty, 32, 34, 49, 87, 111, 143-49; glorification of the modern, 32, 47, 49, 68, 87, 141, 144, 147, 152, 182; his attacks on the imitation of nature, 33, 135, 163; reputation as a critic established by "Salon de 1846," 33; on the variable nature of beauty, 34, 87; foundations of criticism laid before contact with Poe, 34; borrowings, 34, 49, 178 (amounting to plagiarism, 51); glorification of the imagination, 38, 107, 117, 118-33, 175, 184,